"Action, adventure, supernatural bass players and a real self-deprecating sense of humor..."
—*The Brazen Bull*

"...feels like meeting up with an old mate for a pint...both heartfelt and hilarious."
—*Big Comic Page*

"The intricate layering is just one more jewel in the crown of a visually stunning, completely engrossing read."
—*Comic Watch*

"...keeps the punk in all of us alive with this excellent genre-bending series."
—*Multiversity*

"Witty, weird and wonderful, a gob of fresh phlegm for fans of edgy, cape-free comics...a riot of technicolour and tentacles."
—*Hero Collector*

"A great, fun, dark humoured book that mixes the rebellious cultures of music and youth with a story of horror and the supernatural. And all to a kicking soundtrack."
—*Comicon.com*

"A wild walk on the wild side with supernatural spectacles and musical nods."
—*Major Spoilers*

"...a vibe and energy all its own."
—*Bleeding Cool*

"Think *The X-Files* directed by early-career Danny Boyle, and you're about there. Ghost stories and deep government conspiracy, soppy teen romance and kitchen sink drama, all of it guided by an elemental spirit that belongs ...e queen."
—*Doom* ...lthq.com

LONDON

WHAT I WANT YOU TO *SEE* IS JUST OUT *HERE.*

OH. NOT WHAT I WAS EXPECTING...

Written by **David Barnett**
Art, covers & logo by **Martin Simmonds**

Lettering by **Aditya Bidikar**
Flats by **Dee Cunniffe**

Editorial Assistance by **Megan Brown**
Edited by **Shelly Bond**
Publication Design by **PopGum**
PUNKS NOT DEAD is created by **Barnett & Simmonds**

BLACK CROWN HQ
Shelly Bond, Editor • **Megan Brown,** Editorial Assistant • **Aditya Bidikar,** Letterer
Arlene Lo, Proofreader • **Philip Bond,** logo, publication design and general dogsbody
Chris Ryall, President, Publisher & Chief Creative Officer

BLACK CROWN is a fully functioning curation operation based in Los Angeles by way of IDW Publishing.
Accept No Substitutes!

For international rights, contact **licensing@idwpublishing.com**

ISBN: 978-1-68405-496-1

22 21 20 19   1 2 3 4

IDW®
www.IDWPUBLISHING.com

Chris Ryall, President & Publisher/CCO • **John Barber,** Editor-in-Chief • **Cara Morrison,** Chief Financial Officer • **Matthew Ruzicka,** Chief Accounting Officer •
David Hedgecock, Associate Publisher • **Jerry Bennington,** VP of New Product Development • **Lorelei Bunjes,** VP of Digital Services • **Justin Eisinger,** Editorial
Director, Graphic Novels and Collections • **Eric Moss,** Sr. Director, Licensing & Business Development
Ted Adams and Robbie Robbins, IDW Founders

Facebook: **facebook.com/idwpublishing** • Twitter: **@idwpublishing** • YouTube: **youtube.com/idwpublishing**
Tumblr: **tumblr.idwpublishing.com** • Instagram: **instagram.com/idwpublishing**

CALLing

SID!
WILL YOU
MOVE IT?!

CONTENTS

Introduction by Ian Rankin

blackcrown.pub

INTRODUCTION
by IAN RANKIN

Suddenly everyone wanted in on the act.

Competent musicians were making a pretence of basic skills; Mick Jagger was wearing a Destroy T-shirt; Fee Waybill of music-hall-meets-big-top performance group The Tubes wagged a finger and sang "I was a punk before you were."

Everyone wanted in on the act — and maybe that's why punk's trajectory was as short as it was fiery.

I was the right age — 17 in 1977. My high school even boasted punk royalty in Skids guitarist Stuart Adamson. Club nights sprang up in the unlikeliest spots. My own punk band, the Dancing Pigs, rehearsed in the local YWCA. We were probably doomed by the fact that some of us were more proficient than strictly necessary, and new wave with its added synths and studio trickery was calling.

The Sex Pistols lasted the merest blink of an eye; others soldiered on, morphing into the mainstream or treading an increasingly lonely if principled path.

And then there was Sid.

Every musical era seems to demand its sacrifice. Sid Vicious climbed gleefully into the wicker man and lit the match himself, damaged from the start and damaged to the end. Yet here he is (spoiler alert: kinda), resurrected and returned from the afterlife within the pages of the book you're holding and keen to play merry hell with our teenage protagonist Fergie Ferguson in present-day unmerrie England.

LONDON CALLING is the second volume in the series, and it turns the amplification all the way up as Fergie and Sid head to London in search of Fergie's father and answers to uncomfortably occult questions. Pursued by both demons and the wonderful Dorothy Culpepper (of the government's shadowy Department for Extra-Usual Affairs), Fergie is in for the gig of his life.

Writer David Barnett and artist Martin Simmonds give us all the right notes in the right order, aided and abetted by Dee Cunniffe and Aditya Bidikar.

Even if you don't remember punk (and if you *do* remember it, you probably weren't there), this chunk of blitzkrieg bop will have your senses pogoing like never before.

Never trust an old hippie they say, but you can trust me on this. I wasn't a hippie. **I was a punk.**

Ian Rankin
Edinburgh

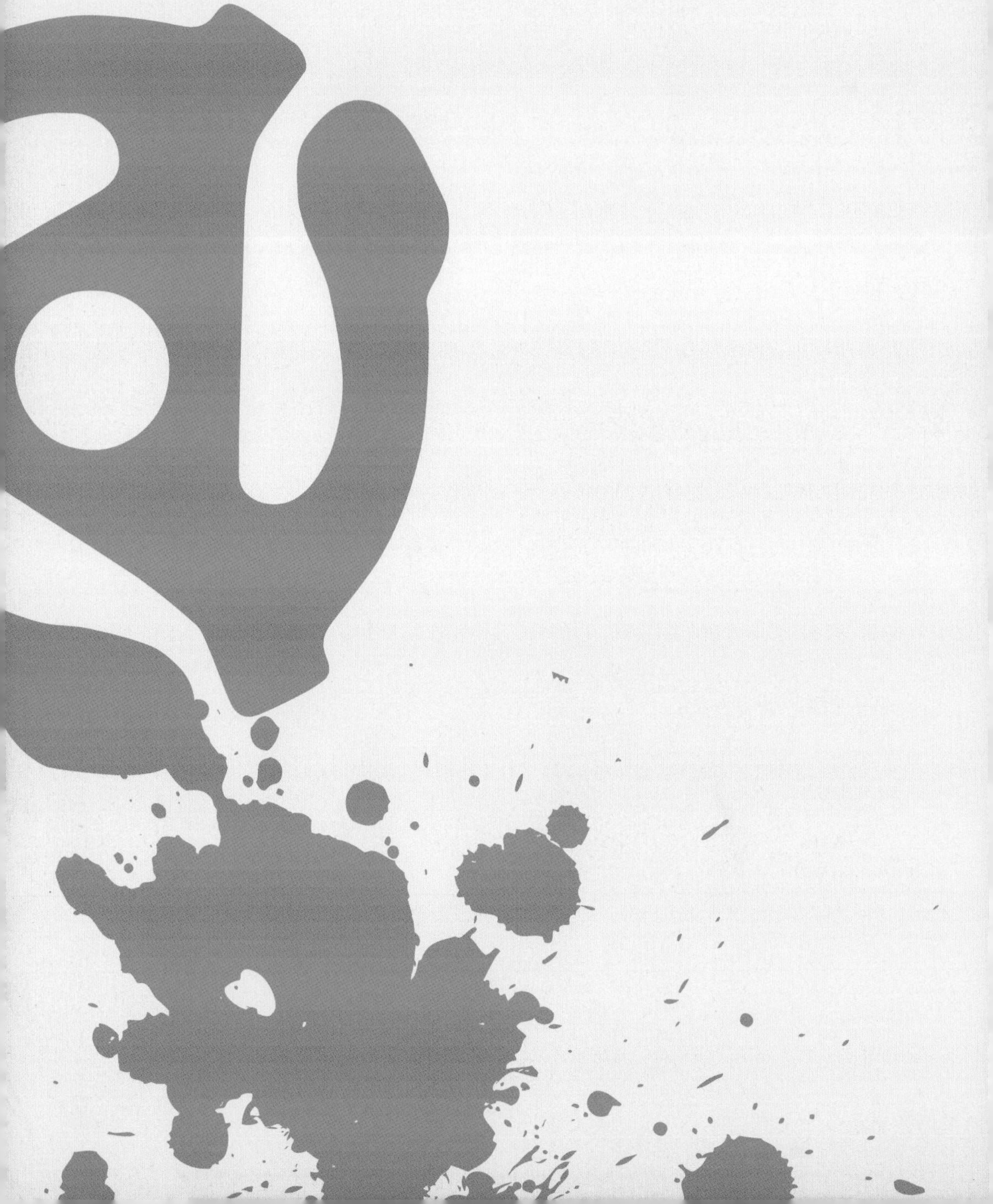

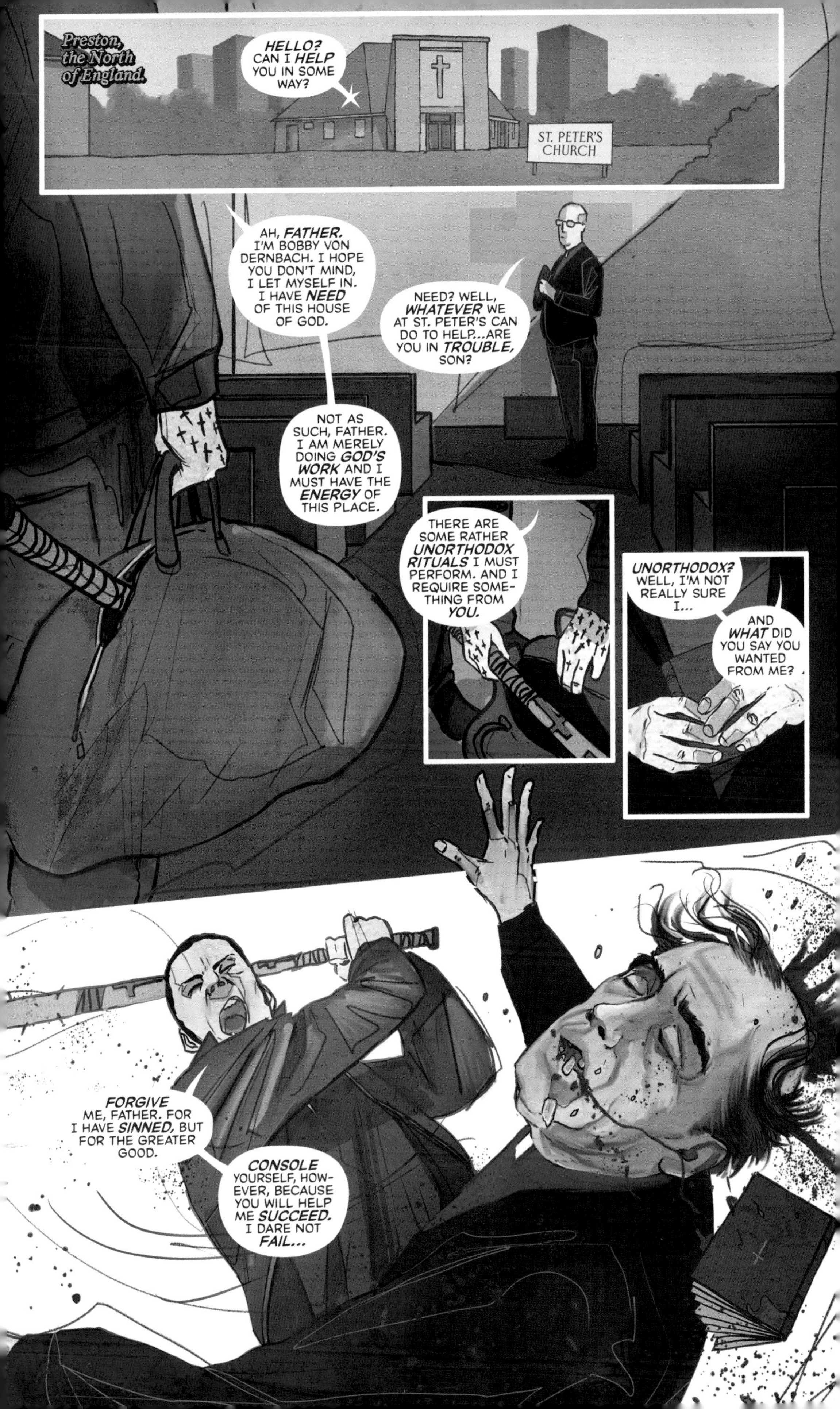
Preston, the North of England.
HELLO? CAN I HELP YOU IN SOME WAY?
ST. PETER'S CHURCH
AH, FATHER. I'M BOBBY VON DERNBACH. I HOPE YOU DON'T MIND, I LET MYSELF IN. I HAVE NEED OF THIS HOUSE OF GOD.
NEED? WELL, WHATEVER WE AT ST. PETER'S CAN DO TO HELP...ARE YOU IN TROUBLE, SON?
NOT AS SUCH, FATHER. I AM MERELY DOING GOD'S WORK AND I MUST HAVE THE ENERGY OF THIS PLACE.
THERE ARE SOME RATHER UNORTHODOX RITUALS I MUST PERFORM. AND I REQUIRE SOMETHING FROM YOU.
UNORTHODOX? WELL, I'M NOT REALLY SURE I...
AND WHAT DID YOU SAY YOU WANTED FROM ME?
FORGIVE ME, FATHER. FOR I HAVE SINNED, BUT FOR THE GREATER GOOD.
CONSOLE YOURSELF, HOWEVER, BECAUSE YOU WILL HELP ME SUCCEED. I DARE NOT FAIL...

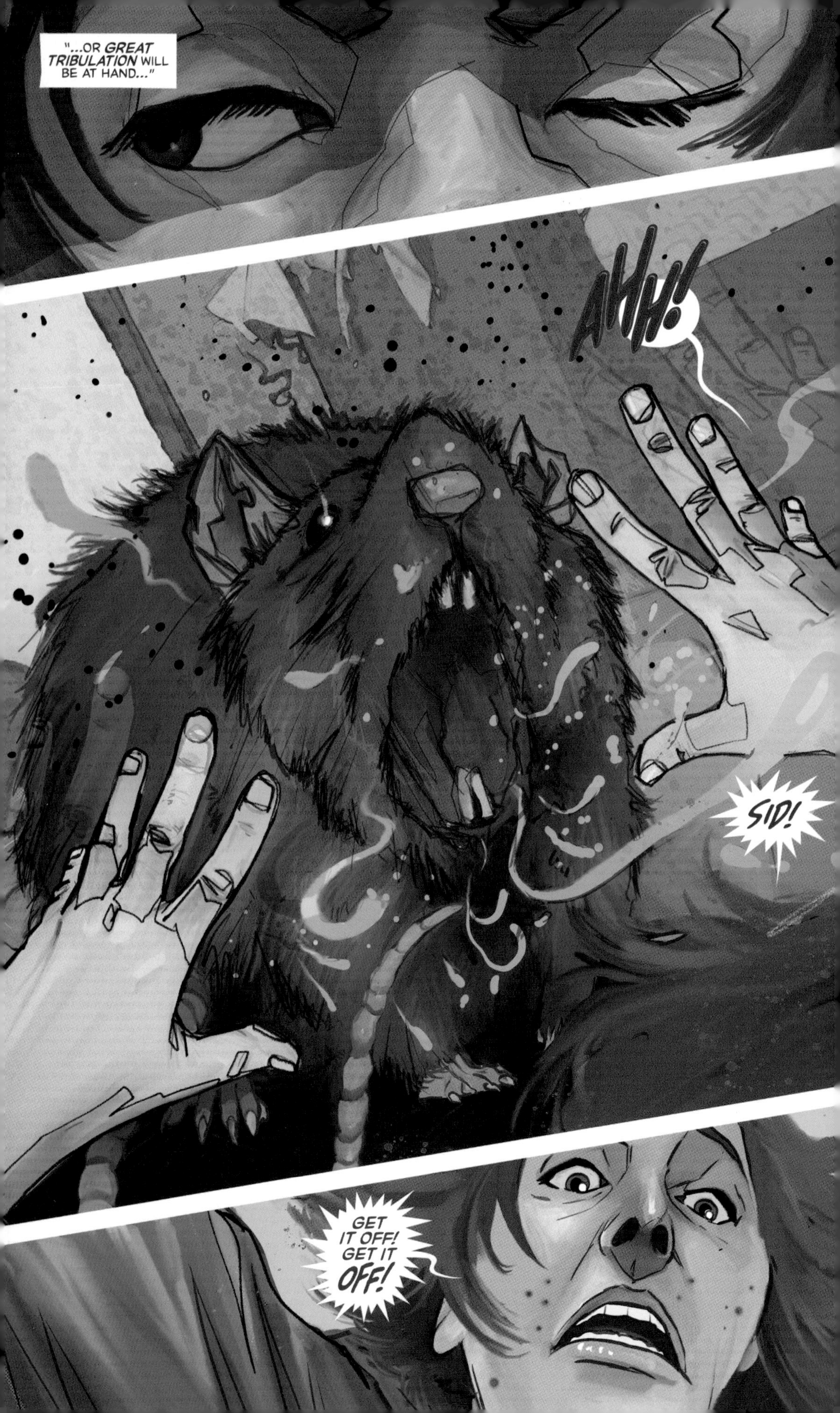
"...OR GREAT TRIBULATION WILL BE AT HAND..."
AHHH!
SID!
GET IT OFF! GET IT OFF!

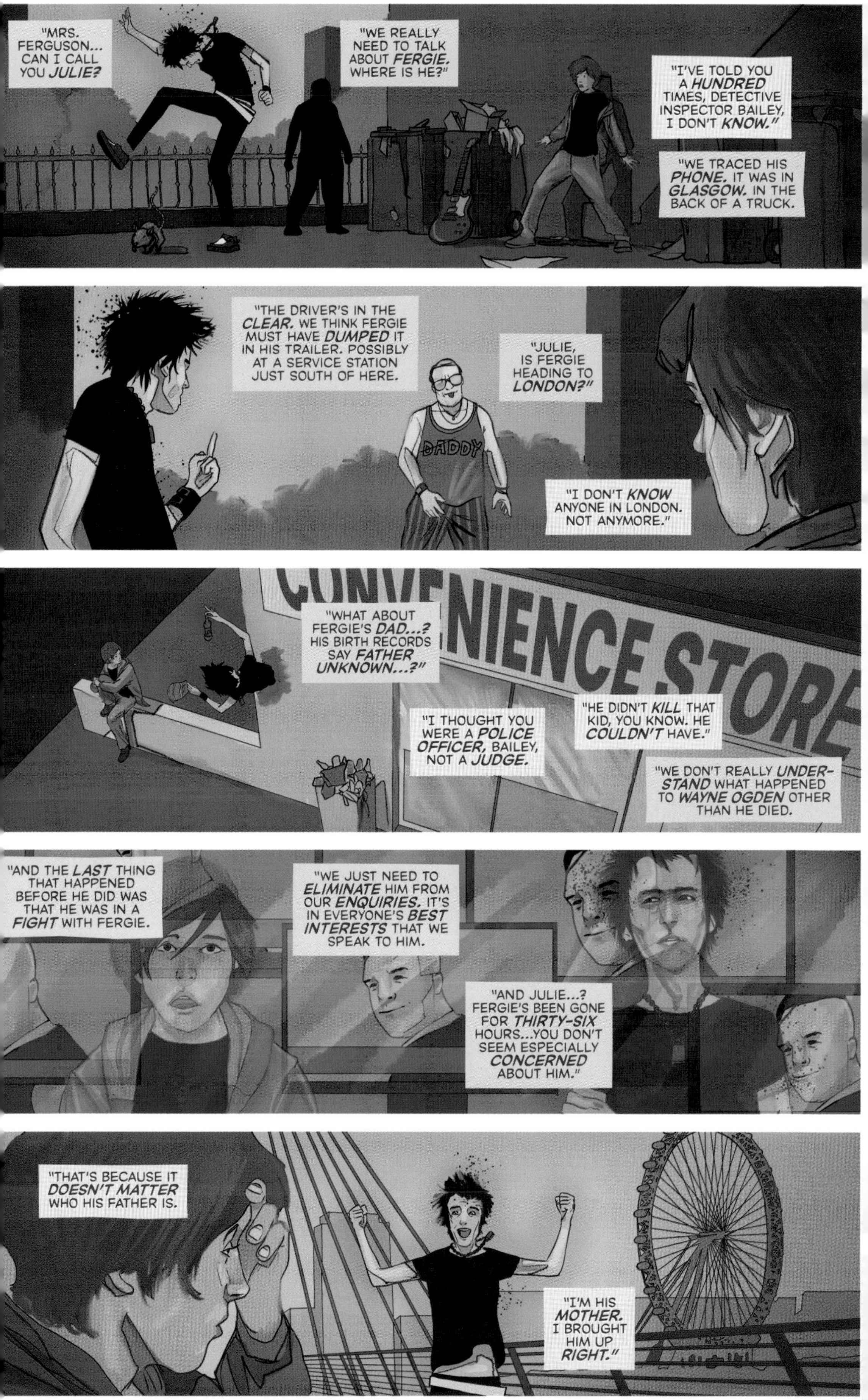
"MRS. FERGUSON... CAN I CALL YOU *JULIE?*
"WE REALLY NEED TO TALK ABOUT *FERGIE.* WHERE IS HE?"
"I'VE TOLD YOU A *HUNDRED* TIMES, DETECTIVE INSPECTOR BAILEY, I DON'T *KNOW."*
"WE TRACED HIS *PHONE.* IT WAS IN *GLASGOW.* IN THE BACK OF A TRUCK.
"THE DRIVER'S IN THE *CLEAR.* WE THINK FERGIE MUST HAVE *DUMPED* IT IN HIS TRAILER. POSSIBLY AT A SERVICE STATION JUST SOUTH OF HERE.
DADDY
"JULIE, IS FERGIE HEADING TO *LONDON?"*
"I DON'T *KNOW* ANYONE IN LONDON. NOT ANYMORE."
CONVENIENCE STORE
"WHAT ABOUT FERGIE'S *DAD...?* HIS BIRTH RECORDS SAY *FATHER UNKNOWN...?"*
"I THOUGHT YOU WERE A *POLICE OFFICER,* BAILEY, NOT A *JUDGE.*
"HE DIDN'T *KILL* THAT KID, YOU KNOW. HE *COULDN'T* HAVE."
"WE DON'T REALLY *UNDERSTAND* WHAT HAPPENED TO *WAYNE OGDEN* OTHER THAN HE DIED.
"AND THE *LAST* THING THAT HAPPENED BEFORE HE DID WAS THAT HE WAS IN A *FIGHT* WITH FERGIE.
"WE JUST NEED TO *ELIMINATE* HIM FROM OUR *ENQUIRIES.* IT'S IN EVERYONE'S *BEST INTERESTS* THAT WE SPEAK TO HIM.
"AND JULIE...? FERGIE'S BEEN GONE FOR *THIRTY-SIX* HOURS...YOU DON'T SEEM ESPECIALLY *CONCERNED* ABOUT HIM."
"THAT'S BECAUSE IT *DOESN'T MATTER* WHO HIS FATHER IS.
"I'M HIS *MOTHER.* I BROUGHT HIM UP *RIGHT."*

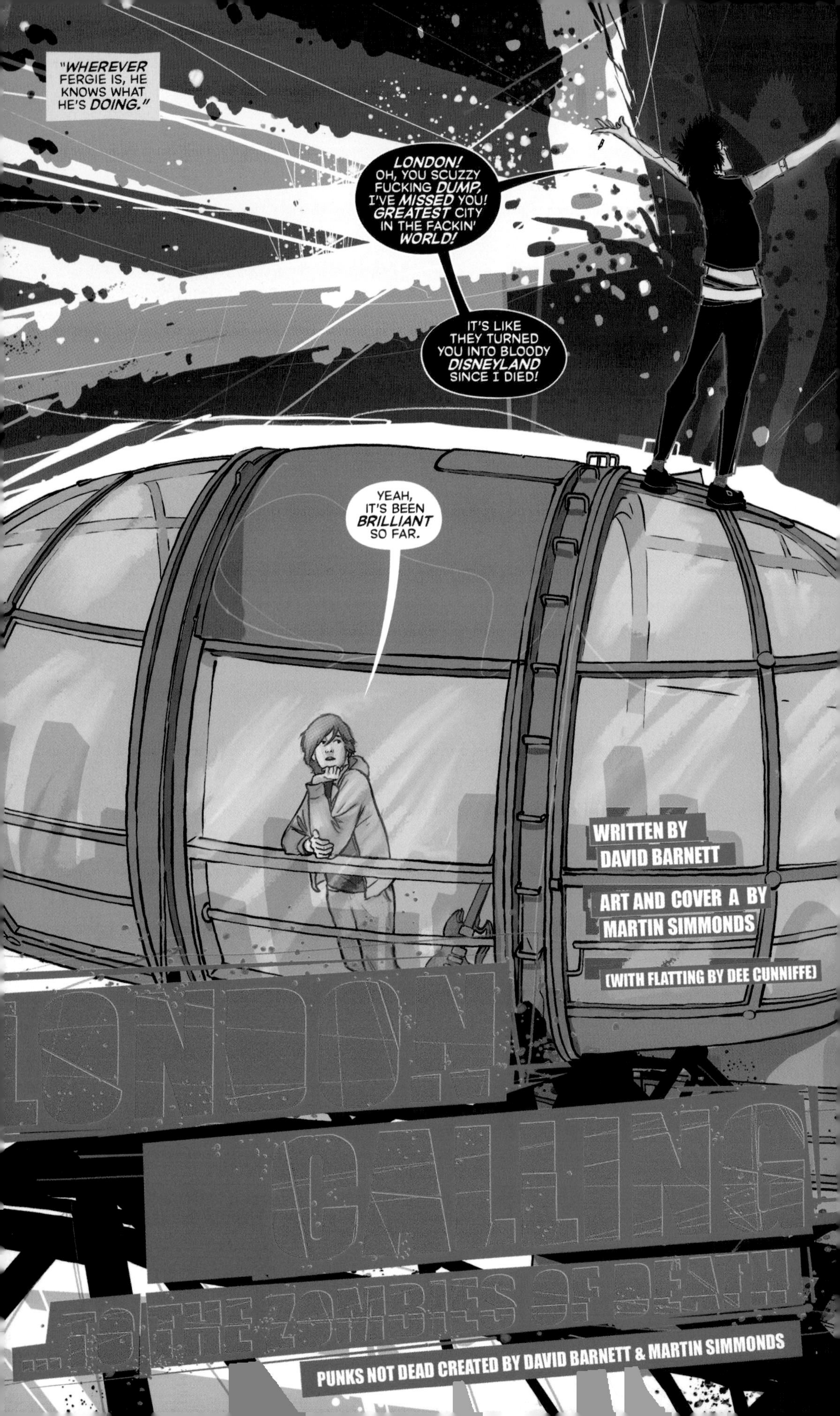
"WHEREVER FERGIE IS, HE KNOWS WHAT HE'S DOING."
LONDON! OH, YOU SCUZZY FUCKING DUMP, I'VE MISSED YOU! GREATEST CITY IN THE FACKIN' WORLD!
IT'S LIKE THEY TURNED YOU INTO BLOODY DISNEYLAND SINCE I DIED!
YEAH, IT'S BEEN BRILLIANT SO FAR.
WRITTEN BY DAVID BARNETT
ART AND COVER A BY MARTIN SIMMONDS
(WITH FLATTING BY DEE CUNNIFFE)
LONDON CALLING TO THE ZOMBIES OF DEATH
PUNKS NOT DEAD CREATED BY DAVID BARNETT & MARTIN SIMMONDS

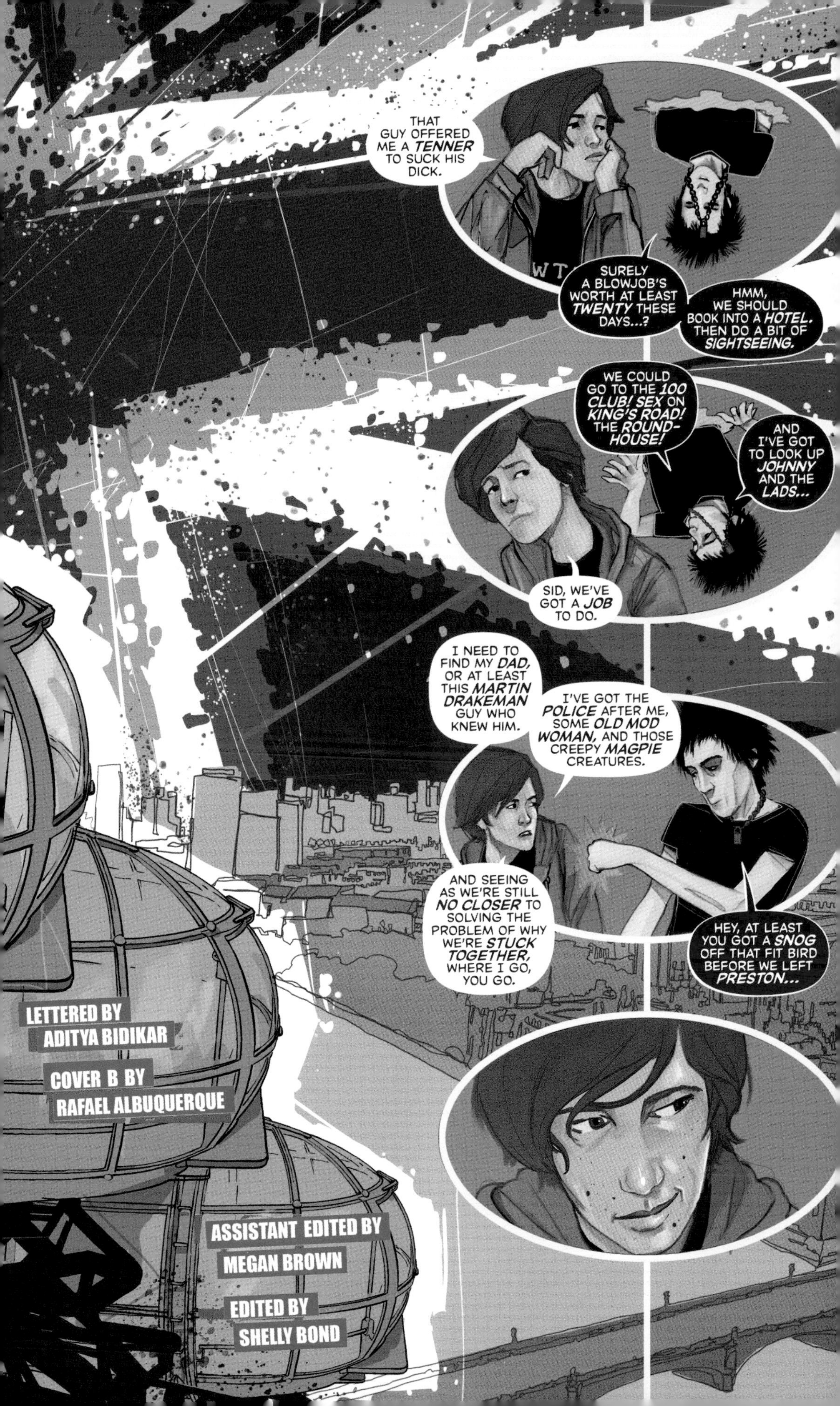
THAT GUY OFFERED ME A TENNER TO SUCK HIS DICK.
SURELY A BLOWJOB'S WORTH AT LEAST TWENTY THESE DAYS...?
HMM, WE SHOULD BOOK INTO A HOTEL. THEN DO A BIT OF SIGHTSEEING.
WE COULD GO TO THE 100 CLUB! SEX ON KING'S ROAD! THE ROUND-HOUSE!
AND I'VE GOT TO LOOK UP JOHNNY AND THE LADS...
SID, WE'VE GOT A JOB TO DO.
I NEED TO FIND MY DAD, OR AT LEAST THIS MARTIN DRAKEMAN GUY WHO KNEW HIM.
I'VE GOT THE POLICE AFTER ME, SOME OLD MOD WOMAN, AND THOSE CREEPY MAGPIE CREATURES.
AND SEEING AS WE'RE STILL NO CLOSER TO SOLVING THE PROBLEM OF WHY WE'RE STUCK TOGETHER, WHERE I GO, YOU GO.
HEY, AT LEAST YOU GOT A SNOG OFF THAT FIT BIRD BEFORE WE LEFT PRESTON...
LETTERED BY ADITYA BIDIKAR
COVER B BY RAFAEL ALBUQUERQUE
ASSISTANT EDITED BY MEGAN BROWN
EDITED BY SHELLY BOND

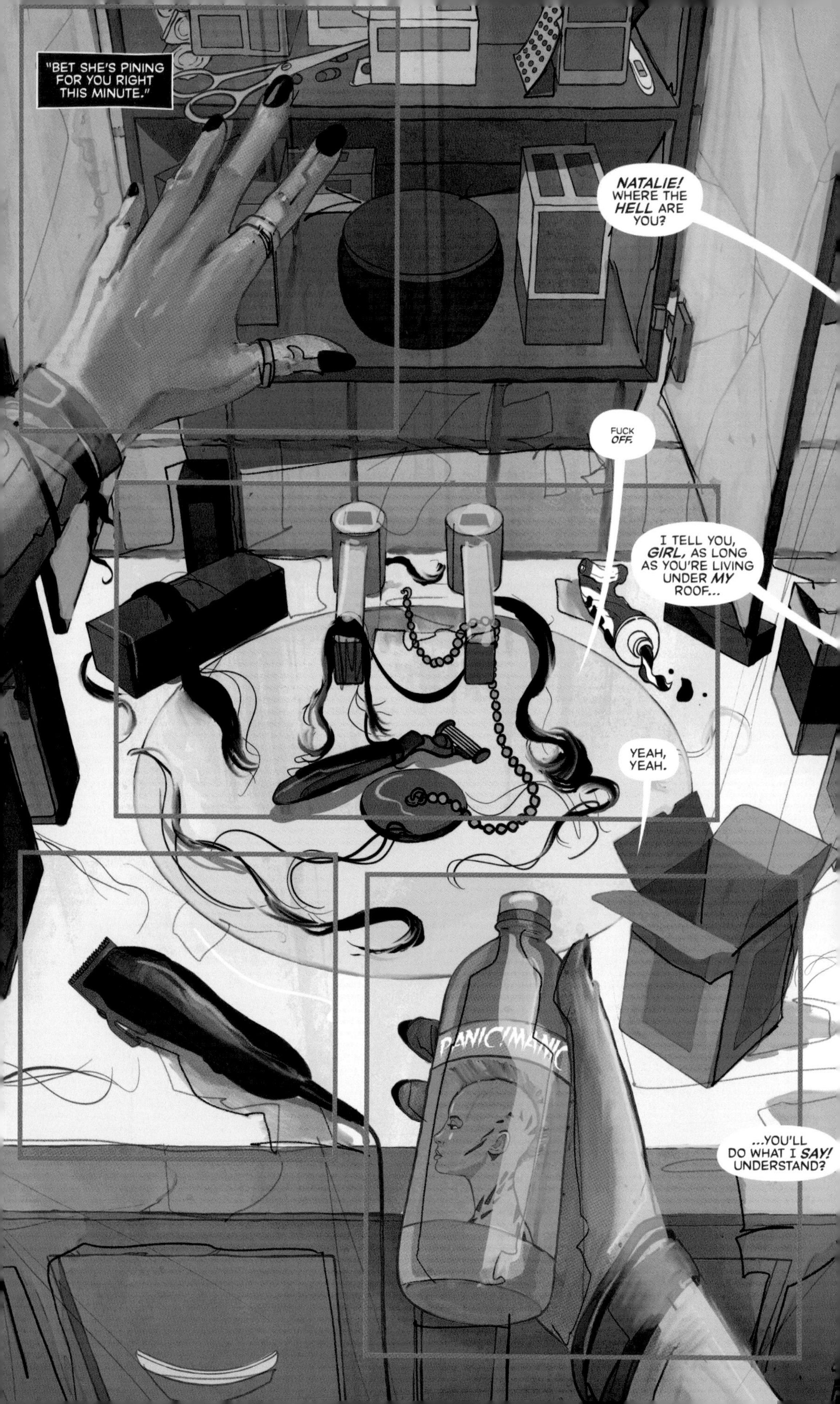
"BET SHE'S PINING FOR YOU RIGHT THIS MINUTE."
NATALIE! WHERE THE HELL ARE YOU?
FUCK OFF.
I TELL YOU, GIRL, AS LONG AS YOU'RE LIVING UNDER MY ROOF...
YEAH, YEAH.
...YOU'LL DO WHAT I SAY! UNDERSTAND?
PANIC!MANIC

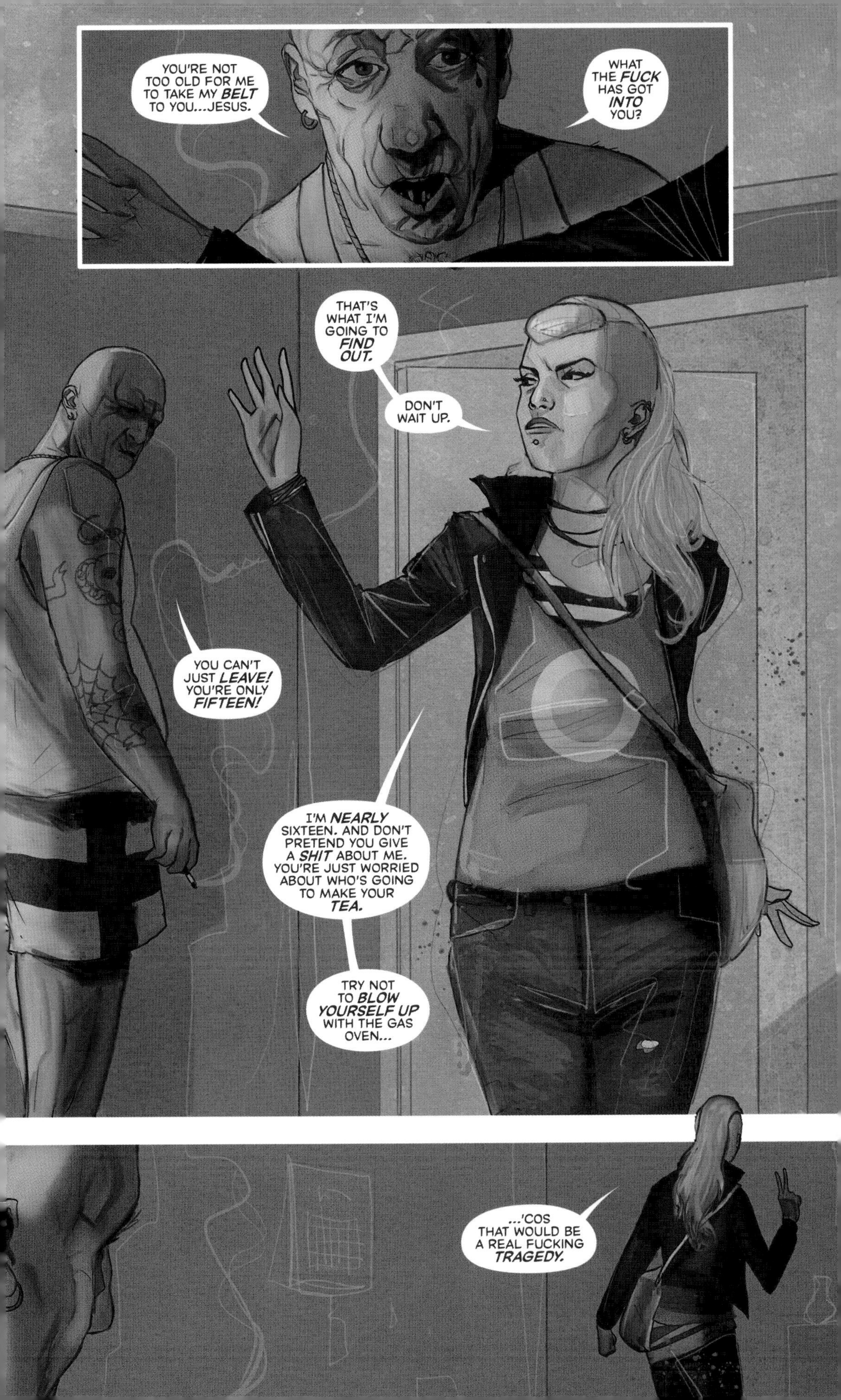
YOU'RE NOT TOO OLD FOR ME TO TAKE MY *BELT* TO YOU...JESUS.
WHAT THE *FUCK* HAS GOT *INTO* YOU?
THAT'S WHAT I'M GOING TO *FIND OUT.*
DON'T WAIT UP.
YOU CAN'T JUST *LEAVE!* YOU'RE ONLY *FIFTEEN!*
I'M *NEARLY* SIXTEEN. AND DON'T PRETEND YOU GIVE A *SHIT* ABOUT ME. YOU'RE JUST WORRIED ABOUT WHO'S GOING TO MAKE YOUR *TEA.*
TRY NOT TO *BLOW YOURSELF UP* WITH THE GAS OVEN...
...'COS THAT WOULD BE A REAL FUCKING *TRAGEDY.*

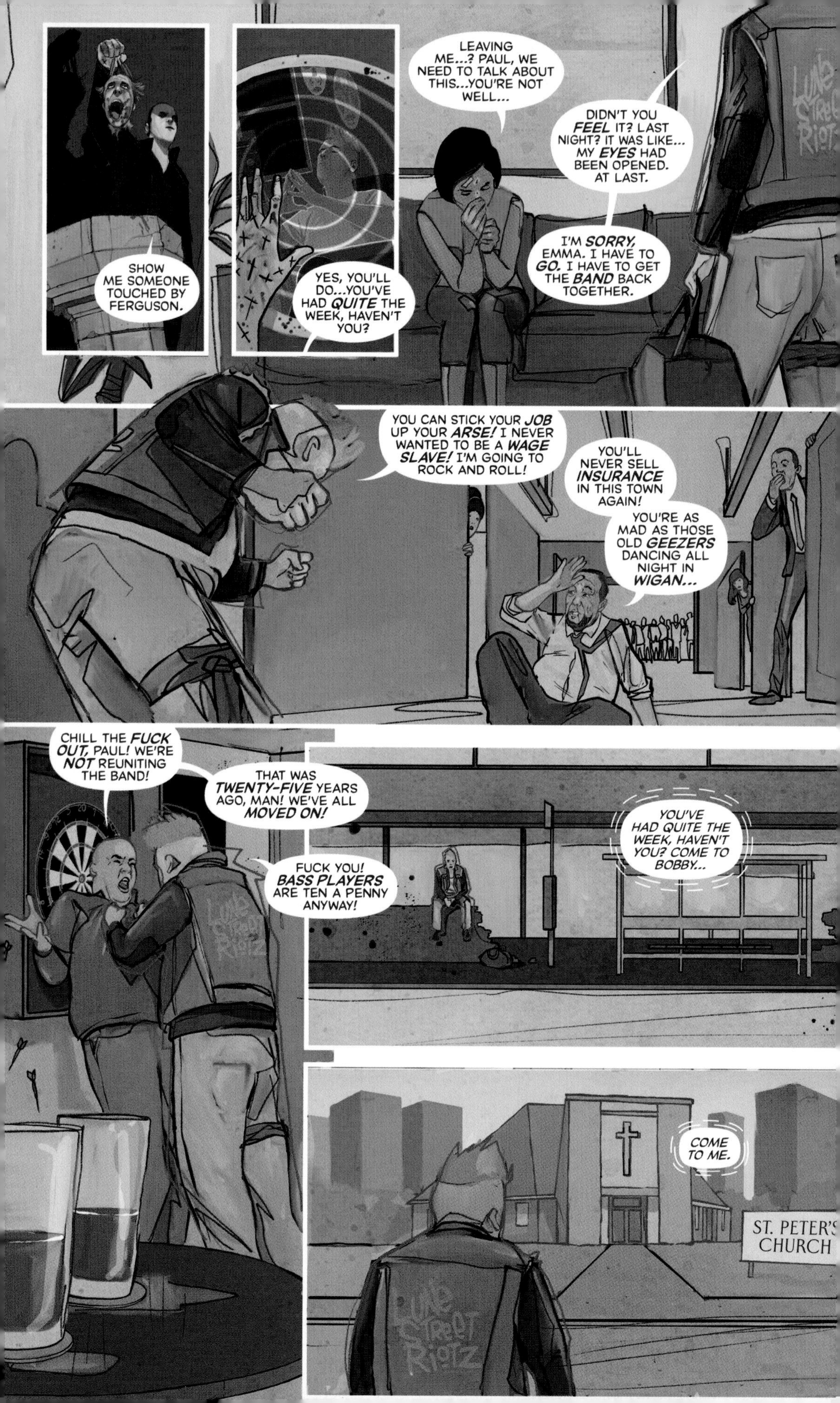
SHOW ME SOMEONE TOUCHED BY FERGUSON.
YES, YOU'LL DO...YOU'VE HAD QUITE THE WEEK, HAVEN'T YOU?
LEAVING ME...? PAUL, WE NEED TO TALK ABOUT THIS...YOU'RE NOT WELL...
DIDN'T YOU FEEL IT? LAST NIGHT? IT WAS LIKE... MY EYES HAD BEEN OPENED. AT LAST.
I'M SORRY, EMMA. I HAVE TO GO. I HAVE TO GET THE BAND BACK TOGETHER.
LUNE STREET RIOTZ
YOU CAN STICK YOUR JOB UP YOUR ARSE! I NEVER WANTED TO BE A WAGE SLAVE! I'M GOING TO ROCK AND ROLL!
YOU'LL NEVER SELL INSURANCE IN THIS TOWN AGAIN!
YOU'RE AS MAD AS THOSE OLD GEEZERS DANCING ALL NIGHT IN WIGAN...
CHILL THE FUCK OUT, PAUL! WE'RE NOT REUNITING THE BAND!
THAT WAS TWENTY-FIVE YEARS AGO, MAN! WE'VE ALL MOVED ON!
FUCK YOU! BASS PLAYERS ARE TEN A PENNY ANYWAY!
YOU'VE HAD QUITE THE WEEK, HAVEN'T YOU? COME TO BOBBY...
COME TO ME.
ST. PETER'S CHURCH

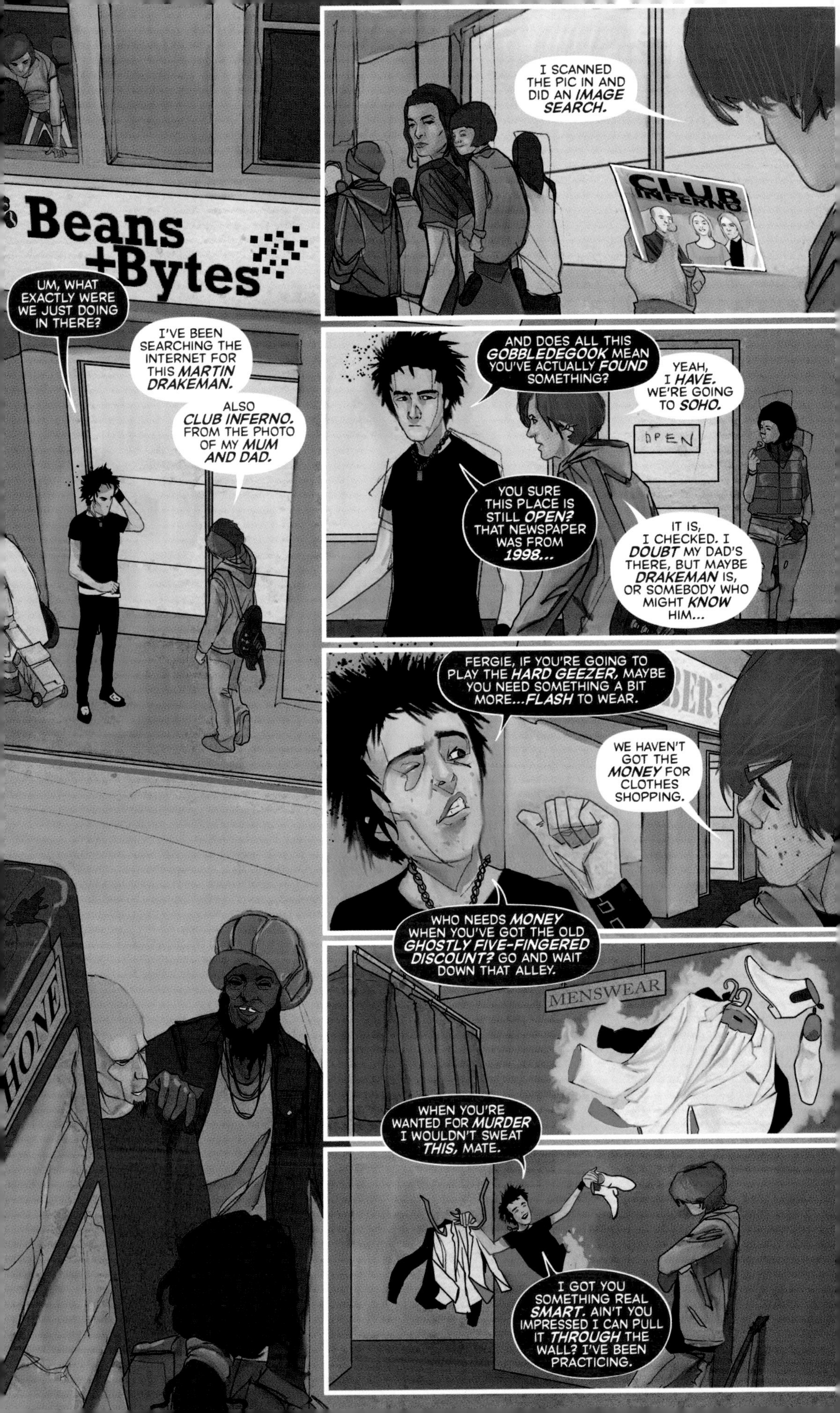

Beans +Bytes
UM, WHAT EXACTLY WERE WE JUST DOING IN THERE?
I'VE BEEN SEARCHING THE INTERNET FOR THIS *MARTIN DRAKEMAN.*
ALSO *CLUB INFERNO.* FROM THE PHOTO OF MY *MUM AND DAD.*
I SCANNED THE PIC IN AND DID AN *IMAGE SEARCH.*
CLUB INFERNO
AND DOES ALL THIS *GOBBLEDEGOOK* MEAN YOU'VE ACTUALLY *FOUND* SOMETHING?
YEAH, I *HAVE.* WE'RE GOING TO *SOHO.*
OPEN
YOU SURE THIS PLACE IS STILL *OPEN?* THAT NEWSPAPER WAS FROM *1998...*
IT IS, I CHECKED. I *DOUBT* MY DAD'S THERE, BUT MAYBE *DRAKEMAN* IS, OR SOMEBODY WHO MIGHT *KNOW* HIM...
FERGIE, IF YOU'RE GOING TO PLAY THE *HARD GEEZER,* MAYBE YOU NEED SOMETHING A BIT MORE...*FLASH* TO WEAR.
WE HAVEN'T GOT THE *MONEY* FOR CLOTHES SHOPPING.
WHO NEEDS *MONEY* WHEN YOU'VE GOT THE OLD *GHOSTLY FIVE-FINGERED DISCOUNT?* GO AND WAIT DOWN THAT ALLEY.
MENSWEAR
WHEN YOU'RE WANTED FOR *MURDER* I WOULDN'T SWEAT *THIS,* MATE.
I GOT YOU SOMETHING REAL *SMART.* AIN'T YOU IMPRESSED I CAN PULL IT *THROUGH* THE WALL? I'VE BEEN PRACTICING.

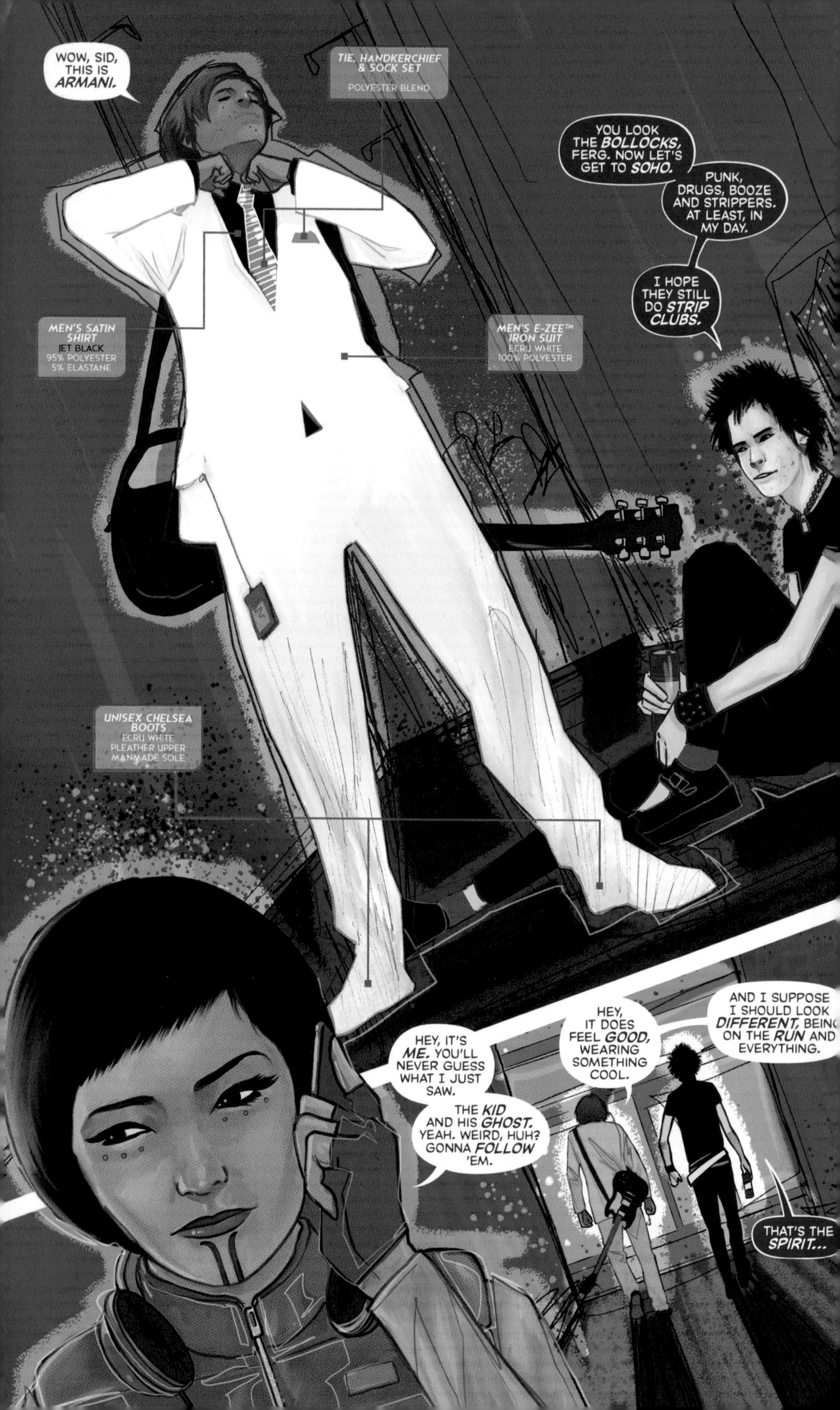
WOW, SID, THIS IS ARMANI.
TIE, HANDKERCHIEF & SOCK SET
POLYESTER BLEND
MEN'S SATIN SHIRT
JET BLACK
95% POLYESTER
5% ELASTANE
MEN'S E-ZEE™ IRON SUIT
ECRU WHITE
100% POLYESTER
UNISEX CHELSEA BOOTS
ECRU WHITE
PLEATHER UPPER
MANMADE SOLE
YOU LOOK THE BOLLOCKS, FERG. NOW LET'S GET TO SOHO.
PUNK, DRUGS, BOOZE AND STRIPPERS. AT LEAST, IN MY DAY.
I HOPE THEY STILL DO STRIP CLUBS.
HEY, IT'S ME. YOU'LL NEVER GUESS WHAT I JUST SAW.
THE KID AND HIS GHOST. YEAH. WEIRD, HUH? GONNA FOLLOW 'EM.
HEY, IT DOES FEEL GOOD, WEARING SOMETHING COOL.
AND I SUPPOSE I SHOULD LOOK DIFFERENT, BEIN ON THE RUN AND EVERYTHING.
THAT'S THE SPIRIT...

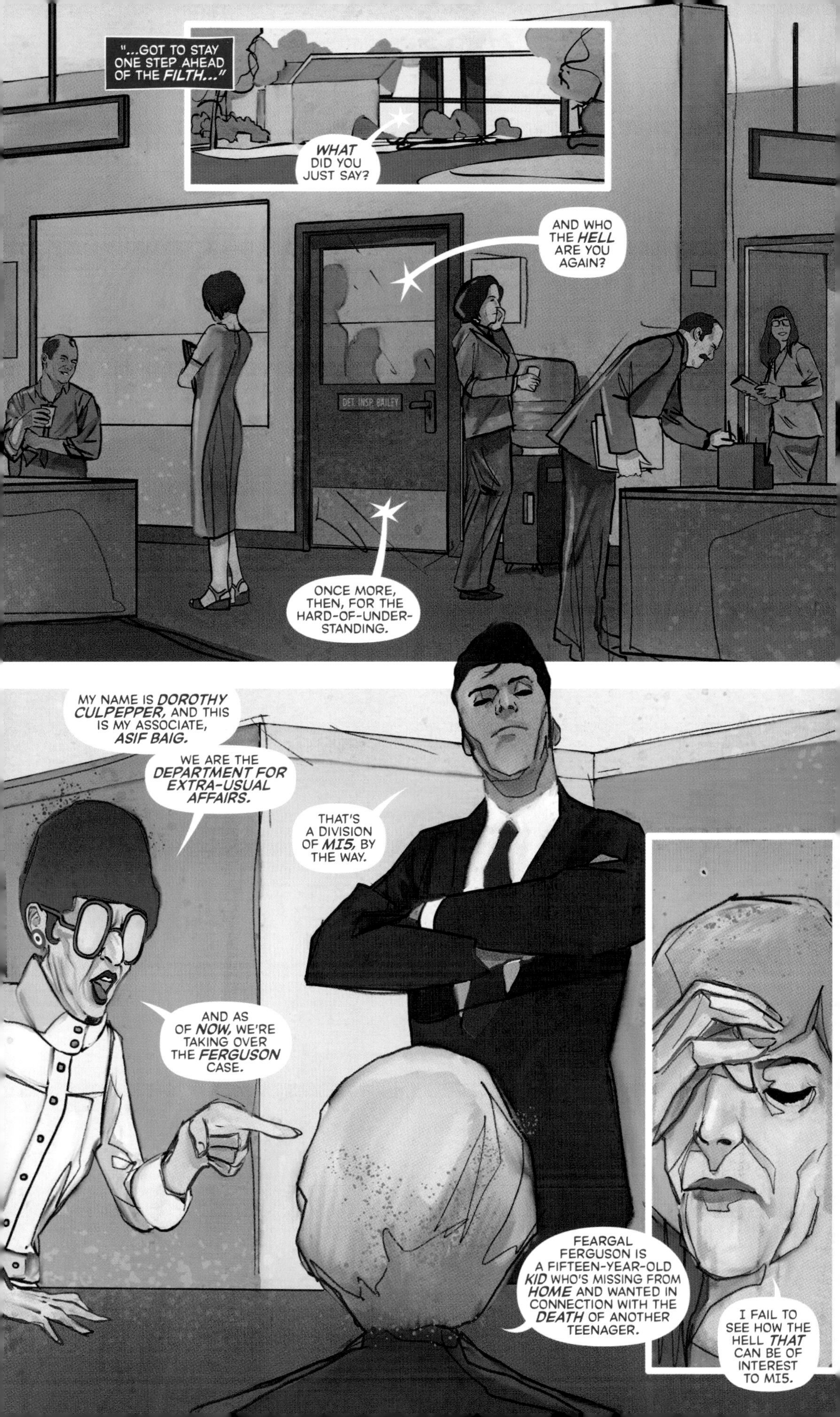
"...GOT TO STAY ONE STEP AHEAD OF THE FILTH..."
WHAT DID YOU JUST SAY?
AND WHO THE HELL ARE YOU AGAIN?
DET. INSP. BAILEY
ONCE MORE, THEN, FOR THE HARD-OF-UNDER-STANDING.
MY NAME IS DOROTHY CULPEPPER, AND THIS IS MY ASSOCIATE, ASIF BAIG.
WE ARE THE DEPARTMENT FOR EXTRA-USUAL AFFAIRS.
THAT'S A DIVISION OF MI5, BY THE WAY.
AND AS OF NOW, WE'RE TAKING OVER THE FERGUSON CASE.
FEARGAL FERGUSON IS A FIFTEEN-YEAR-OLD KID WHO'S MISSING FROM HOME AND WANTED IN CONNECTION WITH THE DEATH OF ANOTHER TEENAGER.
I FAIL TO SEE HOW THE HELL THAT CAN BE OF INTEREST TO MI5.

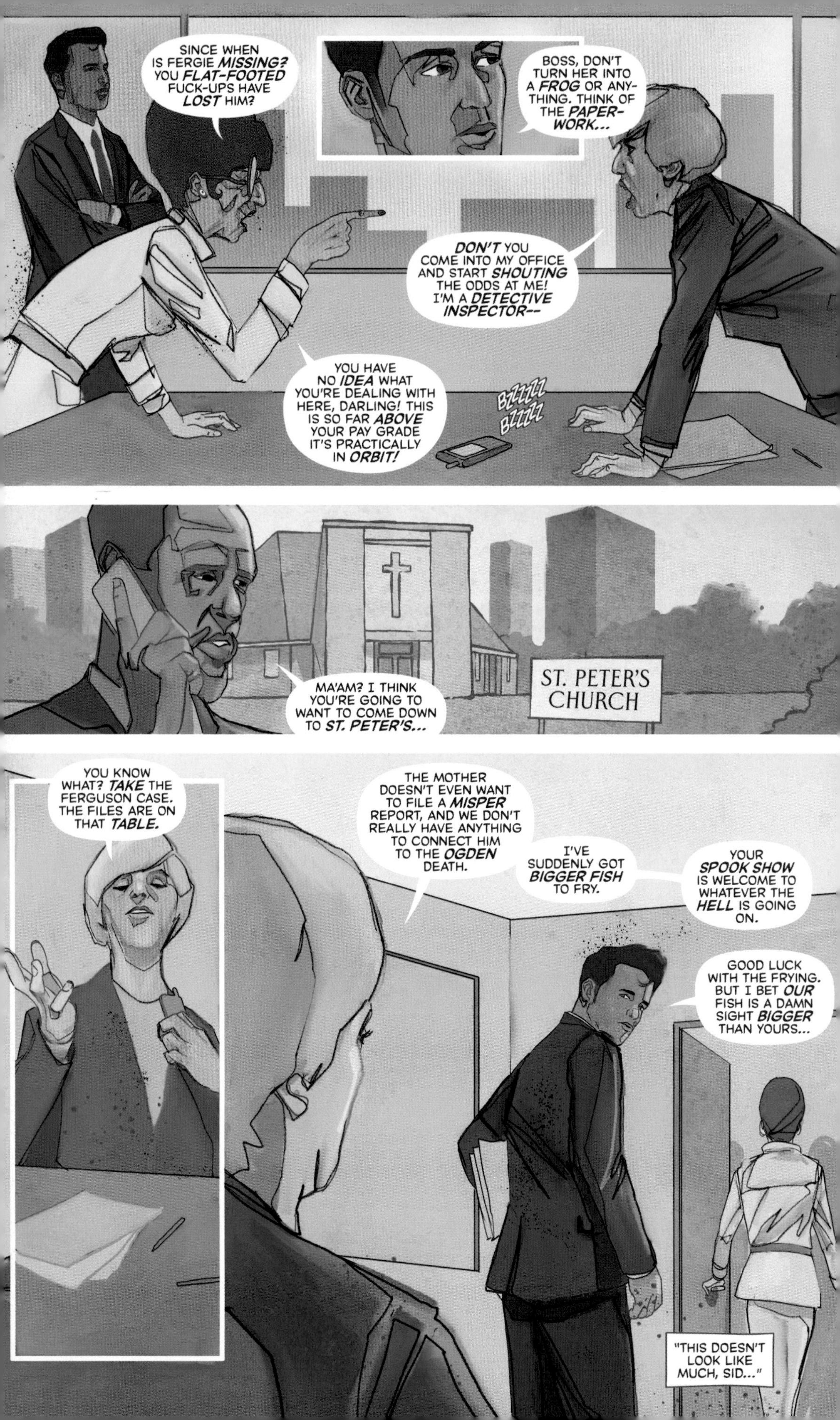
SINCE WHEN IS FERGIE MISSING? YOU FLAT-FOOTED FUCK-UPS HAVE LOST HIM?
BOSS, DON'T TURN HER INTO A FROG OR ANY-THING. THINK OF THE PAPER-WORK...
DON'T YOU COME INTO MY OFFICE AND START SHOUTING THE ODDS AT ME! I'M A DETECTIVE INSPECTOR--
YOU HAVE NO IDEA WHAT YOU'RE DEALING WITH HERE, DARLING! THIS IS SO FAR ABOVE YOUR PAY GRADE IT'S PRACTICALLY IN ORBIT!
BZZZZZZ BZZZZZ
MA'AM? I THINK YOU'RE GOING TO WANT TO COME DOWN TO ST. PETER'S...
ST. PETER'S CHURCH
YOU KNOW WHAT? TAKE THE FERGUSON CASE. THE FILES ARE ON THAT TABLE.
THE MOTHER DOESN'T EVEN WANT TO FILE A MISPER REPORT, AND WE DON'T REALLY HAVE ANYTHING TO CONNECT HIM TO THE OGDEN DEATH.
I'VE SUDDENLY GOT BIGGER FISH TO FRY.
YOUR SPOOK SHOW IS WELCOME TO WHATEVER THE HELL IS GOING ON.
GOOD LUCK WITH THE FRYING. BUT I BET OUR FISH IS A DAMN SIGHT BIGGER THAN YOURS...
"THIS DOESN'T LOOK LIKE MUCH, SID..."

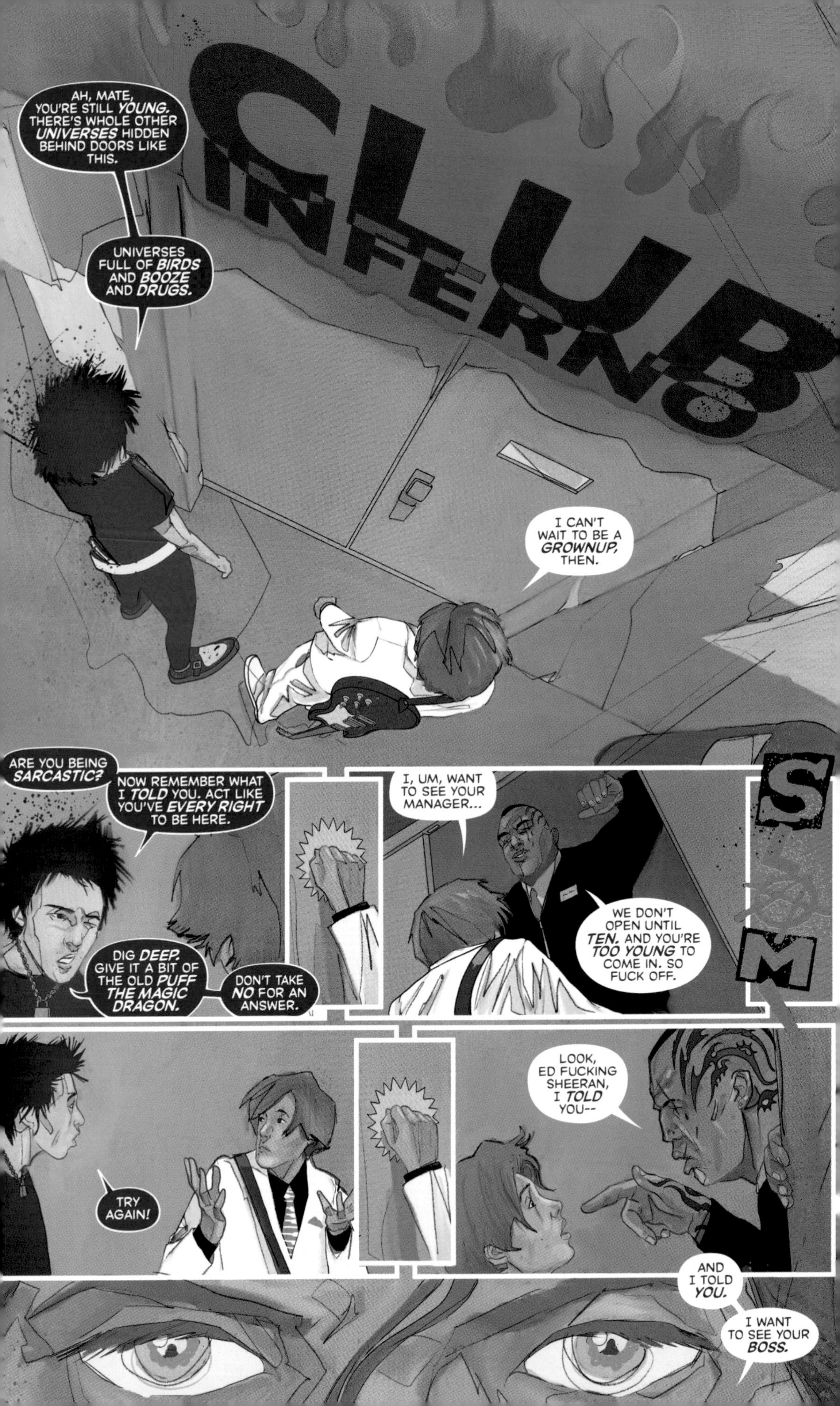

AH, MATE, YOU'RE STILL *YOUNG.* THERE'S WHOLE OTHER *UNIVERSES* HIDDEN BEHIND DOORS LIKE THIS.
UNIVERSES FULL OF *BIRDS* AND *BOOZE* AND *DRUGS.*
CLUB INFERNO
I CAN'T WAIT TO BE A *GROWNUP,* THEN.
ARE YOU BEING *SARCASTIC?*
NOW REMEMBER WHAT I *TOLD* YOU. ACT LIKE YOU'VE *EVERY RIGHT* TO BE HERE.
DIG *DEEP.* GIVE IT A BIT OF THE OLD *PUFF THE MAGIC DRAGON.*
DON'T TAKE *NO* FOR AN ANSWER.
I, UM, WANT TO SEE YOUR MANAGER...
WE DON'T OPEN UNTIL *TEN.* AND YOU'RE *TOO YOUNG* TO COME IN. SO FUCK OFF.
S
M
TRY AGAIN!
LOOK, ED FUCKING SHEERAN, I *TOLD* YOU--
AND I TOLD *YOU.*
I WANT TO SEE YOUR *BOSS.*

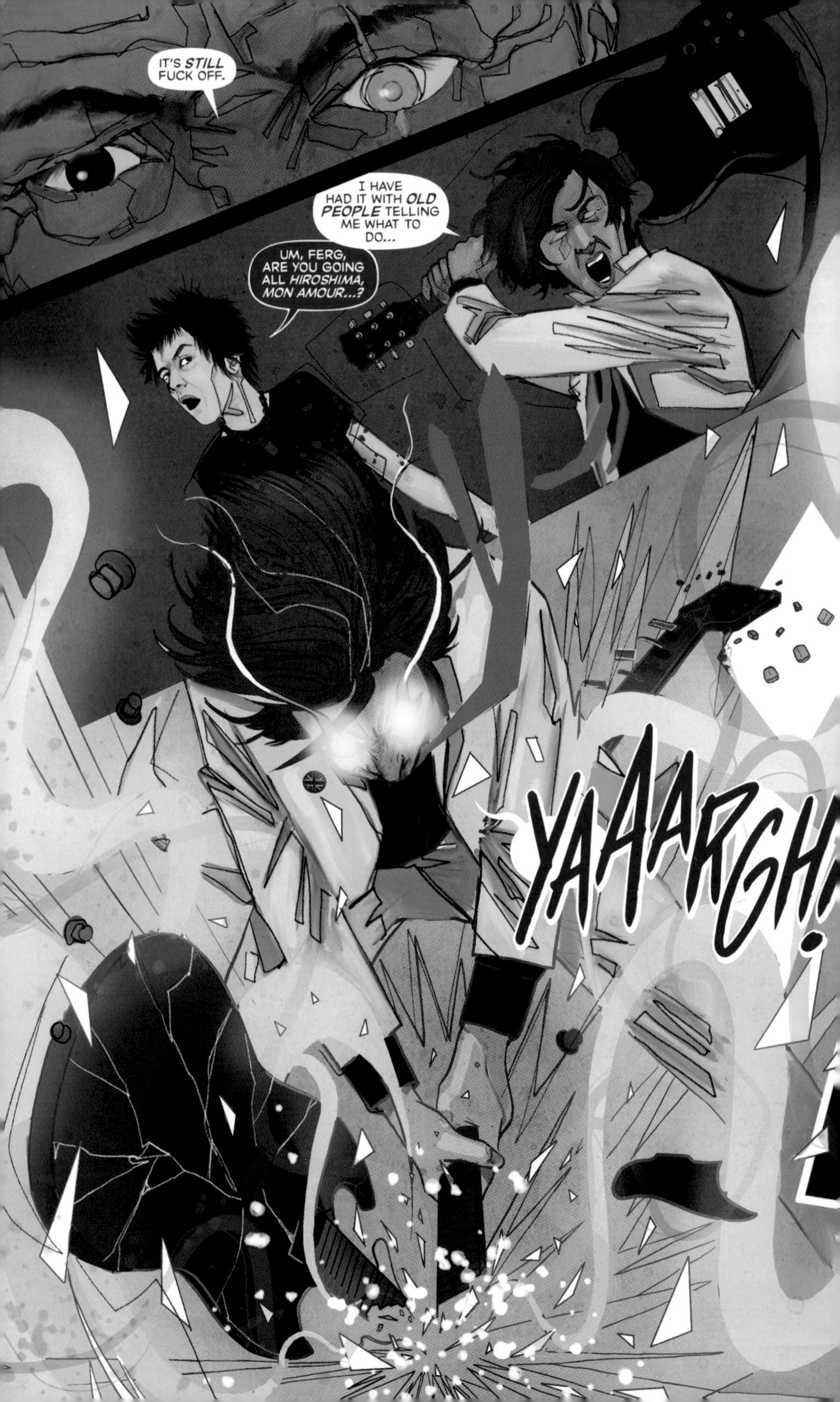
IT'S *STILL* FUCK OFF.
I HAVE HAD IT WITH *OLD PEOPLE* TELLING ME WHAT TO DO...
UM, FERG, ARE YOU GOING ALL *HIROSHIMA, MON AMOUR...?*
YAAARGH!

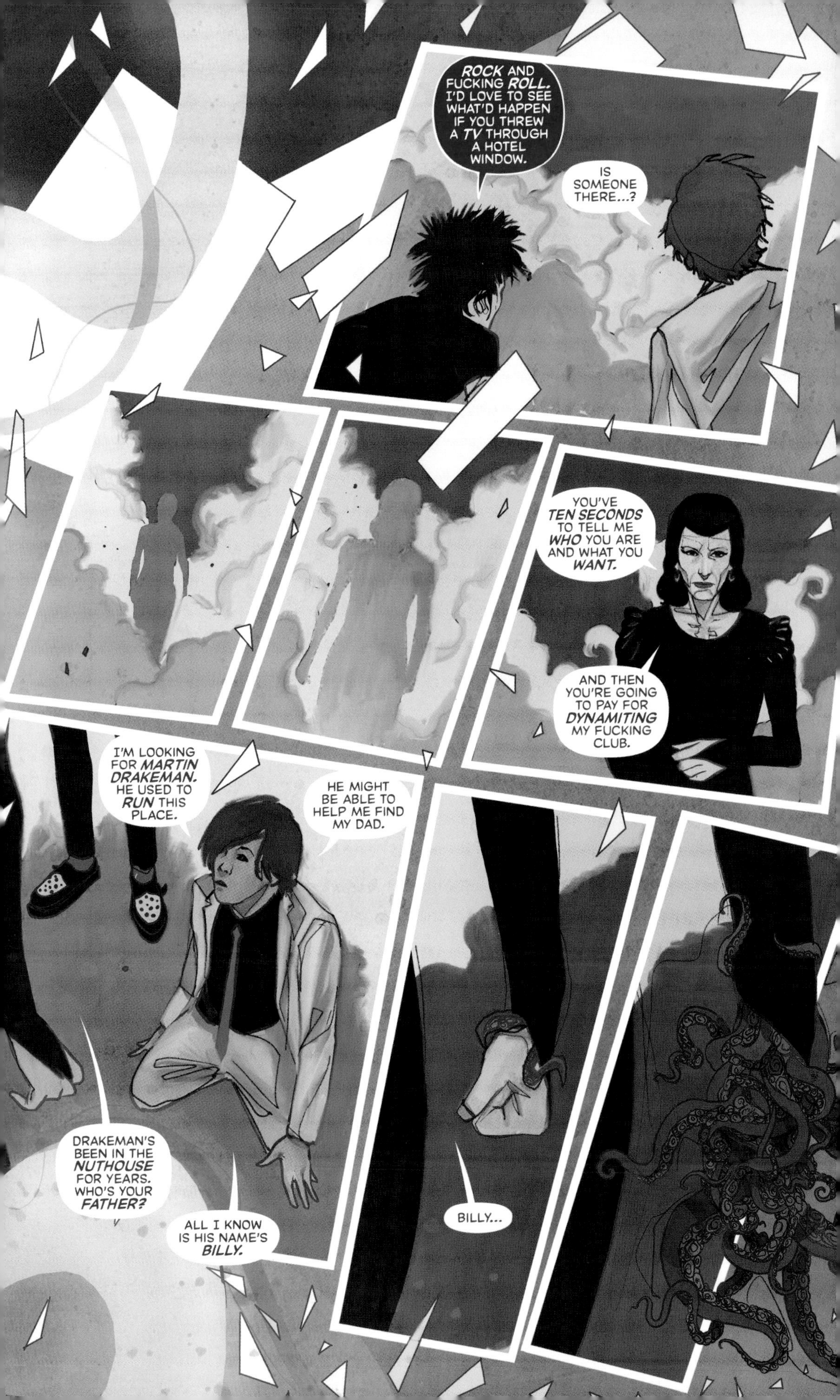

ROCK AND FUCKING ROLL. I'D LOVE TO SEE WHAT'D HAPPEN IF YOU THREW A TV THROUGH A HOTEL WINDOW.
IS SOMEONE THERE...?
YOU'VE TEN SECONDS TO TELL ME WHO YOU ARE AND WHAT YOU WANT.
AND THEN YOU'RE GOING TO PAY FOR DYNAMITING MY FUCKING CLUB.
I'M LOOKING FOR MARTIN DRAKEMAN. HE USED TO RUN THIS PLACE.
HE MIGHT BE ABLE TO HELP ME FIND MY DAD.
DRAKEMAN'S BEEN IN THE NUTHOUSE FOR YEARS. WHO'S YOUR FATHER?
ALL I KNOW IS HIS NAME'S BILLY.
BILLY...

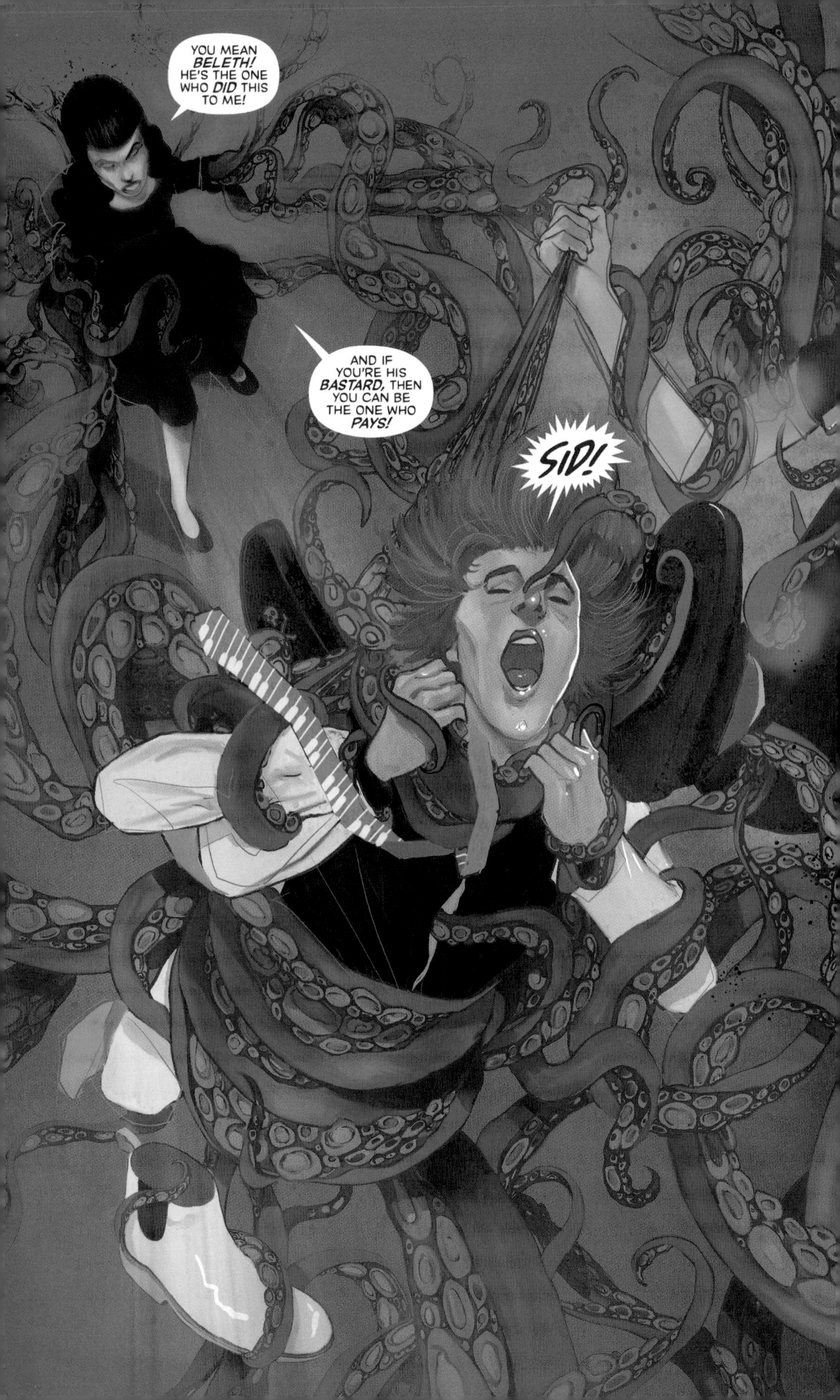
YOU MEAN *BELETH!* HE'S THE ONE WHO *DID* THIS TO ME!
AND IF YOU'RE HIS *BASTARD,* THEN YOU CAN BE THE ONE WHO *PAYS!*
SID!

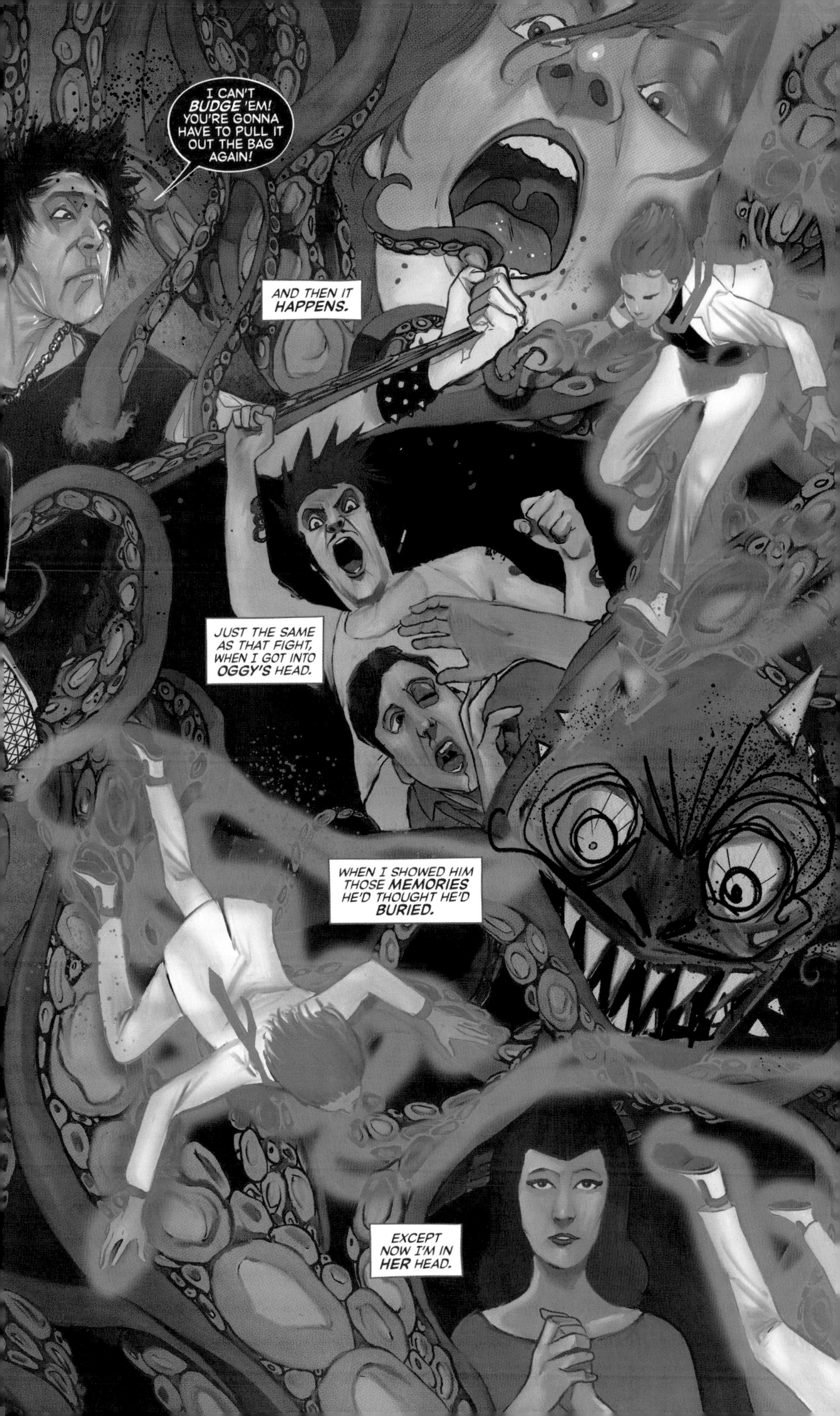
I CAN'T BUDGE 'EM! YOU'RE GONNA HAVE TO PULL IT OUT THE BAG AGAIN!
AND THEN IT HAPPENS.
JUST THE SAME AS THAT FIGHT, WHEN I GOT INTO OGGY'S HEAD.
WHEN I SHOWED HIM THOSE MEMORIES HE'D THOUGHT HE'D BURIED.
EXCEPT NOW I'M IN HER HEAD.

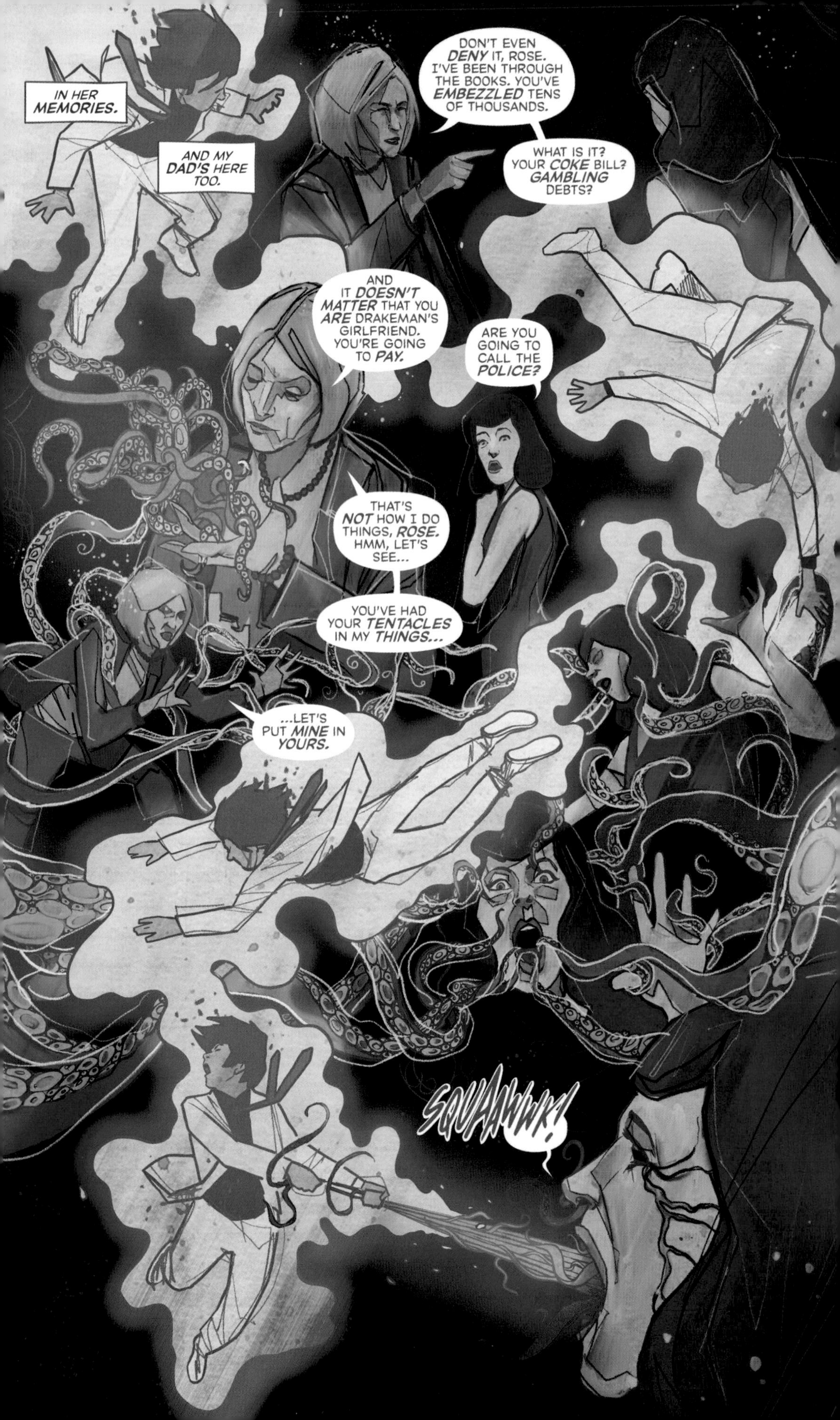

IN HER MEMORIES.
AND MY DAD'S HERE TOO.
DON'T EVEN DENY IT, ROSE. I'VE BEEN THROUGH THE BOOKS. YOU'VE EMBEZZLED TENS OF THOUSANDS.
WHAT IS IT? YOUR COKE BILL? GAMBLING DEBTS?
AND IT DOESN'T MATTER THAT YOU ARE DRAKEMAN'S GIRLFRIEND. YOU'RE GOING TO PAY.
ARE YOU GOING TO CALL THE POLICE?
THAT'S NOT HOW I DO THINGS, ROSE. HMM, LET'S SEE...
YOU'VE HAD YOUR TENTACLES IN MY THINGS...
...LET'S PUT MINE IN YOURS.
SQUAAWWK!

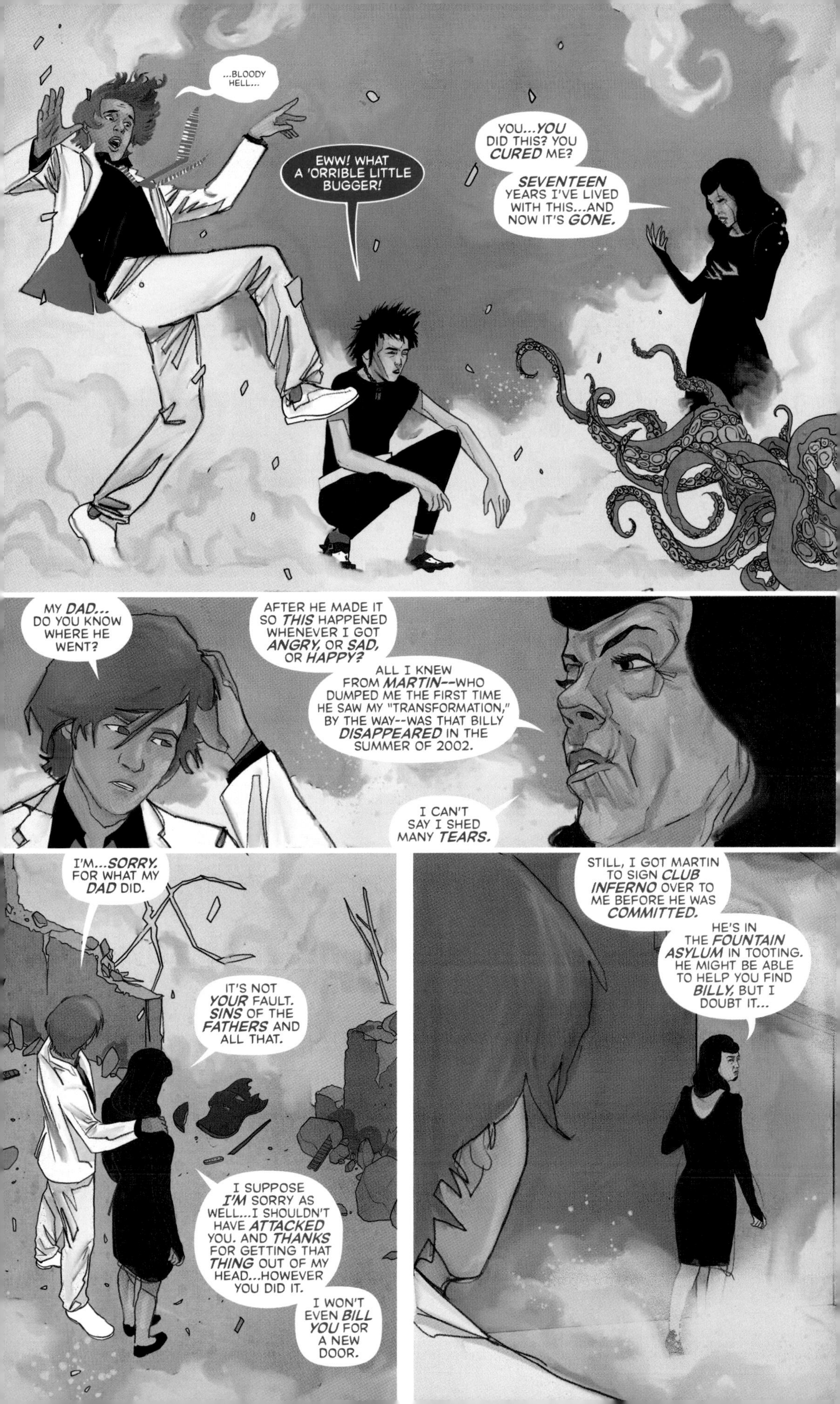
...BLOODY HELL...
EWW! WHAT A 'ORRIBLE LITTLE BUGGER!
YOU...YOU DID THIS? YOU CURED ME?
SEVENTEEN YEARS I'VE LIVED WITH THIS...AND NOW IT'S GONE.
MY DAD... DO YOU KNOW WHERE HE WENT?
AFTER HE MADE IT SO THIS HAPPENED WHENEVER I GOT ANGRY, OR SAD, OR HAPPY?
ALL I KNEW FROM MARTIN--WHO DUMPED ME THE FIRST TIME HE SAW MY "TRANSFORMATION," BY THE WAY--WAS THAT BILLY DISAPPEARED IN THE SUMMER OF 2002.
I CAN'T SAY I SHED MANY TEARS.
I'M...SORRY. FOR WHAT MY DAD DID.
IT'S NOT YOUR FAULT. SINS OF THE FATHERS AND ALL THAT.
I SUPPOSE I'M SORRY AS WELL...I SHOULDN'T HAVE ATTACKED YOU. AND THANKS FOR GETTING THAT THING OUT OF MY HEAD...HOWEVER YOU DID IT.
I WON'T EVEN BILL YOU FOR A NEW DOOR.
STILL, I GOT MARTIN TO SIGN CLUB INFERNO OVER TO ME BEFORE HE WAS COMMITTED.
HE'S IN THE FOUNTAIN ASYLUM IN TOOTING. HE MIGHT BE ABLE TO HELP YOU FIND BILLY, BUT I DOUBT IT...

I WAS *RIGHT.* HE *IS* ONE OF US.

AND THE GHOST IS *MORE* THAN THAT. *MUCH* MORE.

YEAH. THERE'S DEFINITELY A *MUSIC THING* GOING ON HERE.

"PUNK, THOUGH. DID ANYTHING EVER SO *SPECTACULARLY* FAIL TO LIVE UP TO ITS PROMISE?"

...IT WAS LIKE, I DON'T KNOW, AN *EXPLOSION* GOING OFF IN MY *HEAD.*

AND ALL I COULD THINK ABOUT WAS *MUSIC*... I WAS IN A *BAND,* SEE. IN THE NINETIES. *LUNE STREET RIOTZ.*

"MAN, OLD PEOPLE *PISS ME OFF.*"

THAT'S QUITE A NEW... *LOOK* YOU'VE GOT.

I MAINLY DID IT TO SCREW WITH MY *DAD.* HE'S SUCH A *DICK.* I'VE LEFT HOME.

"THEY HAD THEIR *CHANCE.* THEY *BLEW* IT. AND SCREWED UP EVERYTHING FOR *US* IN THE PROCESS."

"BUT IT'S TIME FOR US TO TAKE *CONTROL.* TO LET GO OF THE *PAST.* TO WIPE IT ALL AWAY AND START OVER."

FERGIE'S IN MY *HEAD* AND I DON'T KNOW IF IT'S SOMETHING WEIRD *HE'S* DONE OR IF I...

...IF I REALLY HAVE THESE *FEELINGS...*

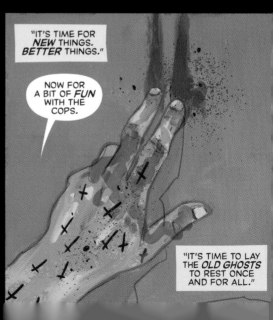

"IT'S TIME FOR *NEW* THINGS. *BETTER* THINGS."

NOW FOR A BIT OF *FUN* WITH THE COPS.

"IT'S TIME TO LAY THE *OLD GHOSTS* TO REST ONCE AND FOR ALL."

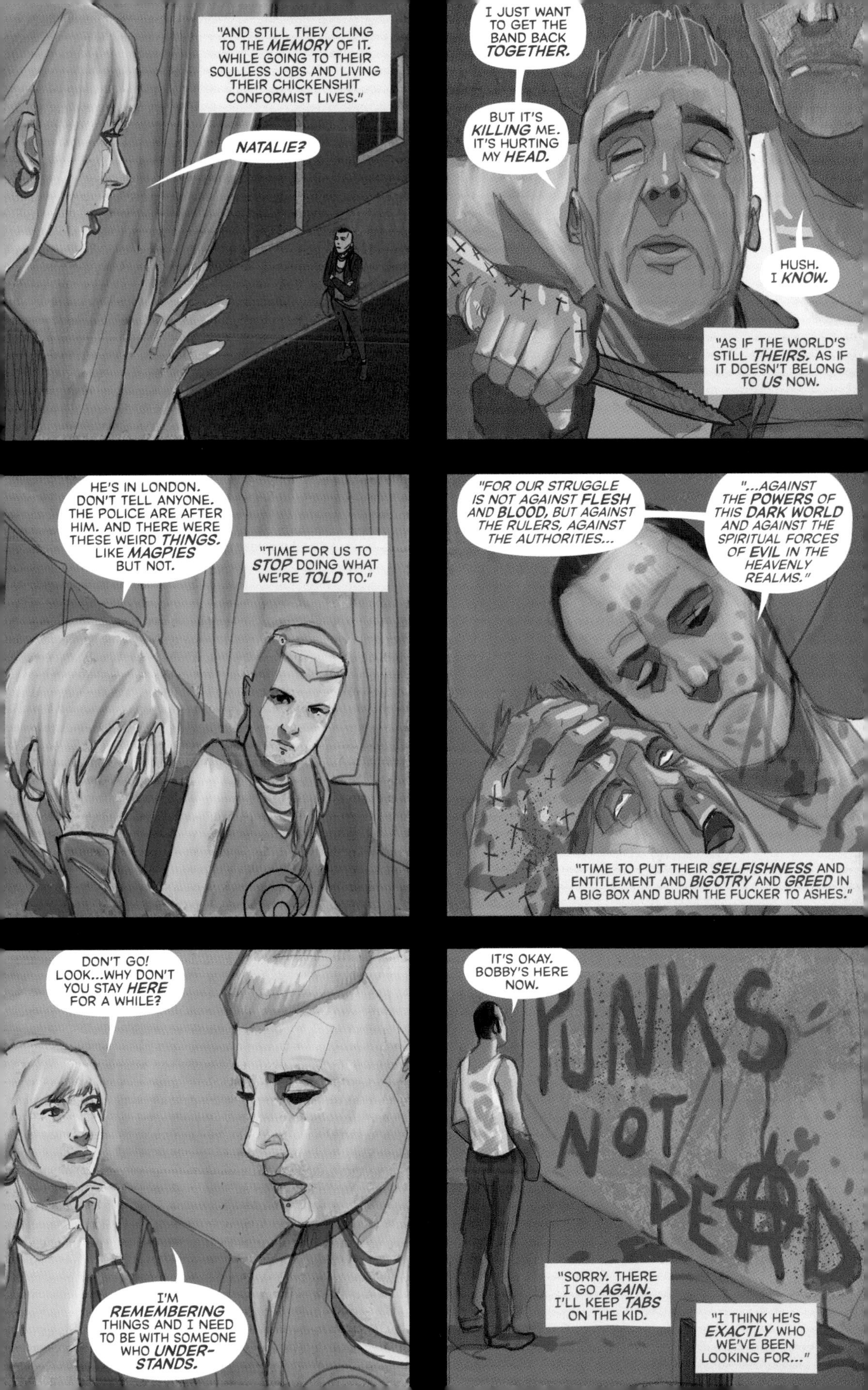
"AND STILL THEY CLING TO THE MEMORY OF IT. WHILE GOING TO THEIR SOULLESS JOBS AND LIVING THEIR CHICKENSHIT CONFORMIST LIVES."
NATALIE?
I JUST WANT TO GET THE BAND BACK TOGETHER.
BUT IT'S KILLING ME. IT'S HURTING MY HEAD.
HUSH. I KNOW.
"AS IF THE WORLD'S STILL THEIRS. AS IF IT DOESN'T BELONG TO US NOW.
HE'S IN LONDON. DON'T TELL ANYONE. THE POLICE ARE AFTER HIM. AND THERE WERE THESE WEIRD THINGS. LIKE MAGPIES BUT NOT.
"TIME FOR US TO STOP DOING WHAT WE'RE TOLD TO."
"FOR OUR STRUGGLE IS NOT AGAINST FLESH AND BLOOD, BUT AGAINST THE RULERS, AGAINST THE AUTHORITIES...
"...AGAINST THE POWERS OF THIS DARK WORLD AND AGAINST THE SPIRITUAL FORCES OF EVIL IN THE HEAVENLY REALMS."
"TIME TO PUT THEIR SELFISHNESS AND ENTITLEMENT AND BIGOTRY AND GREED IN A BIG BOX AND BURN THE FUCKER TO ASHES."
DON'T GO! LOOK...WHY DON'T YOU STAY HERE FOR A WHILE?
I'M REMEMBERING THINGS AND I NEED TO BE WITH SOMEONE WHO UNDER-STANDS.
IT'S OKAY. BOBBY'S HERE NOW.
PUNKS NOT DEAD
"SORRY. THERE I GO AGAIN. I'LL KEEP TABS ON THE KID.
"I THINK HE'S EXACTLY WHO WE'VE BEEN LOOKING FOR..."

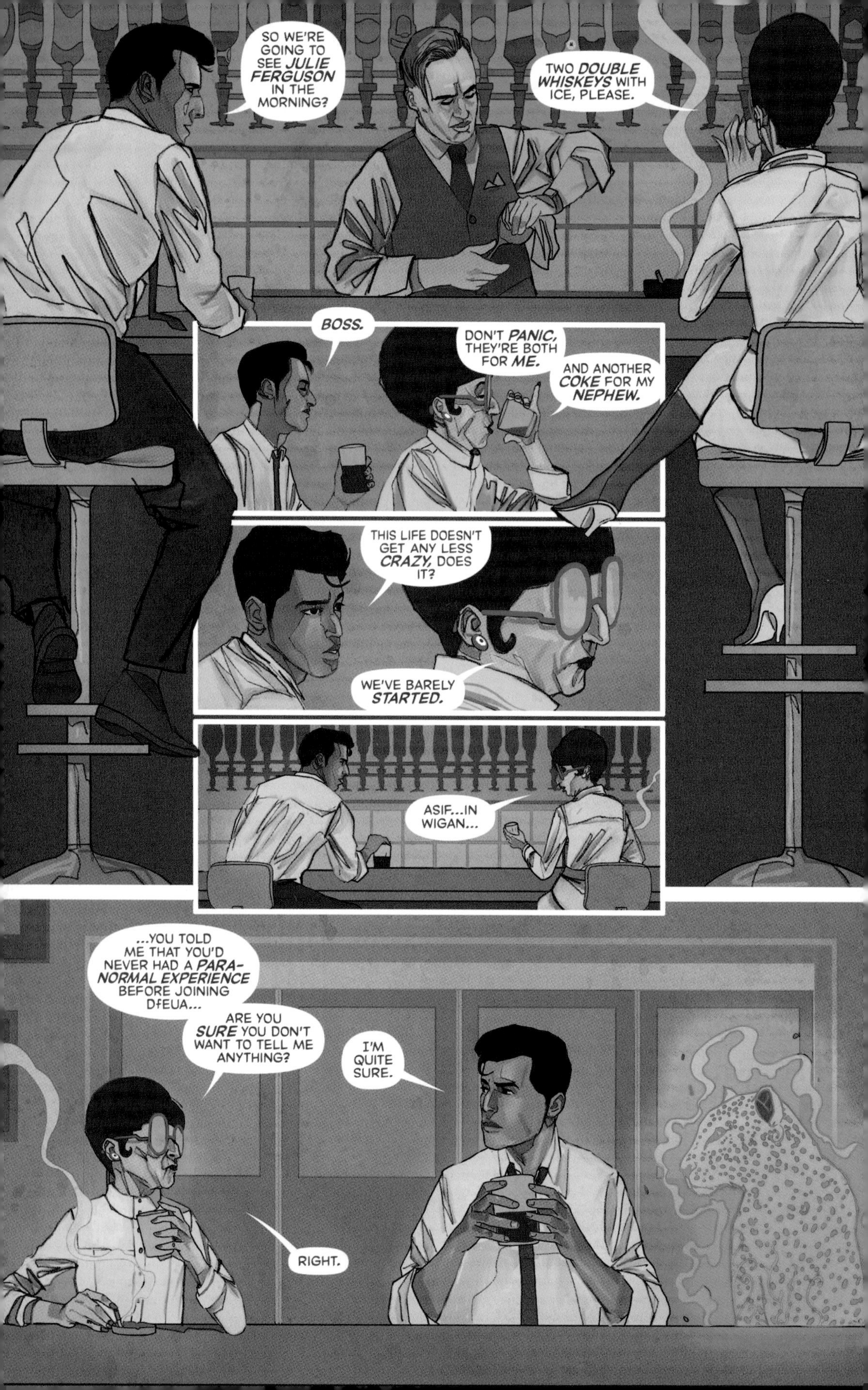
SO WE'RE GOING TO SEE JULIE FERGUSON IN THE MORNING?
TWO DOUBLE WHISKEYS WITH ICE, PLEASE.
BOSS.
DON'T PANIC, THEY'RE BOTH FOR ME.
AND ANOTHER COKE FOR MY NEPHEW.
THIS LIFE DOESN'T GET ANY LESS CRAZY, DOES IT?
WE'VE BARELY STARTED.
ASIF...IN WIGAN...
...YOU TOLD ME THAT YOU'D NEVER HAD A PARA-NORMAL EXPERIENCE BEFORE JOINING DfEUA...
ARE YOU SURE YOU DON'T WANT TO TELL ME ANYTHING?
I'M QUITE SURE.
RIGHT.

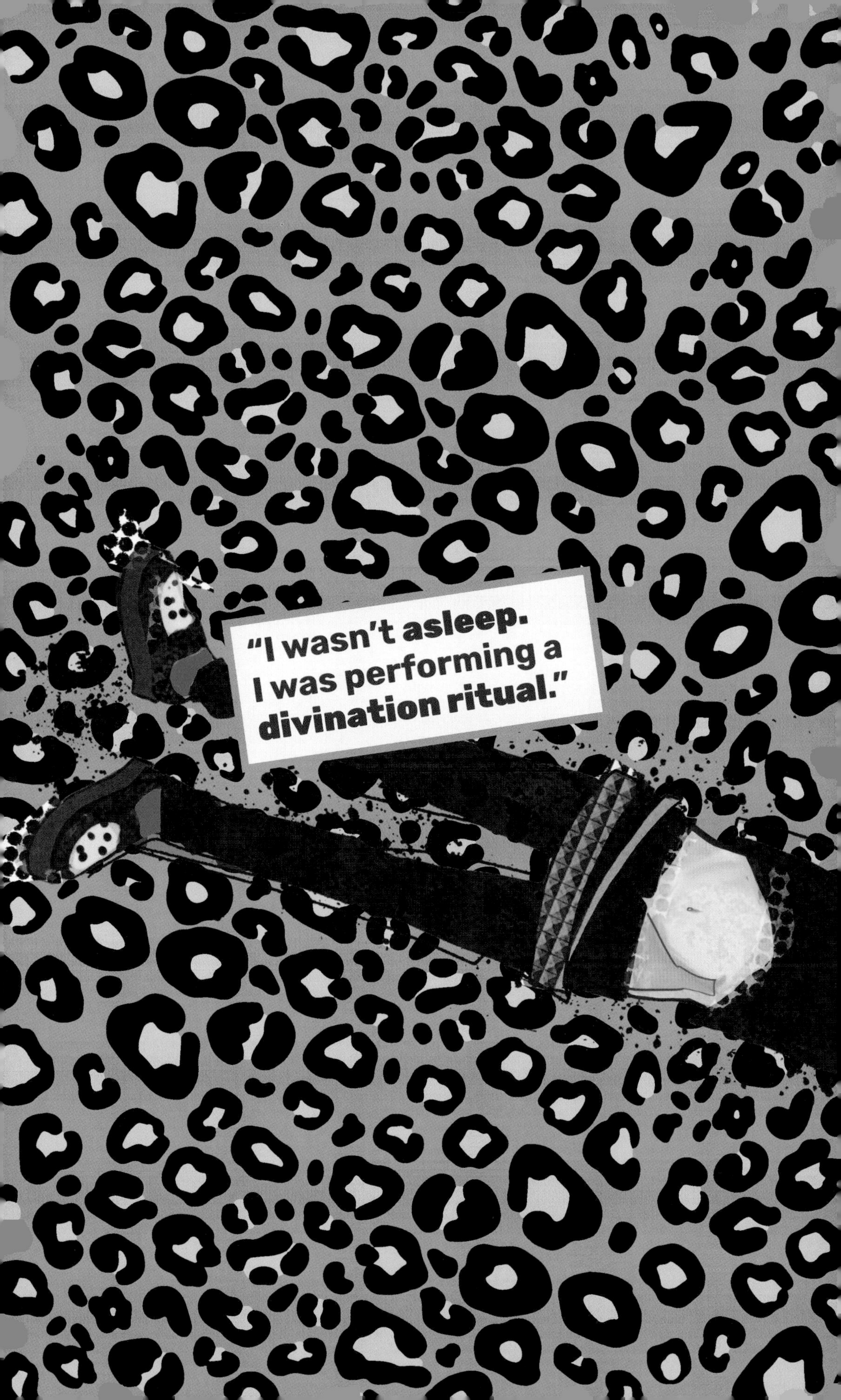
"I wasn't asleep.
I was performing a
divination ritual."

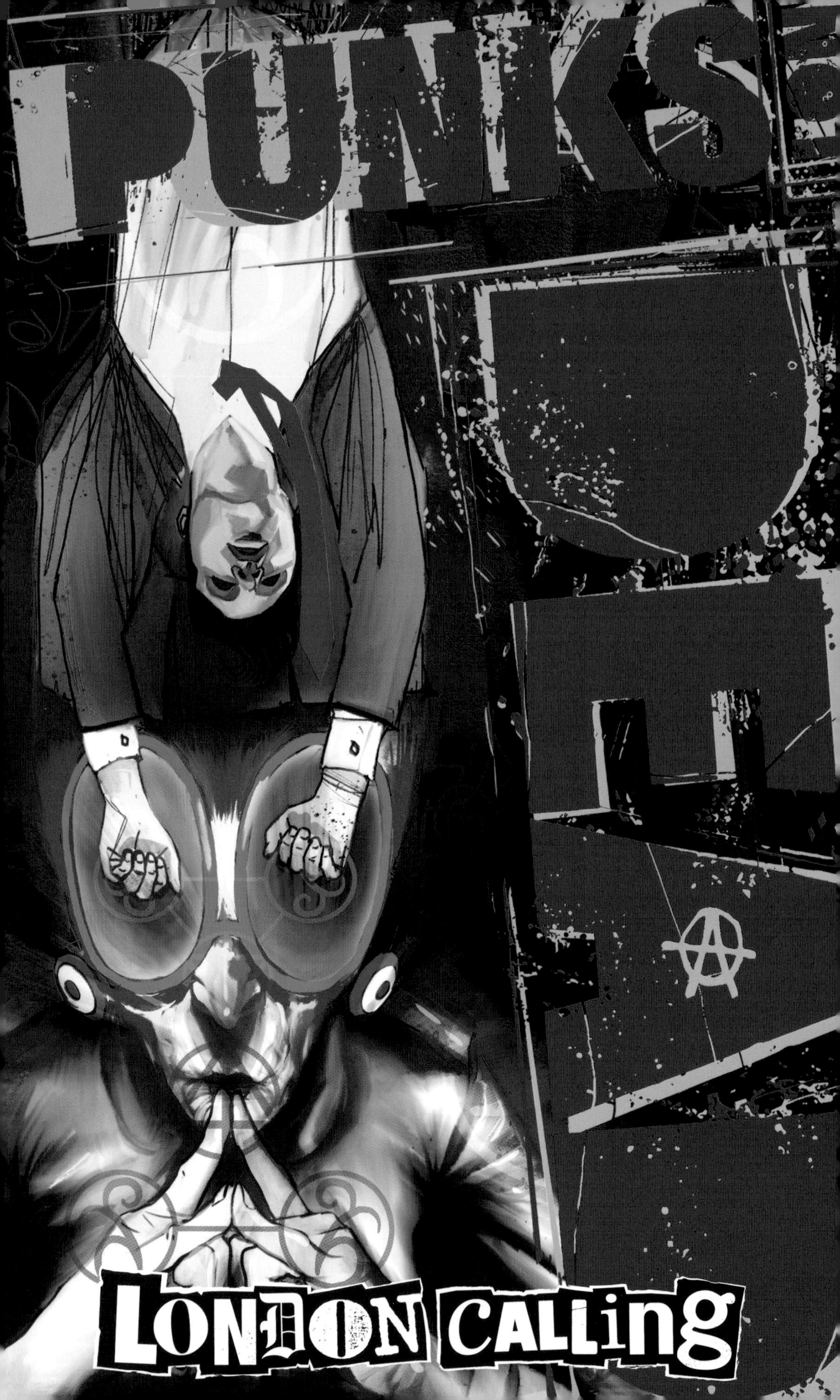
PUNKS
LONDON CALLING

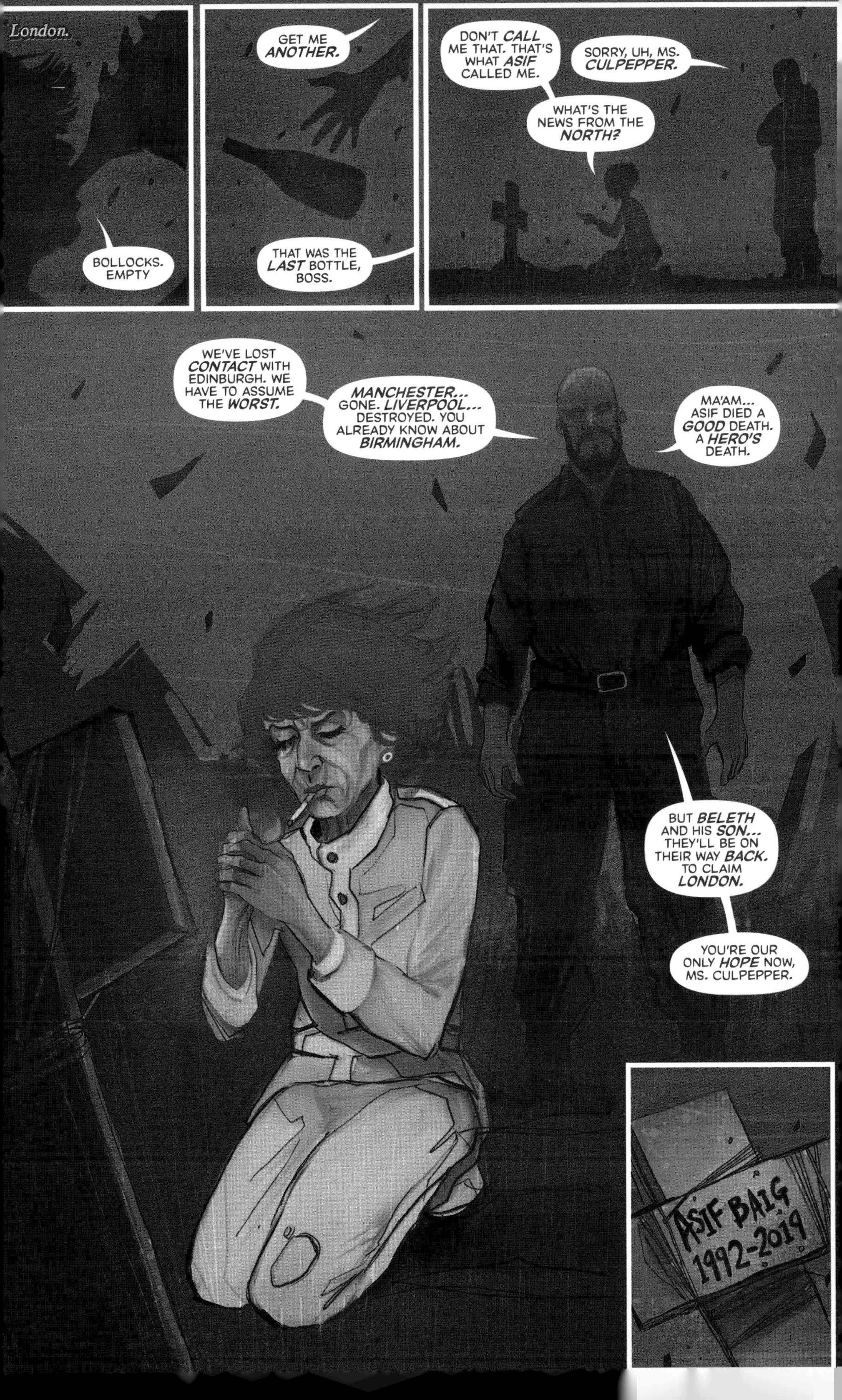

London.
BOLLOCKS. EMPTY
GET ME ANOTHER.
THAT WAS THE LAST BOTTLE, BOSS.
DON'T CALL ME THAT. THAT'S WHAT ASIF CALLED ME.
SORRY, UH, MS. CULPEPPER.
WHAT'S THE NEWS FROM THE NORTH?
WE'VE LOST CONTACT WITH EDINBURGH. WE HAVE TO ASSUME THE WORST.
MANCHESTER... GONE. LIVERPOOL... DESTROYED. YOU ALREADY KNOW ABOUT BIRMINGHAM.
MA'AM... ASIF DIED A GOOD DEATH. A HERO'S DEATH.
BUT BELETH AND HIS SON... THEY'LL BE ON THEIR WAY BACK. TO CLAIM LONDON.
YOU'RE OUR ONLY HOPE NOW, MS. CULPEPPER.
ASIF BAIG 1992-2019

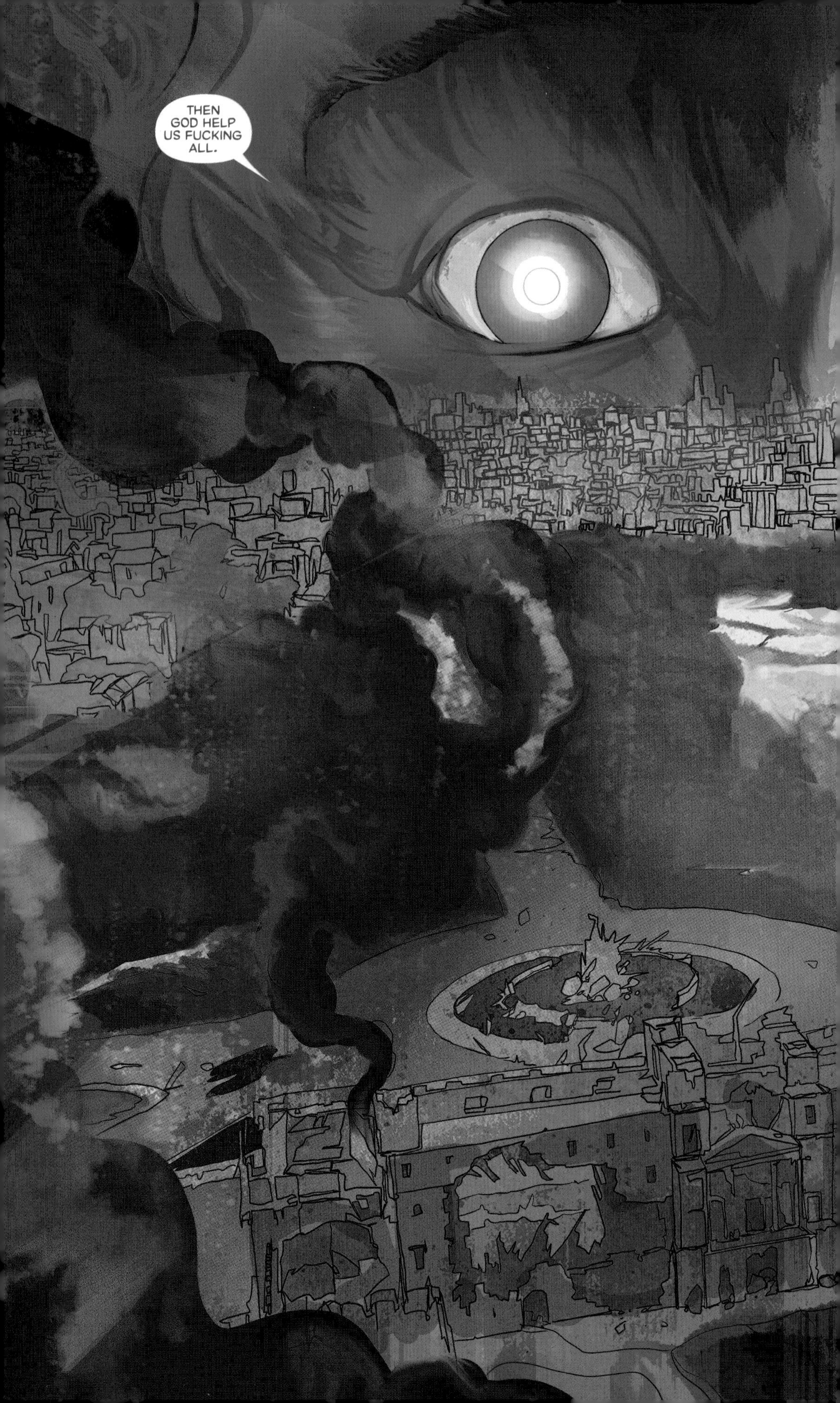
THEN GOD HELP US FUCKING ALL.

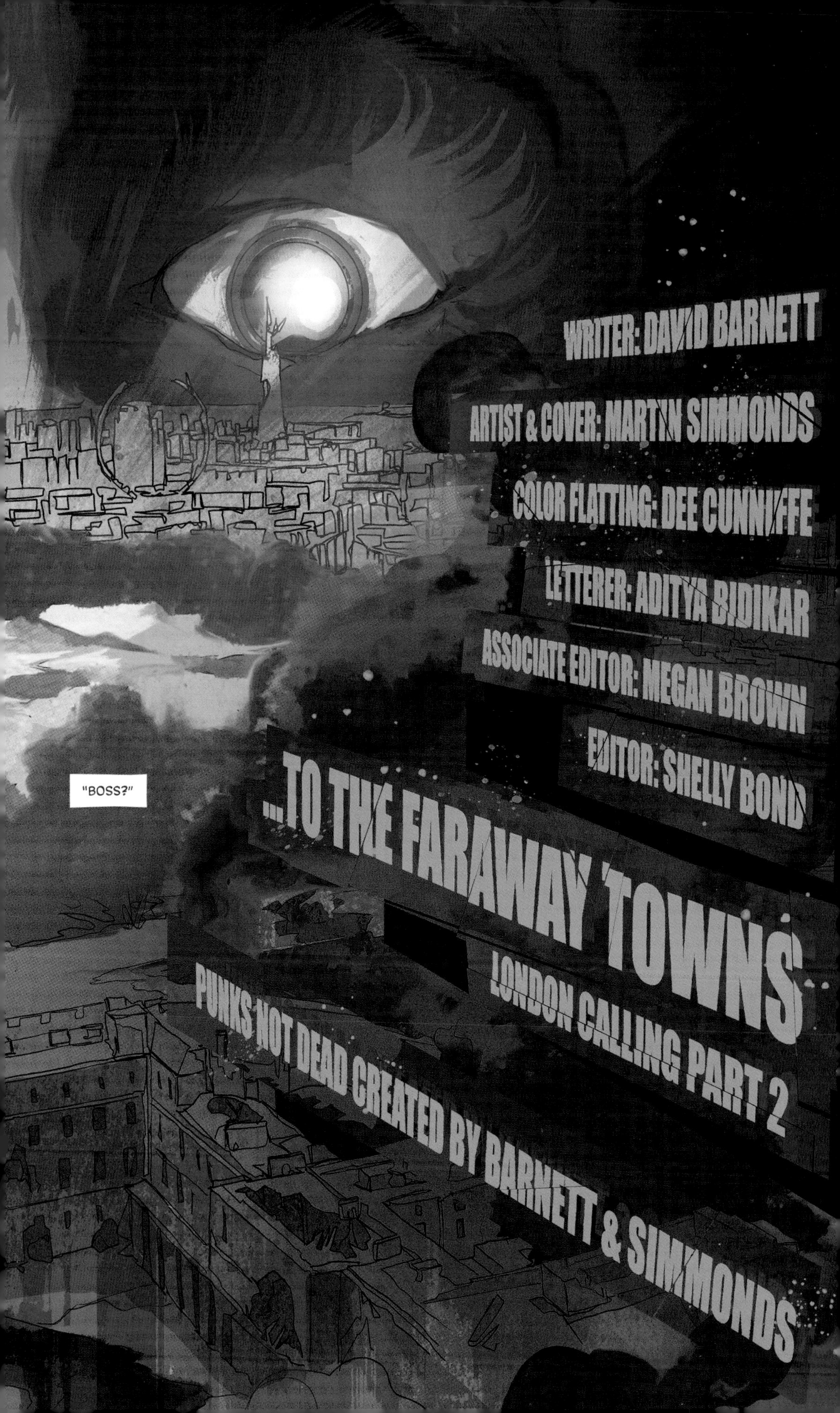
WRITER: DAVID BARNETT
ARTIST & COVER: MARTIN SIMMONDS
COLOR FLATTING: DEE CUNNIFFE
LETTERER: ADITYA BIDIKAR
ASSOCIATE EDITOR: MEGAN BROWN
EDITOR: SHELLY BOND
"BOSS?"
...TO THE FARAWAY TOWNS
LONDON CALLING PART 2
PUNKS NOT DEAD CREATED BY BARNETT & SIMMONDS

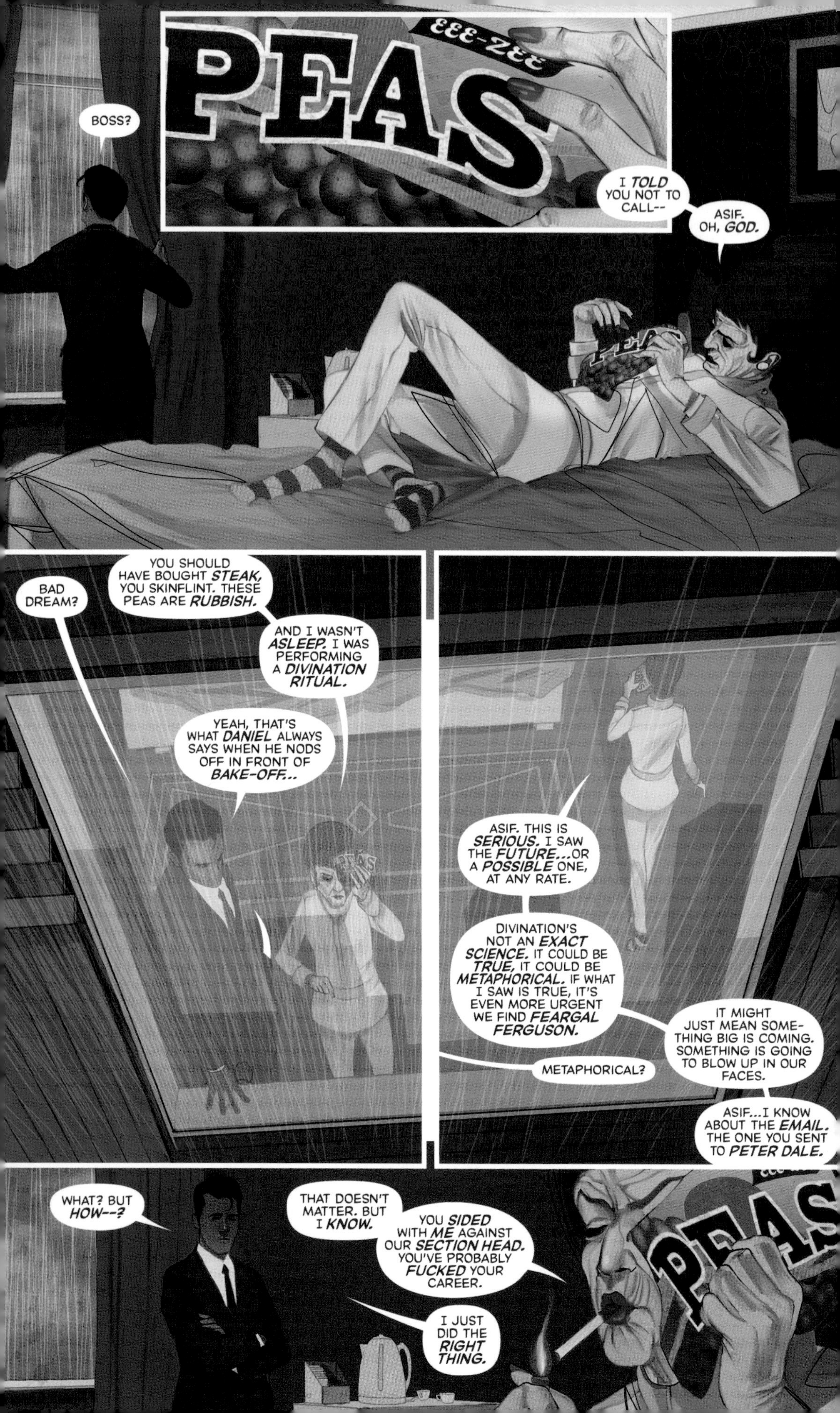
PEAS
332-333
BOSS?
I TOLD YOU NOT TO CALL--
ASIF. OH, GOD.
BAD DREAM?
YOU SHOULD HAVE BOUGHT STEAK, YOU SKINFLINT. THESE PEAS ARE RUBBISH.
AND I WASN'T ASLEEP. I WAS PERFORMING A DIVINATION RITUAL.
YEAH, THAT'S WHAT DANIEL ALWAYS SAYS WHEN HE NODS OFF IN FRONT OF BAKE-OFF...
ASIF. THIS IS SERIOUS. I SAW THE FUTURE...OR A POSSIBLE ONE, AT ANY RATE.
DIVINATION'S NOT AN EXACT SCIENCE. IT COULD BE TRUE, IT COULD BE METAPHORICAL. IF WHAT I SAW IS TRUE, IT'S EVEN MORE URGENT WE FIND FEARGAL FERGUSON.
METAPHORICAL?
IT MIGHT JUST MEAN SOME-THING BIG IS COMING. SOMETHING IS GOING TO BLOW UP IN OUR FACES.
ASIF...I KNOW ABOUT THE EMAIL. THE ONE YOU SENT TO PETER DALE.
WHAT? BUT HOW--?
THAT DOESN'T MATTER. BUT I KNOW.
YOU SIDED WITH ME AGAINST OUR SECTION HEAD. YOU'VE PROBABLY FUCKED YOUR CAREER.
I JUST DID THE RIGHT THING.
PEAS

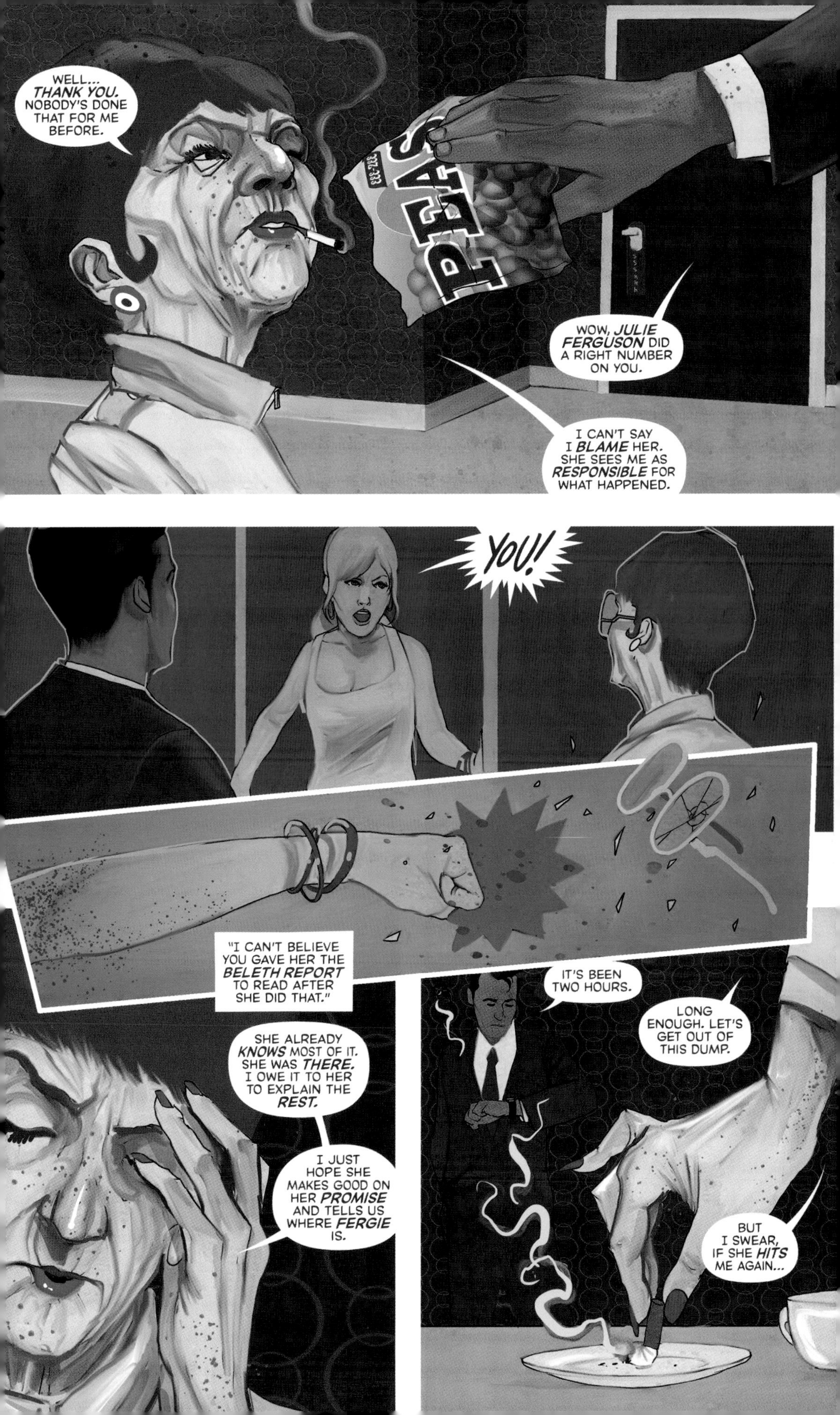

WELL... THANK YOU. NOBODY'S DONE THAT FOR ME BEFORE.
PEAS
WOW, JULIE FERGUSON DID A RIGHT NUMBER ON YOU.
I CAN'T SAY I BLAME HER. SHE SEES ME AS RESPONSIBLE FOR WHAT HAPPENED.
YOU!
"I CAN'T BELIEVE YOU GAVE HER THE BELETH REPORT TO READ AFTER SHE DID THAT."
SHE ALREADY KNOWS MOST OF IT. SHE WAS THERE. I OWE IT TO HER TO EXPLAIN THE REST.
I JUST HOPE SHE MAKES GOOD ON HER PROMISE AND TELLS US WHERE FERGIE IS.
IT'S BEEN TWO HOURS.
LONG ENOUGH. LET'S GET OUT OF THIS DUMP.
BUT I SWEAR, IF SHE HITS ME AGAIN...

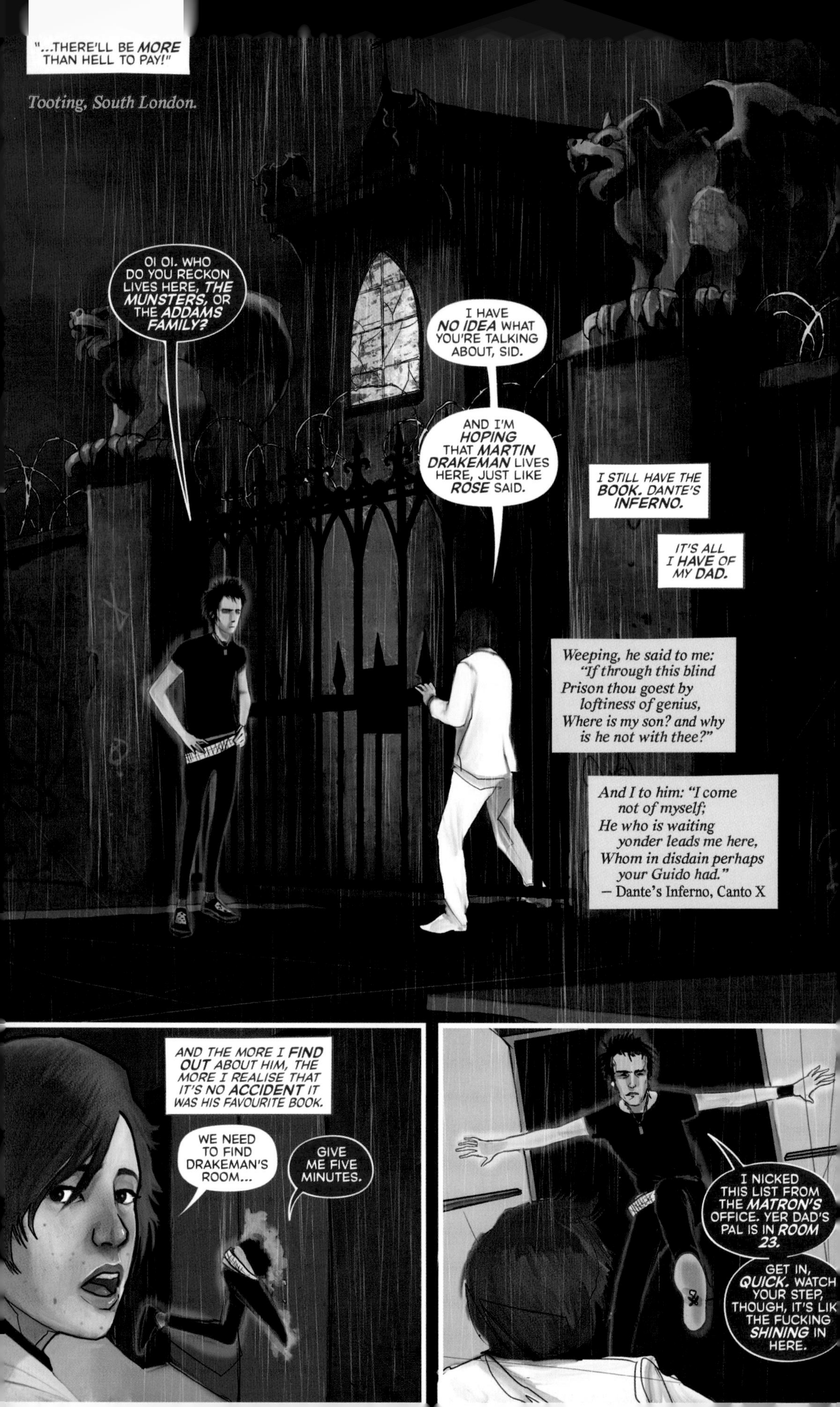
"...THERE'LL BE MORE THAN HELL TO PAY!"
Tooting, South London.
OI OI. WHO DO YOU RECKON LIVES HERE, THE MUNSTERS, OR THE ADDAMS FAMILY?
I HAVE NO IDEA WHAT YOU'RE TALKING ABOUT, SID.
AND I'M HOPING THAT MARTIN DRAKEMAN LIVES HERE, JUST LIKE ROSE SAID.
I STILL HAVE THE BOOK. DANTE'S INFERNO.
IT'S ALL I HAVE OF MY DAD.
Weeping, he said to me: "If through this blind Prison thou goest by loftiness of genius, Where is my son? and why is he not with thee?"
And I to him: "I come not of myself; He who is waiting yonder leads me here, Whom in disdain perhaps your Guido had."
– Dante's Inferno, Canto X
AND THE MORE I FIND OUT ABOUT HIM, THE MORE I REALISE THAT IT'S NO ACCIDENT IT WAS HIS FAVOURITE BOOK.
WE NEED TO FIND DRAKEMAN'S ROOM...
GIVE ME FIVE MINUTES.
I NICKED THIS LIST FROM THE MATRON'S OFFICE. YER DAD'S PAL IS IN ROOM 23.
GET IN, QUICK. WATCH YOUR STEP, THOUGH, IT'S LIK THE FUCKING SHINING IN HERE.

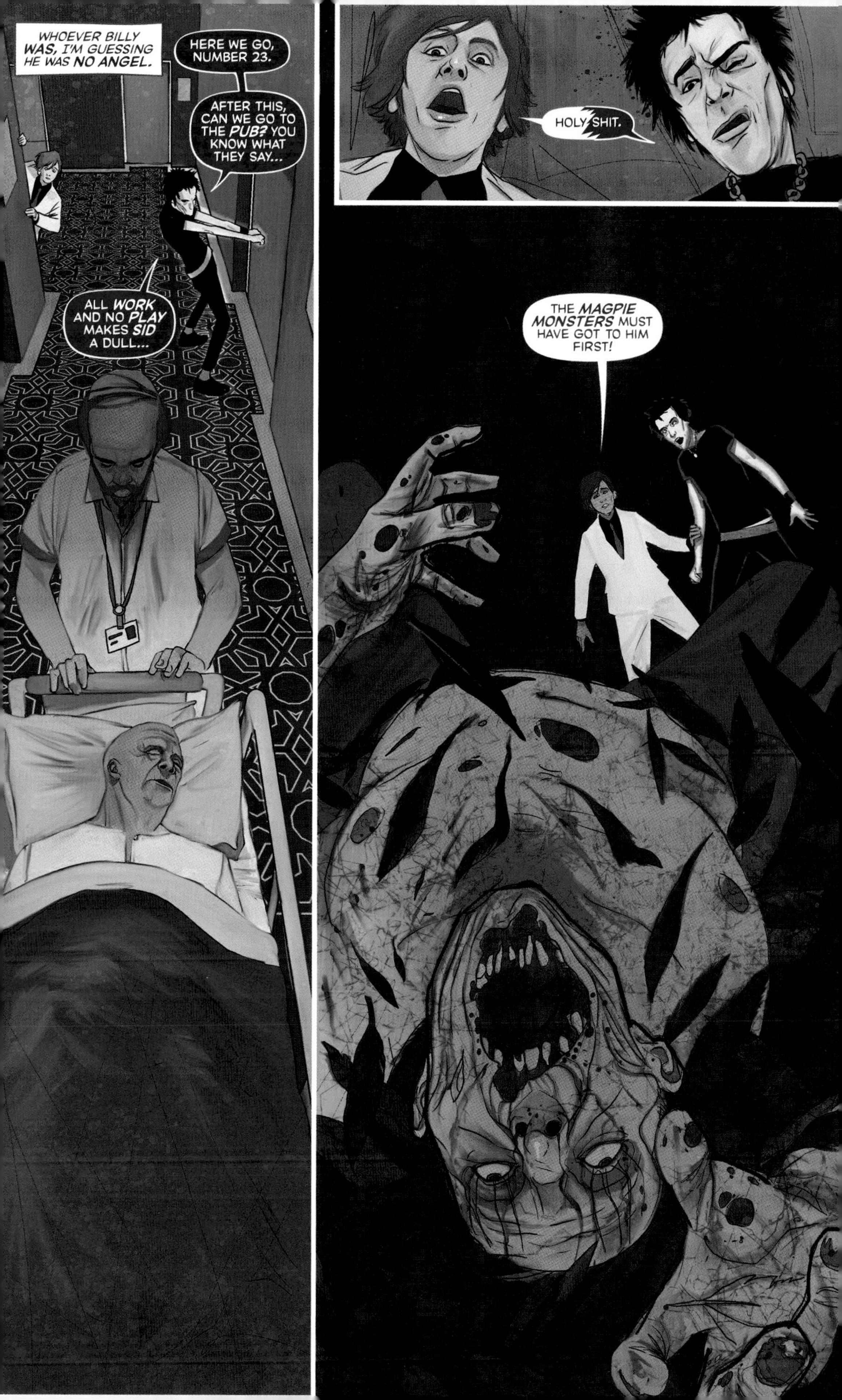
WHOEVER BILLY WAS, I'M GUESSING HE WAS NO ANGEL.
HERE WE GO, NUMBER 23.
AFTER THIS, CAN WE GO TO THE PUB? YOU KNOW WHAT THEY SAY...
ALL WORK AND NO PLAY MAKES SID A DULL...
HOLY SHIT.
THE MAGPIE MONSTERS MUST HAVE GOT TO HIM FIRST!

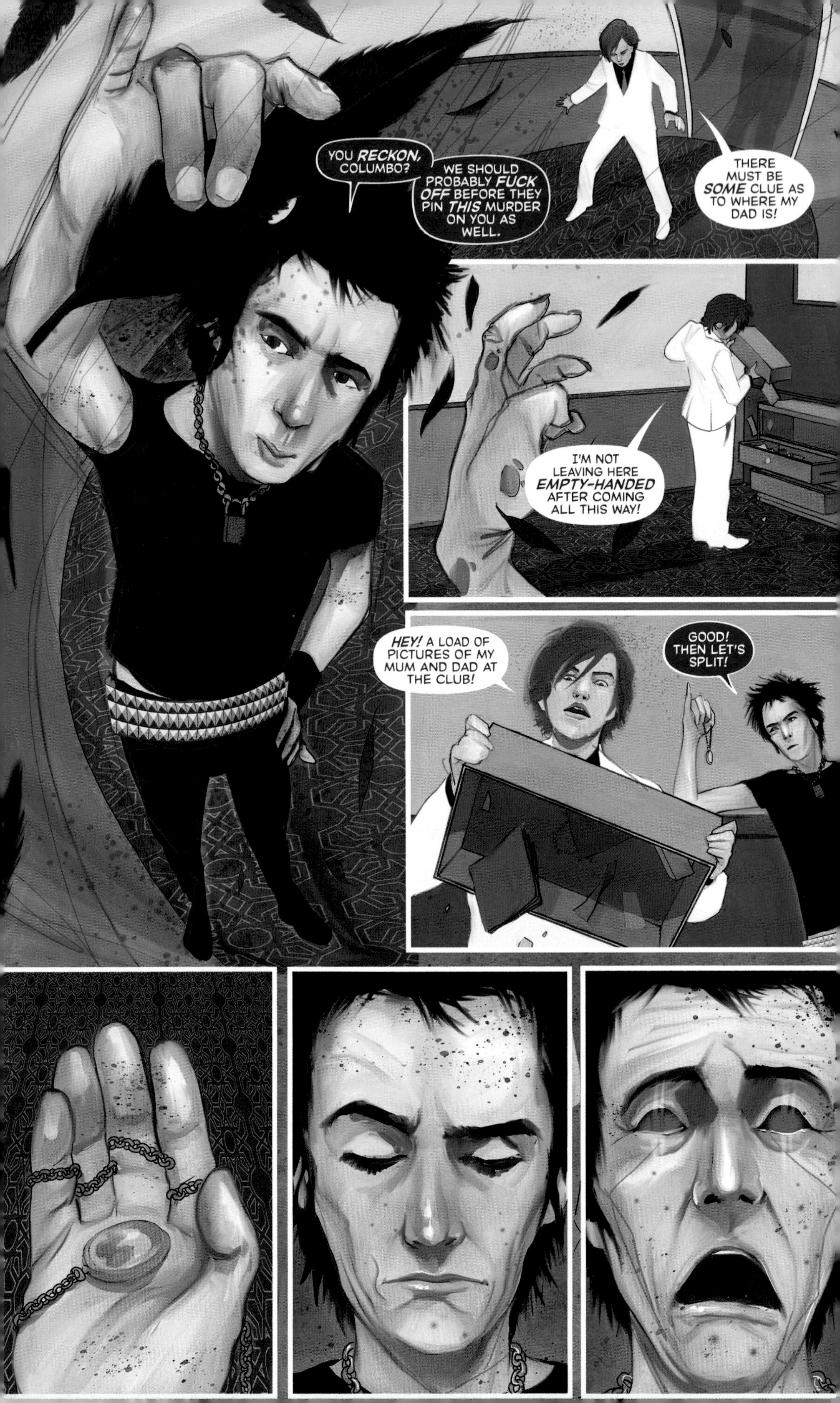

YOU RECKON, COLUMBO?
WE SHOULD PROBABLY FUCK OFF BEFORE THEY PIN THIS MURDER ON YOU AS WELL.
THERE MUST BE SOME CLUE AS TO WHERE MY DAD IS!
I'M NOT LEAVING HERE EMPTY-HANDED AFTER COMING ALL THIS WAY!
HEY! A LOAD OF PICTURES OF MY MUM AND DAD AT THE CLUB!
GOOD! THEN LET'S SPLIT!

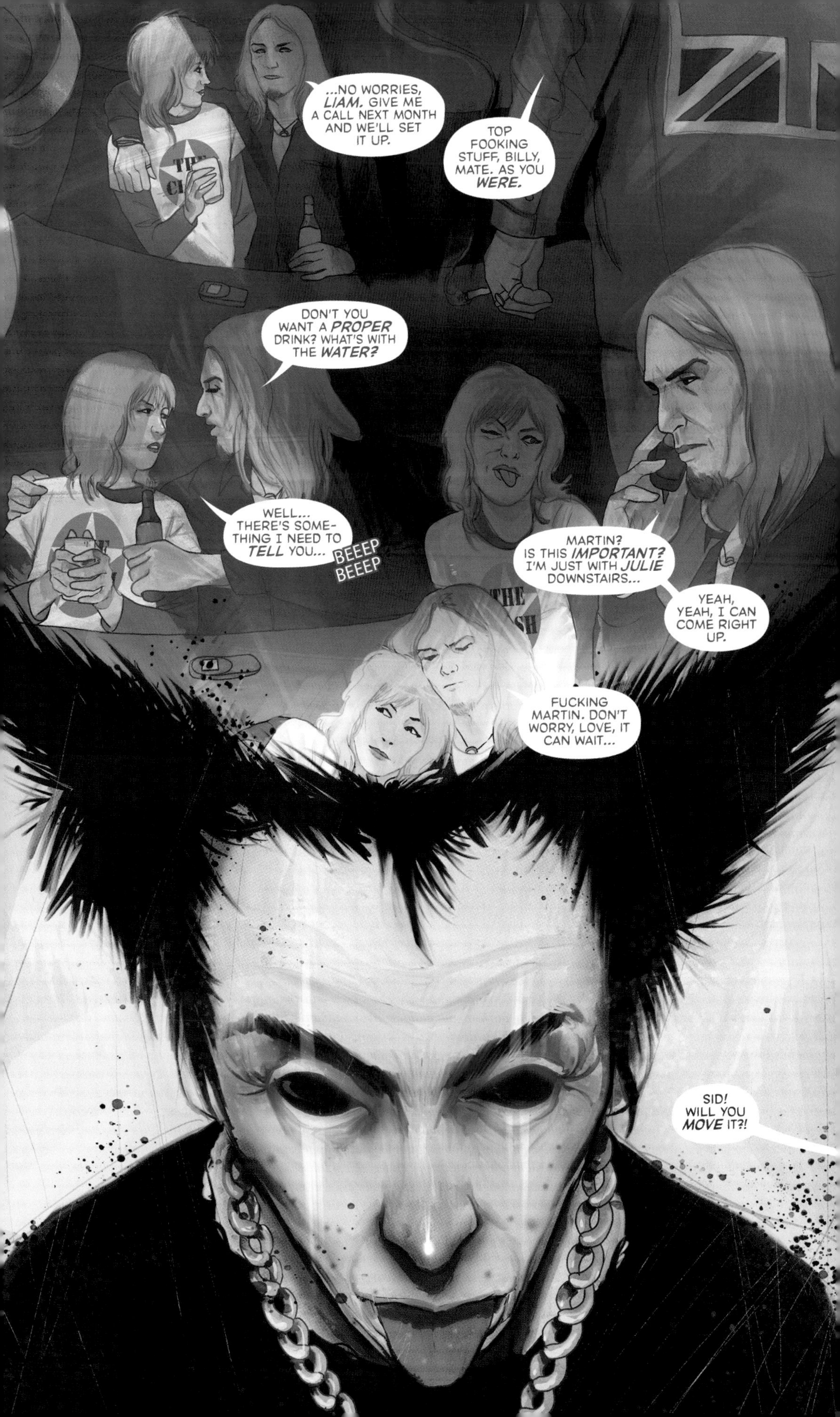
...NO WORRIES, LIAM. GIVE ME A CALL NEXT MONTH AND WE'LL SET IT UP.
TOP FOOKING STUFF, BILLY, MATE. AS YOU WERE.
DON'T YOU WANT A PROPER DRINK? WHAT'S WITH THE WATER?
WELL... THERE'S SOME-THING I NEED TO TELL YOU...
BEEEP BEEEP
MARTIN? IS THIS IMPORTANT? I'M JUST WITH JULIE DOWNSTAIRS...
YEAH, YEAH, I CAN COME RIGHT UP.
FUCKING MARTIN. DON'T WORRY, LOVE, IT CAN WAIT...
SID! WILL YOU MOVE IT?!

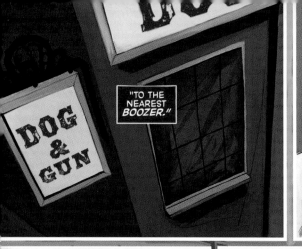

"TO THE NEAREST *BOOZER*."

DOG & GUN

"RIGHT, THE *EDUCATION* OF FEARGAL FERGUSON *CONTINUES*."

YES, SON?

DON'T BE *APOLOGETIC*, LIKE YOU WERE AT THE *CLUB*.

YOU ARE A *YOUNG MAN* OF THE WORLD AND *STRONG CONTINENTAL LAGER* IS YOUR FUCKING *BIRTH-RIGHT!*

PINT OF *STELLA*, PLEASE.

BY *GEORGE*, HE'S FUCKING *GOT* IT!

YOU KNOW... I ALWAYS THOUGHT I'D HAVE MY *FIRST* PINT WITH MY *DAD*.

INSTEAD YOU'RE HAVING IT WITH OLD *SID*. NEXT BEST THING, EH?

I SUPPOSE...

LOOK, MATE, I KNOW IT'S NOT *EASY*. GOD KNOWS, MY *OWN* DAD WAS A BIT OF A *LOSER*.

I JUST WANT YOU TO BE *SURE* WHAT YOU'RE DOING, LOOKING FOR HIM. *SLEEPING DOGS*, AND ALL THAT...

BILLY AND MY *MUM*...THEY LOOK SO *HAPPY* TOGETHER...

I *MISS* HIM, SID. I MISS NOT *KNOWING* HIM.

SHE'S *ALL RIGHT*, YOUR MUM. REMINDS ME OF *MY* OLD LADY. SHE ALWAYS *LOOKED OUT* FOR ME.

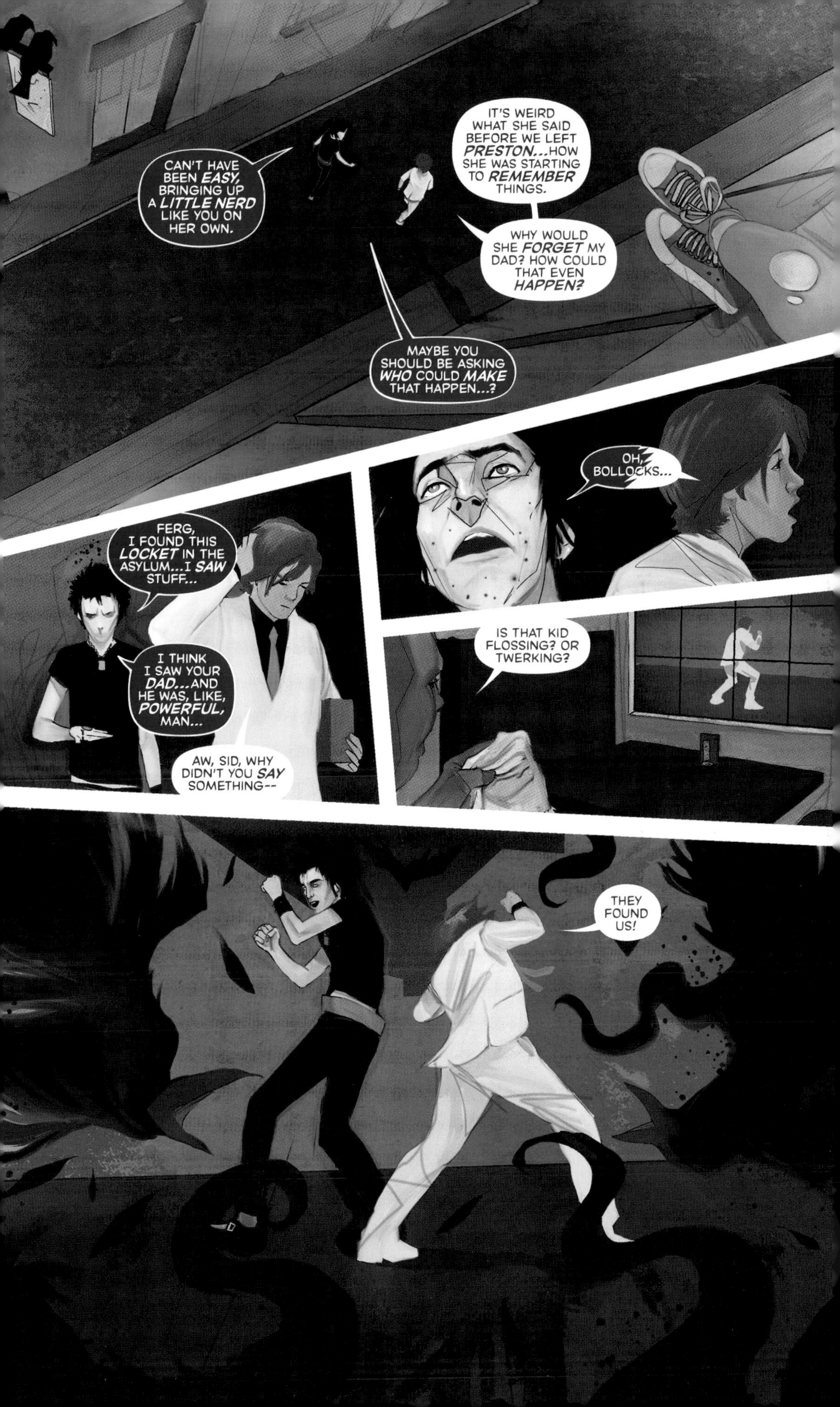
CAN'T HAVE BEEN EASY, BRINGING UP A LITTLE NERD LIKE YOU ON HER OWN.
IT'S WEIRD WHAT SHE SAID BEFORE WE LEFT PRESTON...HOW SHE WAS STARTING TO REMEMBER THINGS.
WHY WOULD SHE FORGET MY DAD? HOW COULD THAT EVEN HAPPEN?
MAYBE YOU SHOULD BE ASKING WHO COULD MAKE THAT HAPPEN...?
FERG, I FOUND THIS LOCKET IN THE ASYLUM...I SAW STUFF...
I THINK I SAW YOUR DAD...AND HE WAS, LIKE, POWERFUL, MAN...
AW, SID, WHY DIDN'T YOU SAY SOMETHING--
OH, BOLLOCKS...
IS THAT KID FLOSSING? OR TWERKING?
THEY FOUND US!

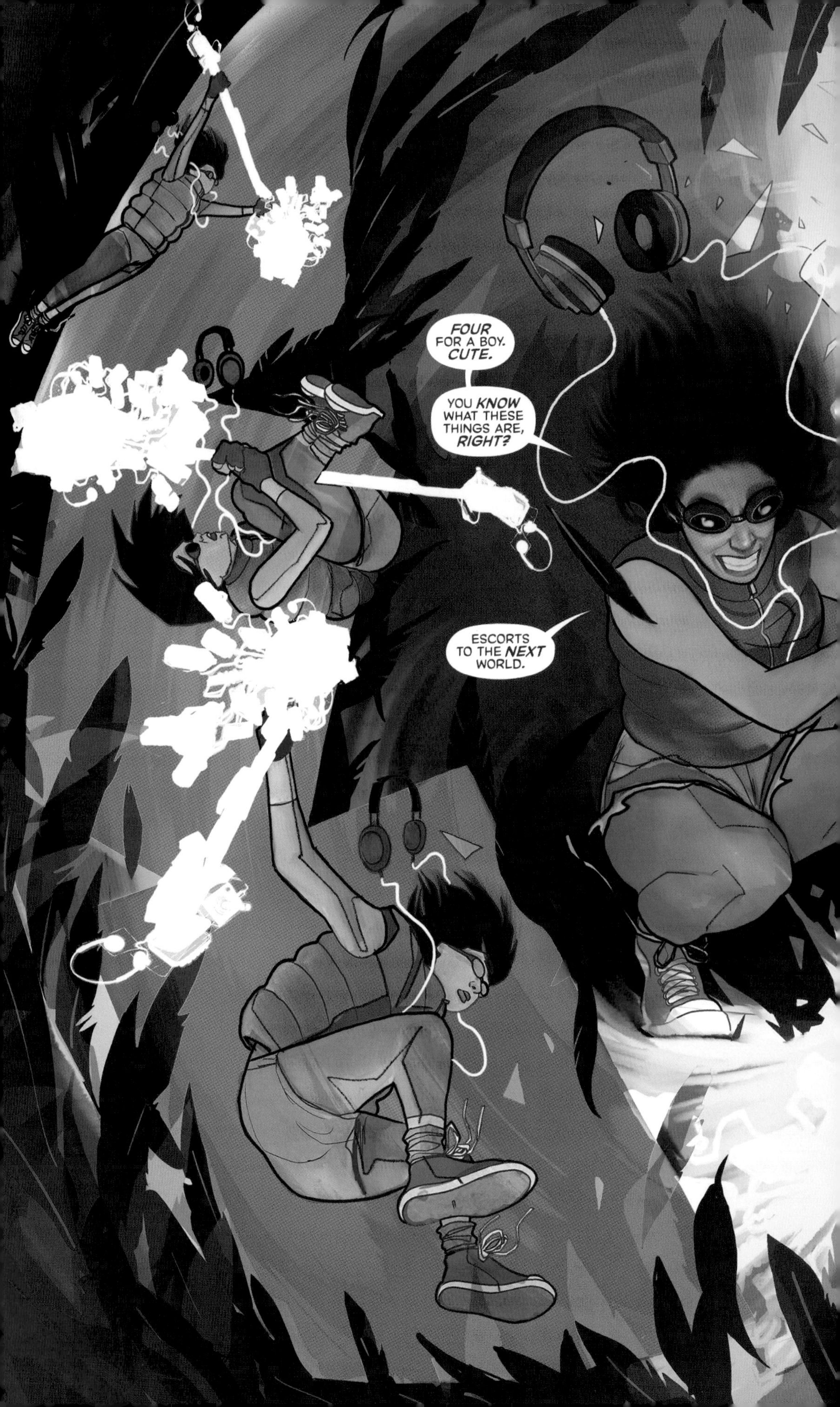
FOUR FOR A BOY. CUTE.
YOU KNOW WHAT THESE THINGS ARE, RIGHT?
ESCORTS TO THE NEXT WORLD.

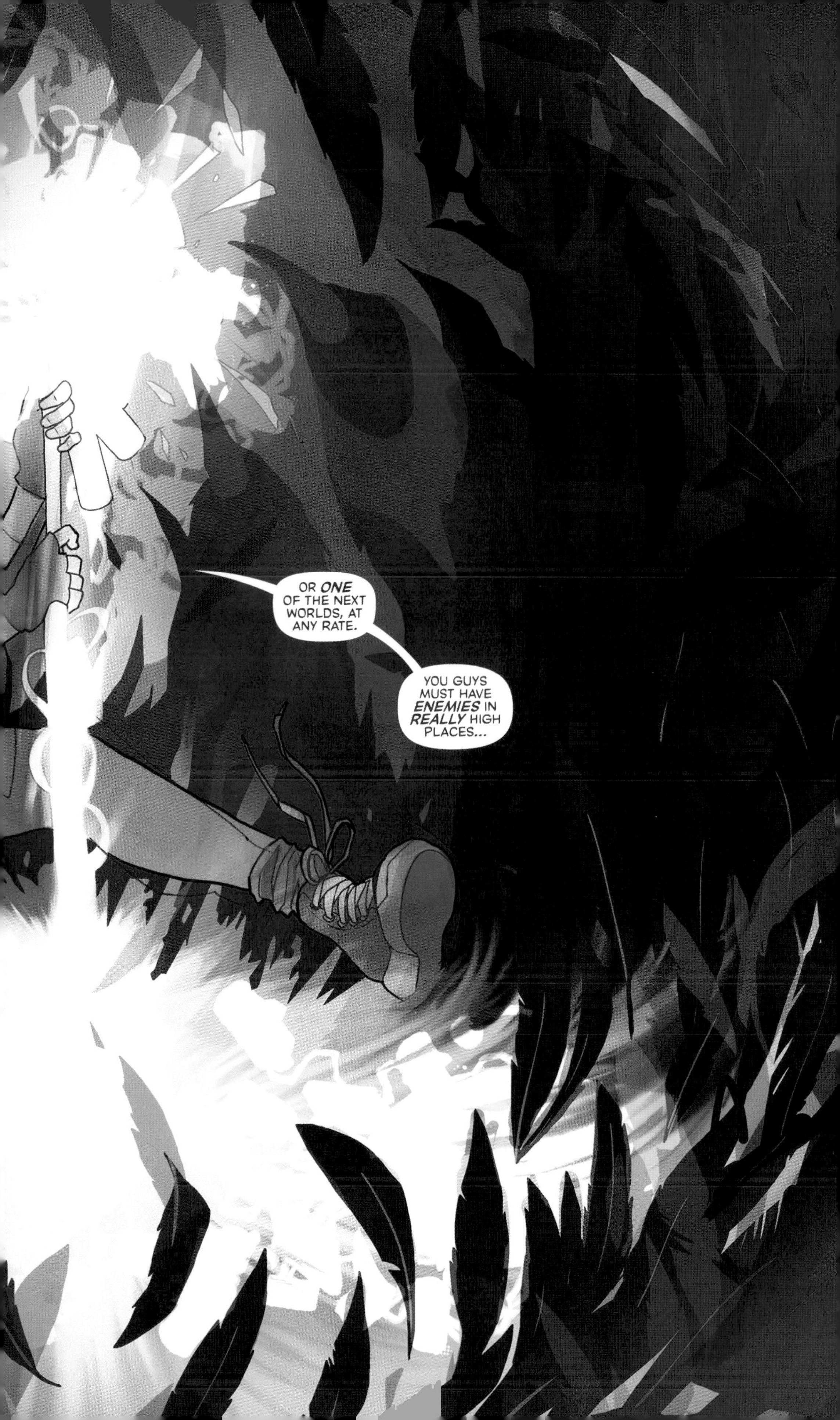
OR ONE OF THE NEXT WORLDS, AT ANY RATE.
YOU GUYS MUST HAVE ENEMIES IN REALLY HIGH PLACES...

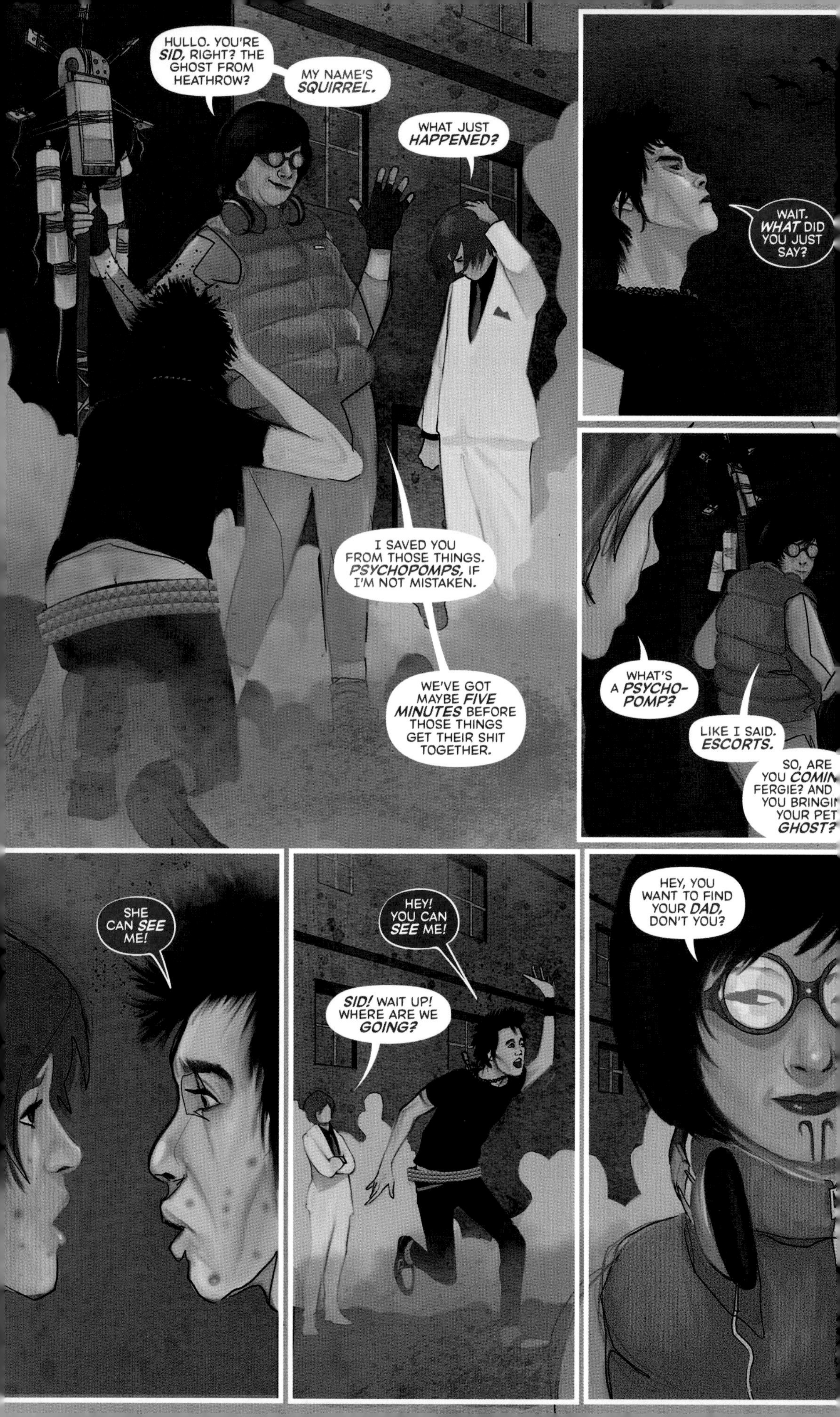

HULLO. YOU'RE SID, RIGHT? THE GHOST FROM HEATHROW?
MY NAME'S SQUIRREL.
WHAT JUST HAPPENED?
I SAVED YOU FROM THOSE THINGS. PSYCHOPOMPS, IF I'M NOT MISTAKEN.
WE'VE GOT MAYBE FIVE MINUTES BEFORE THOSE THINGS GET THEIR SHIT TOGETHER.
WAIT. WHAT DID YOU JUST SAY?
WHAT'S A PSYCHO-POMP?
LIKE I SAID. ESCORTS.
SO, ARE YOU COMIN FERGIE? AND YOU BRINGI YOUR PET GHOST?
SHE CAN SEE ME!
HEY! YOU CAN SEE ME!
SID! WAIT UP! WHERE ARE WE GOING?
HEY, YOU WANT TO FIND YOUR DAD, DON'T YOU?

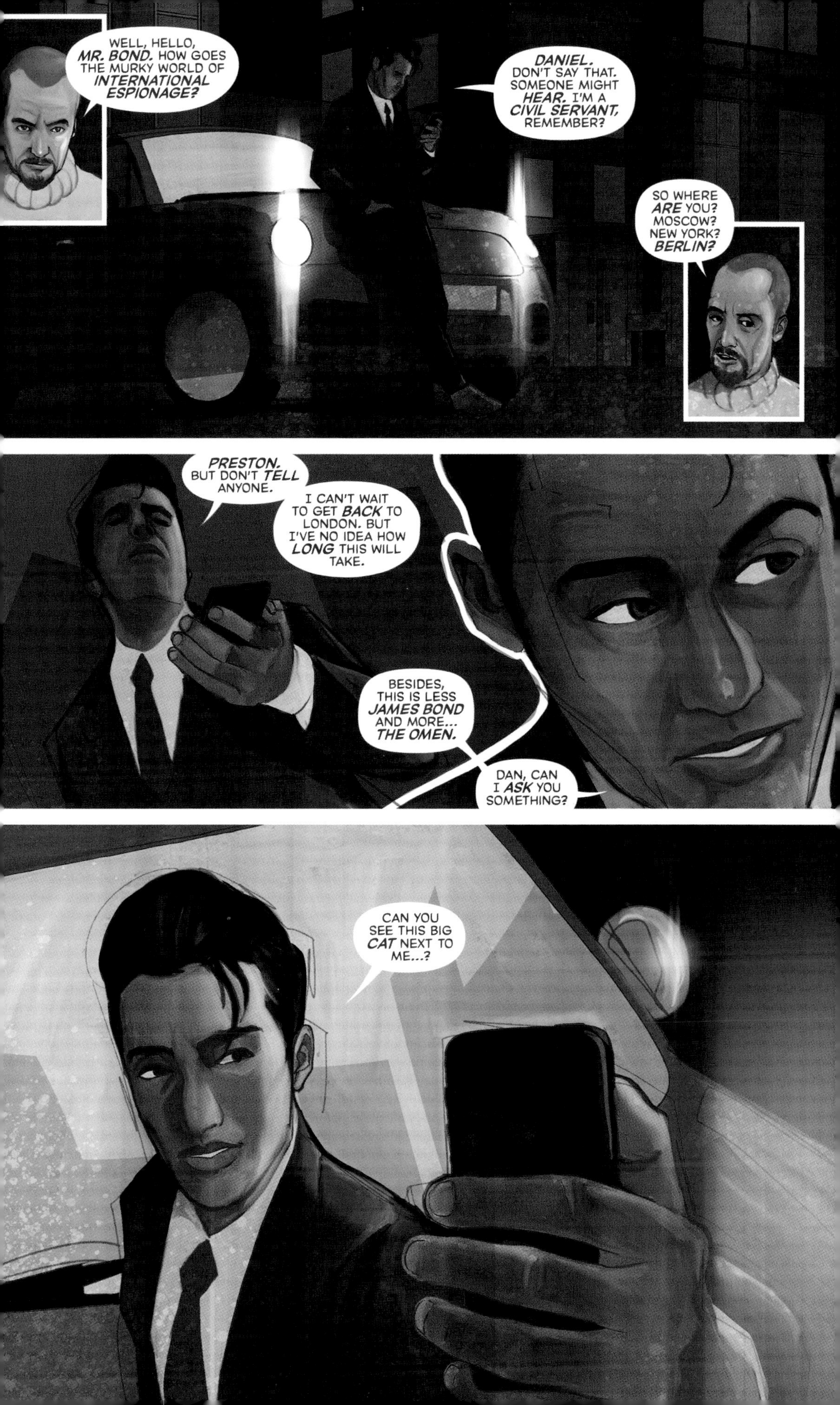
WELL, HELLO, MR. BOND. HOW GOES THE MURKY WORLD OF INTERNATIONAL ESPIONAGE?
DANIEL. DON'T SAY THAT. SOMEONE MIGHT HEAR. I'M A CIVIL SERVANT, REMEMBER?
SO WHERE ARE YOU? MOSCOW? NEW YORK? BERLIN?
PRESTON. BUT DON'T TELL ANYONE.
I CAN'T WAIT TO GET BACK TO LONDON. BUT I'VE NO IDEA HOW LONG THIS WILL TAKE.
BESIDES, THIS IS LESS JAMES BOND AND MORE... THE OMEN.
DAN, CAN I ASK YOU SOMETHING?
CAN YOU SEE THIS BIG CAT NEXT TO ME...?

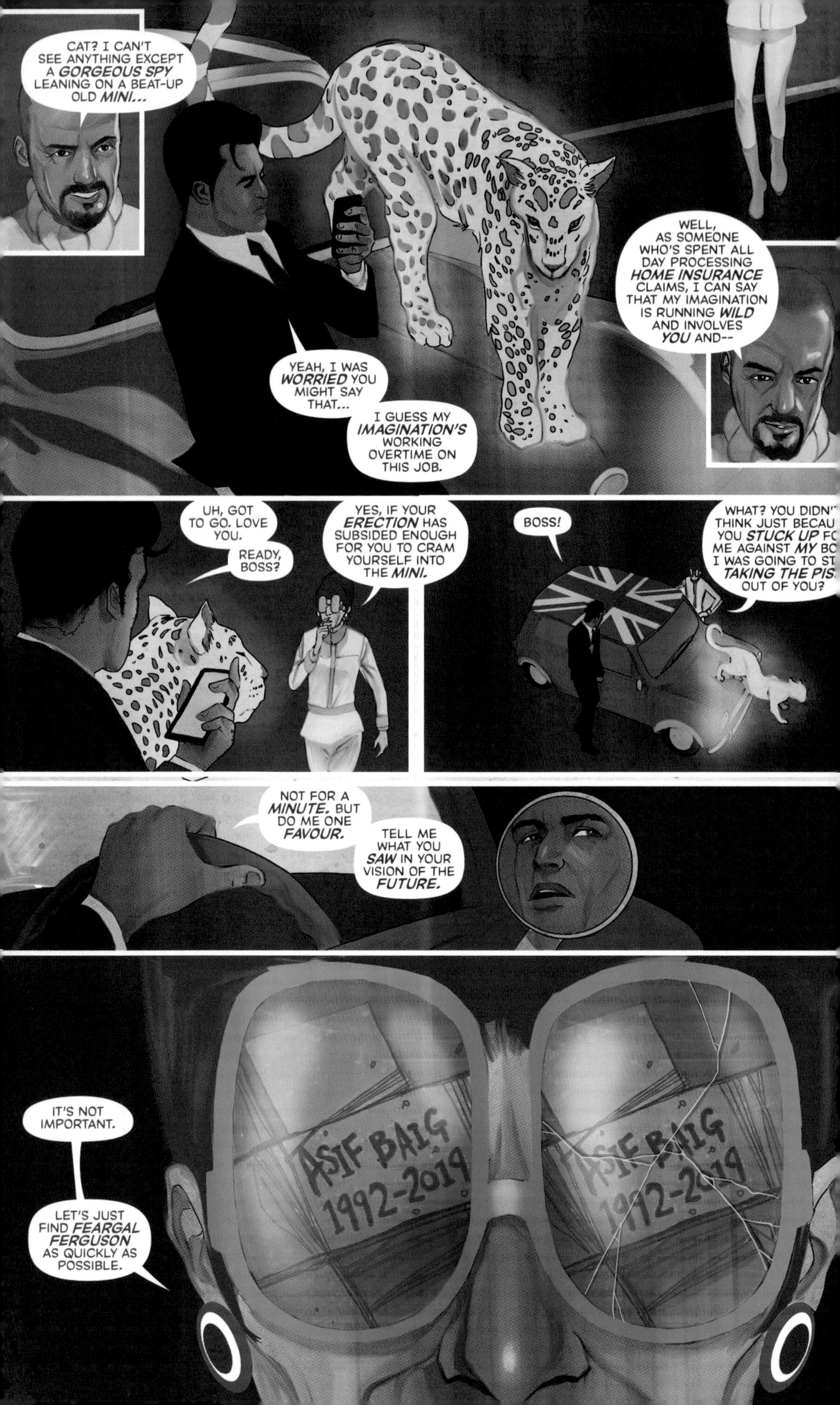

CAT? I CAN'T SEE ANYTHING EXCEPT A *GORGEOUS SPY* LEANING ON A BEAT-UP OLD *MINI...*
YEAH, I WAS *WORRIED* YOU MIGHT SAY THAT...
I GUESS MY *IMAGINATION'S* WORKING OVERTIME ON THIS JOB.
WELL, AS SOMEONE WHO'S SPENT ALL DAY PROCESSING *HOME INSURANCE* CLAIMS, I CAN SAY THAT MY IMAGINATION IS RUNNING *WILD* AND INVOLVES *YOU* AND--
UH, GOT TO GO. LOVE YOU.
READY, BOSS?
YES, IF YOUR *ERECTION* HAS SUBSIDED ENOUGH FOR YOU TO CRAM YOURSELF INTO THE *MINI.*
BOSS!
NOT FOR A *MINUTE.* BUT DO ME ONE *FAVOUR.*
TELL ME WHAT YOU *SAW* IN YOUR VISION OF THE *FUTURE.*
IT'S NOT IMPORTANT.
LET'S JUST FIND *FEARGAL FERGUSON* AS QUICKLY AS POSSIBLE.
ASIF BAIG
1992-2019

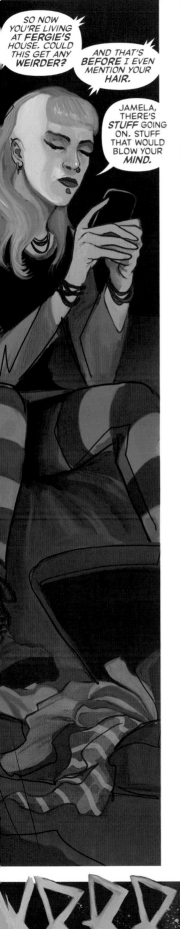

SO NOW YOU'RE LIVING AT *FERGIE'S* HOUSE. COULD THIS GET ANY *WEIRDER?*

AND THAT'S *BEFORE* I EVEN MENTION YOUR *HAIR.*

JAMELA, THERE'S *STUFF* GOING ON. STUFF THAT WOULD BLOW YOUR *MIND.*

"BUT I CAN'T BE WITH MY DAD, AND JULIE NEEDS *SOMEBODY.*

"SHE'S ALL *ALONE* SINCE FERGIE DISAPPEARED. SHE'S REALLY *COOL,* BUT SHE'S SO...*SAD* INSIDE.

"I THINK FERGIE'S... *SPECIAL,* JAM. AND NO, NOT IN *THAT* WAY.

"I MEAN SPECIAL AS IN HE CAN *DO STUFF.* JEEZ, GIRL, NOT *THAT* WAY EITHER!

"UH-OH. SOUNDS LIKE SHE'S *BREAKING* THINGS. I'D BETTER GO.

"HOPE IT'S NOT THE *TELLY.* THEY'VE GOT *NETFLIX."*

KRRRSSH!!

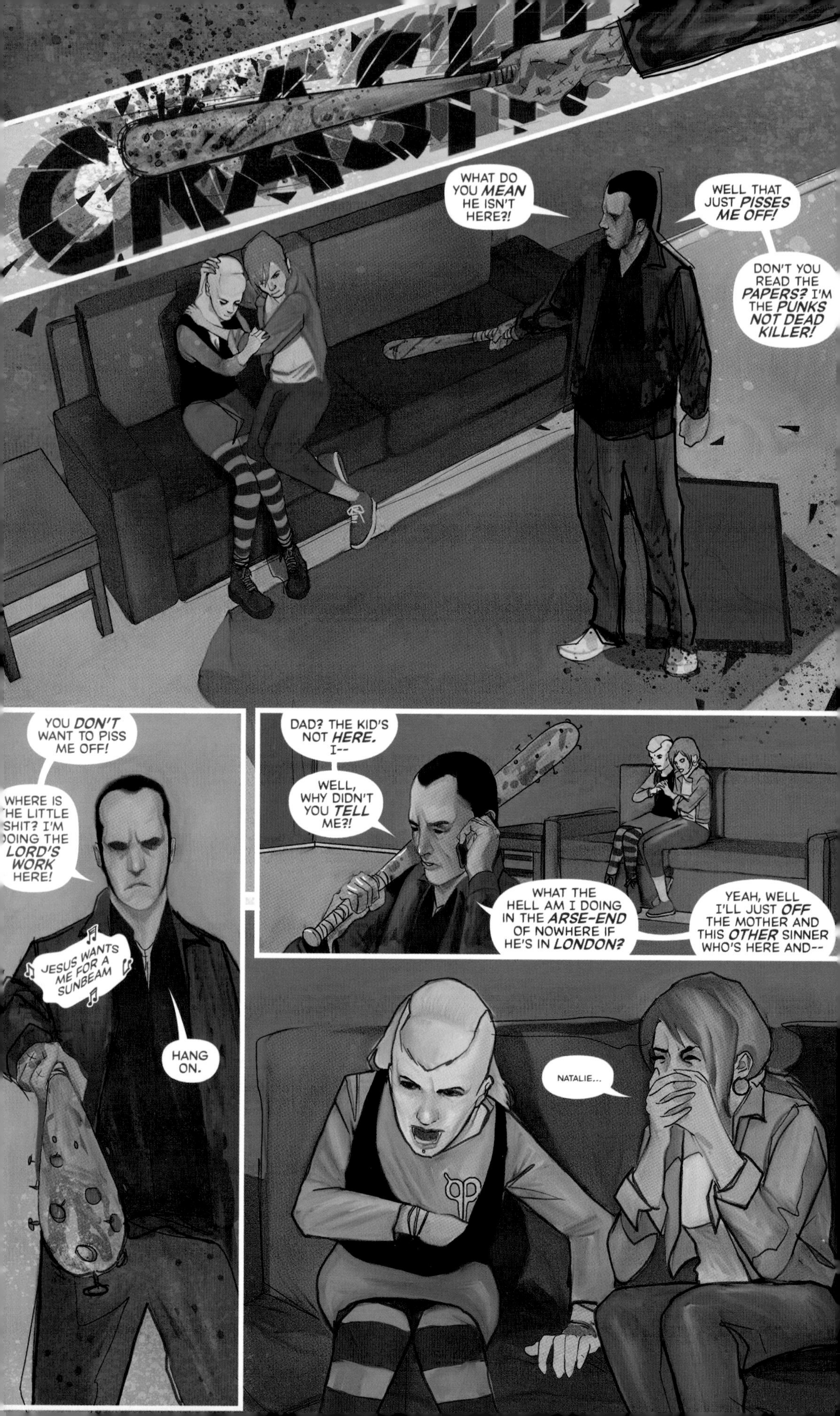
CRASH!!
WHAT DO YOU MEAN HE ISN'T HERE?!
WELL THAT JUST PISSES ME OFF!
DON'T YOU READ THE PAPERS? I'M THE PUNKS NOT DEAD KILLER!
YOU DON'T WANT TO PISS ME OFF!
WHERE IS THE LITTLE SHIT? I'M DOING THE LORD'S WORK HERE!
JESUS WANTS ME FOR A SUNBEAM
HANG ON.
DAD? THE KID'S NOT HERE. I--
WELL, WHY DIDN'T YOU TELL ME?!
WHAT THE HELL AM I DOING IN THE ARSE-END OF NOWHERE IF HE'S IN LONDON?
YEAH, WELL I'LL JUST OFF THE MOTHER AND THIS OTHER SINNER WHO'S HERE AND--
NATALIE...

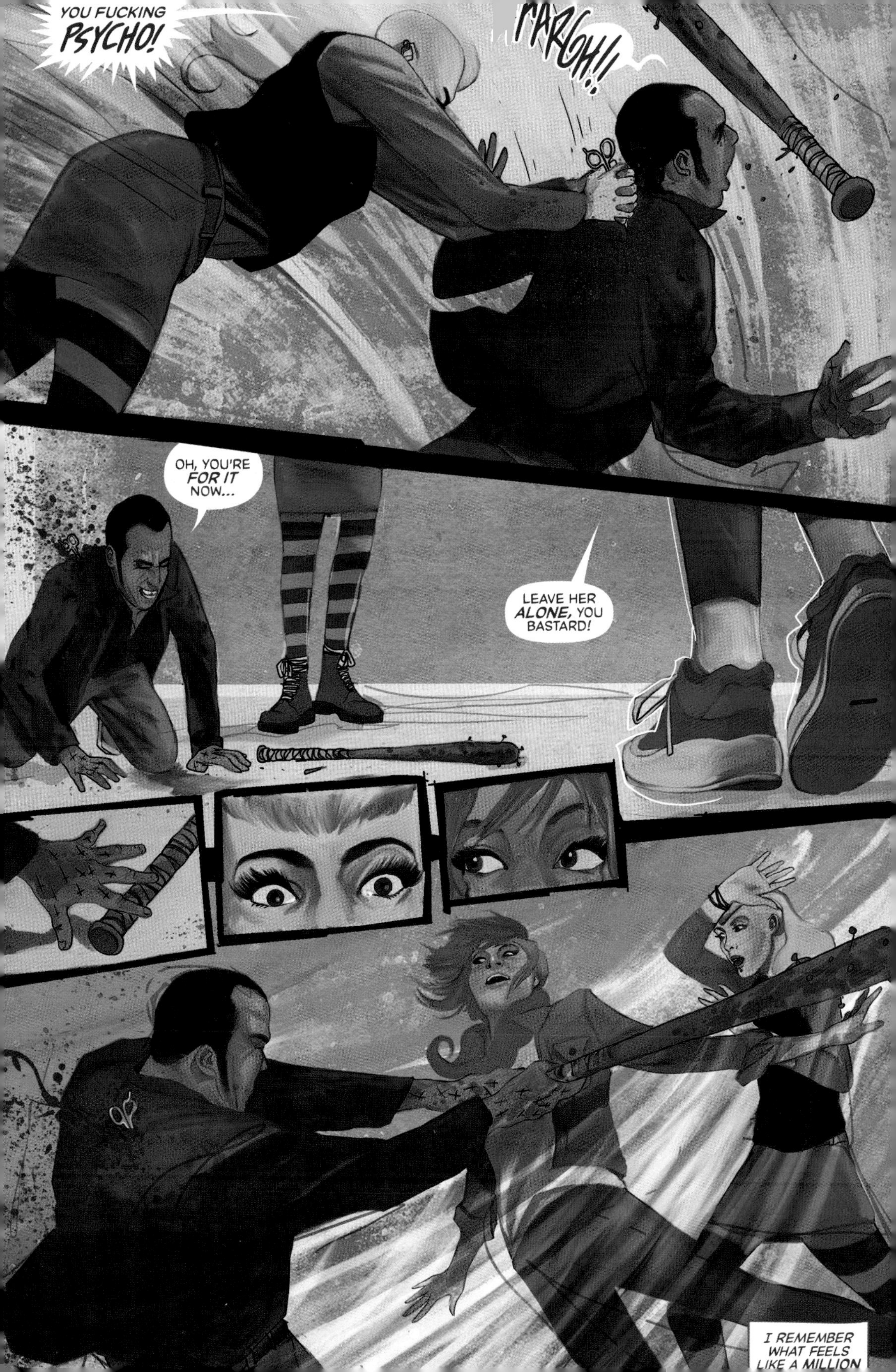
YOU FUCKING PSYCHO!
RARGH!!
OH, YOU'RE FOR IT NOW...
LEAVE HER ALONE, YOU BASTARD!
I REMEMBER WHAT FEELS LIKE A MILLION

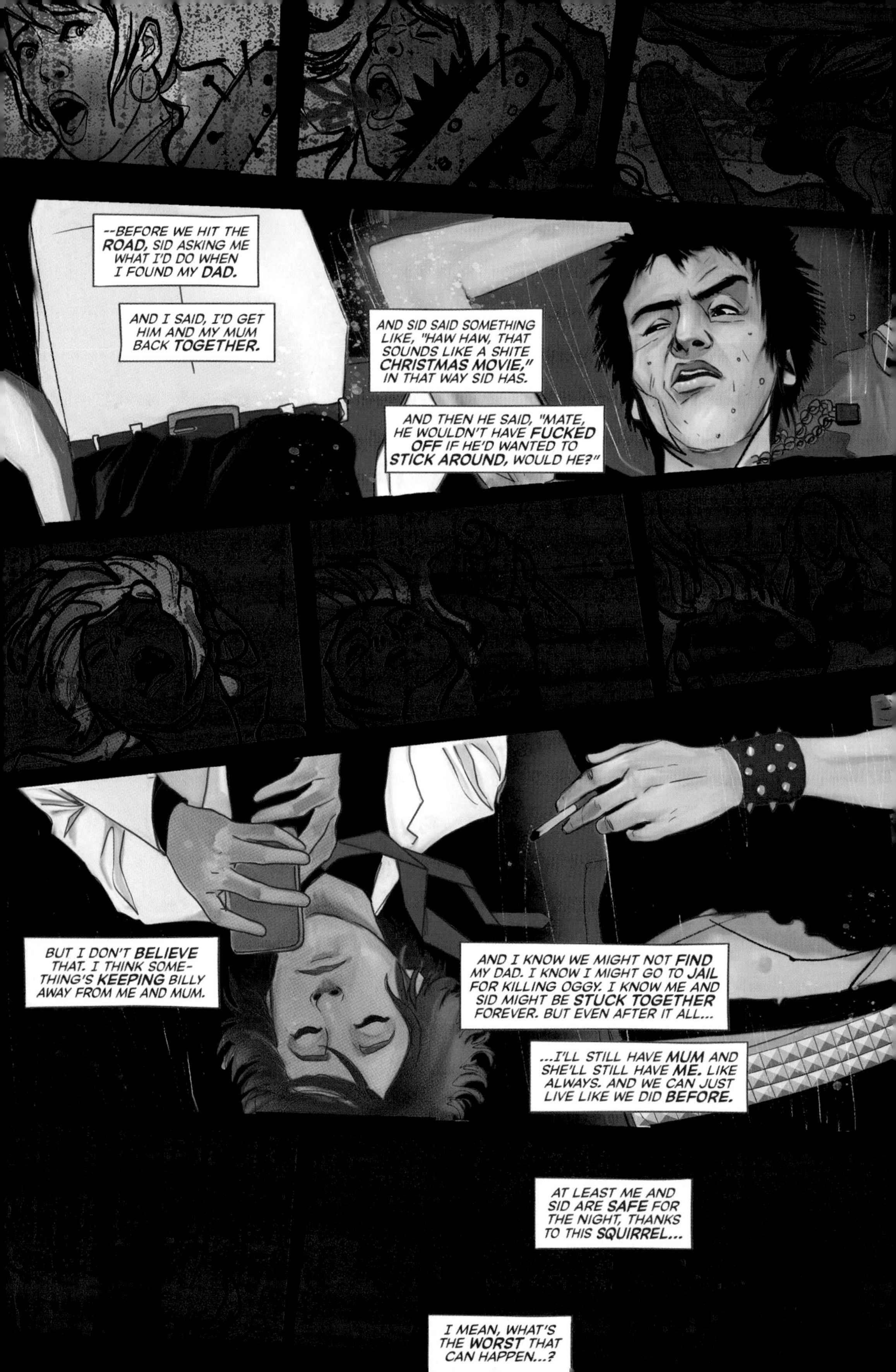
--BEFORE WE HIT THE ROAD, SID ASKING ME WHAT I'D DO WHEN I FOUND MY DAD.
AND I SAID, I'D GET HIM AND MY MUM BACK TOGETHER.
AND SID SAID SOMETHING LIKE, "HAW HAW, THAT SOUNDS LIKE A SHITE CHRISTMAS MOVIE," IN THAT WAY SID HAS.
AND THEN HE SAID, "MATE, HE WOULDN'T HAVE FUCKED OFF IF HE'D WANTED TO STICK AROUND, WOULD HE?"
BUT I DON'T BELIEVE THAT. I THINK SOME-THING'S KEEPING BILLY AWAY FROM ME AND MUM.
AND I KNOW WE MIGHT NOT FIND MY DAD. I KNOW I MIGHT GO TO JAIL FOR KILLING OGGY. I KNOW ME AND SID MIGHT BE STUCK TOGETHER FOREVER. BUT EVEN AFTER IT ALL...
...I'LL STILL HAVE MUM AND SHE'LL STILL HAVE ME. LIKE ALWAYS. AND WE CAN JUST LIVE LIKE WE DID BEFORE.
AT LEAST ME AND SID ARE SAFE FOR THE NIGHT, THANKS TO THIS SQUIRREL...
I MEAN, WHAT'S THE WORST THAT CAN HAPPEN...?

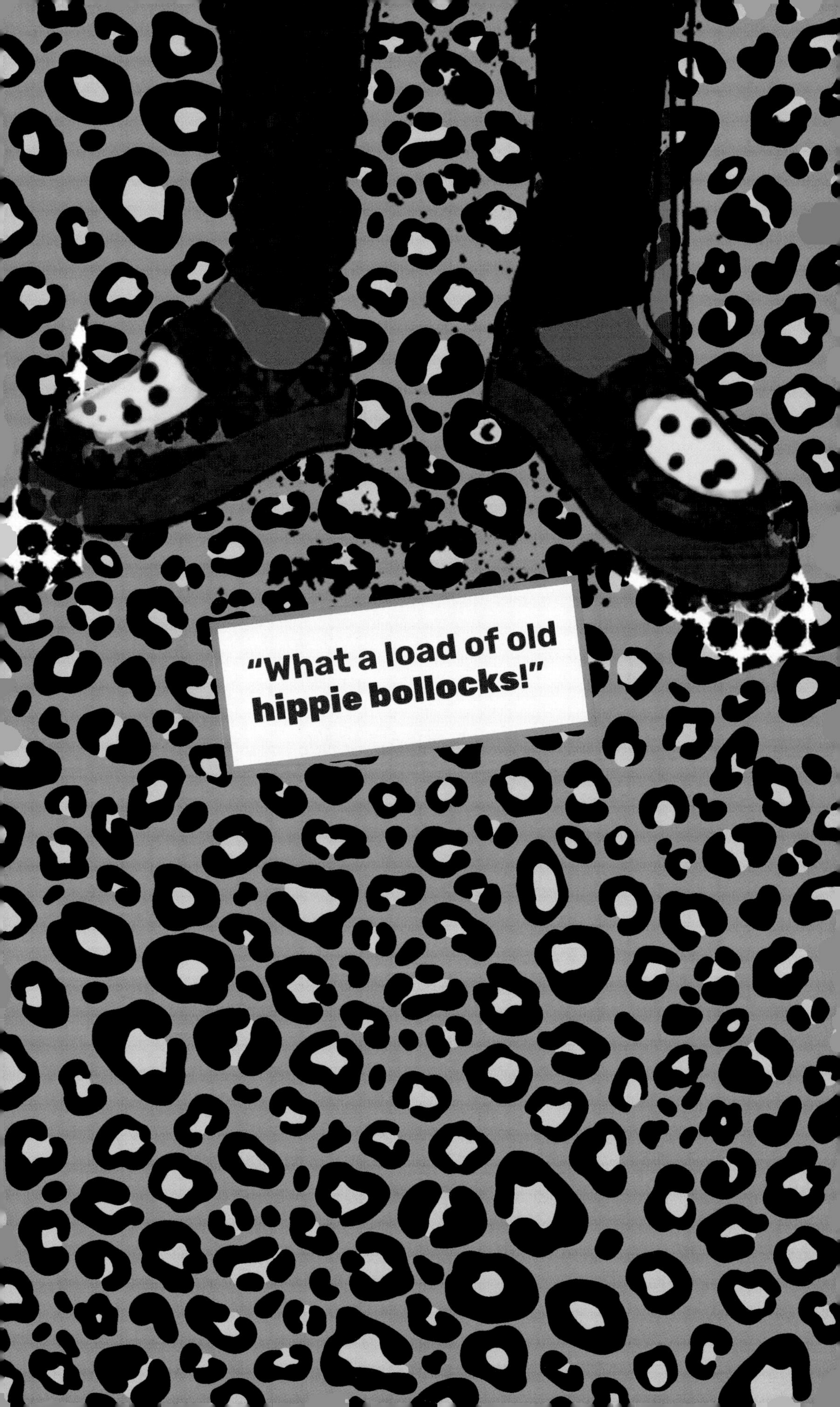
"What a load of old
hippie bollocks!"

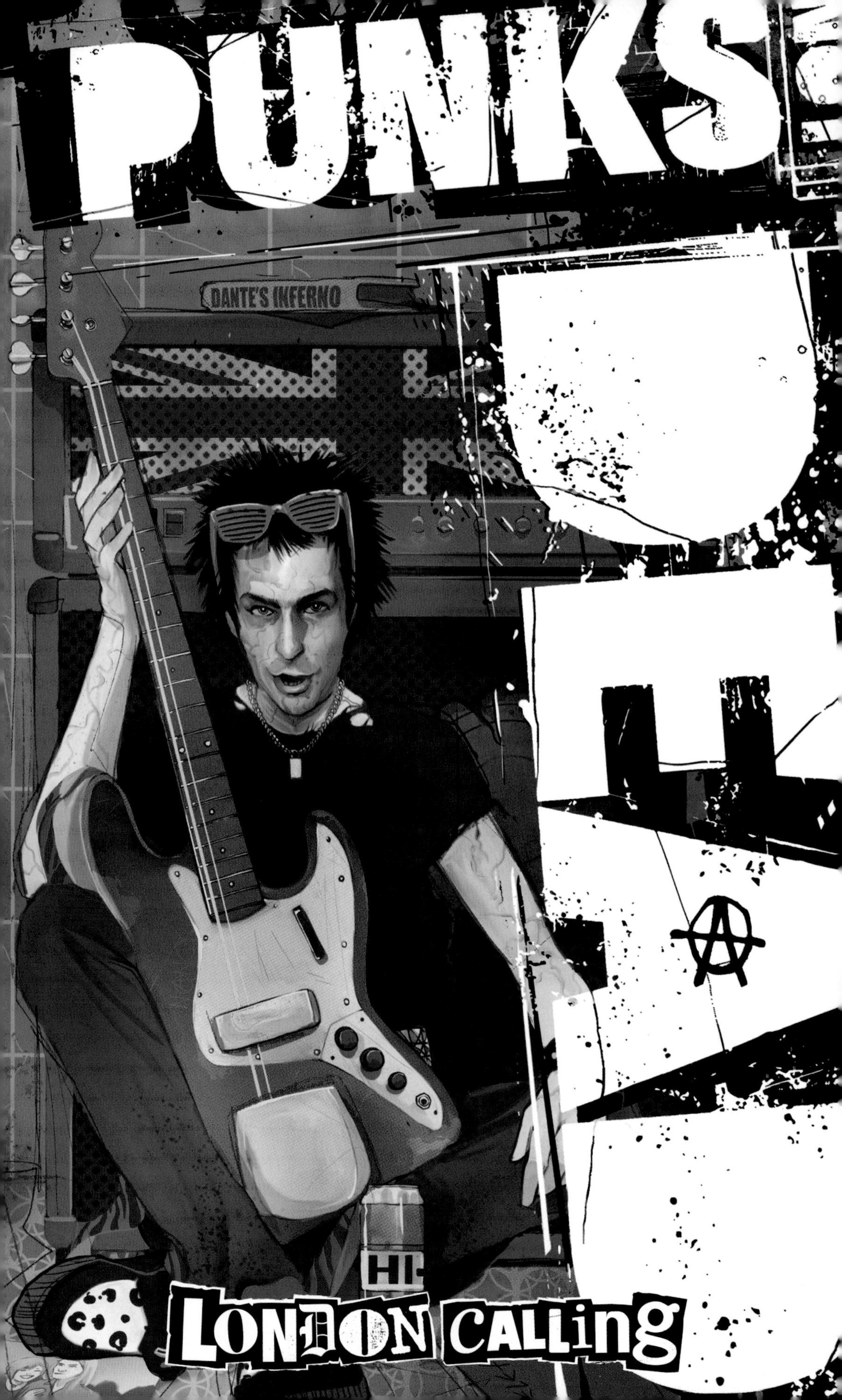
PUNKS
DANTE'S INFERNO
HI
LONDON CALLING

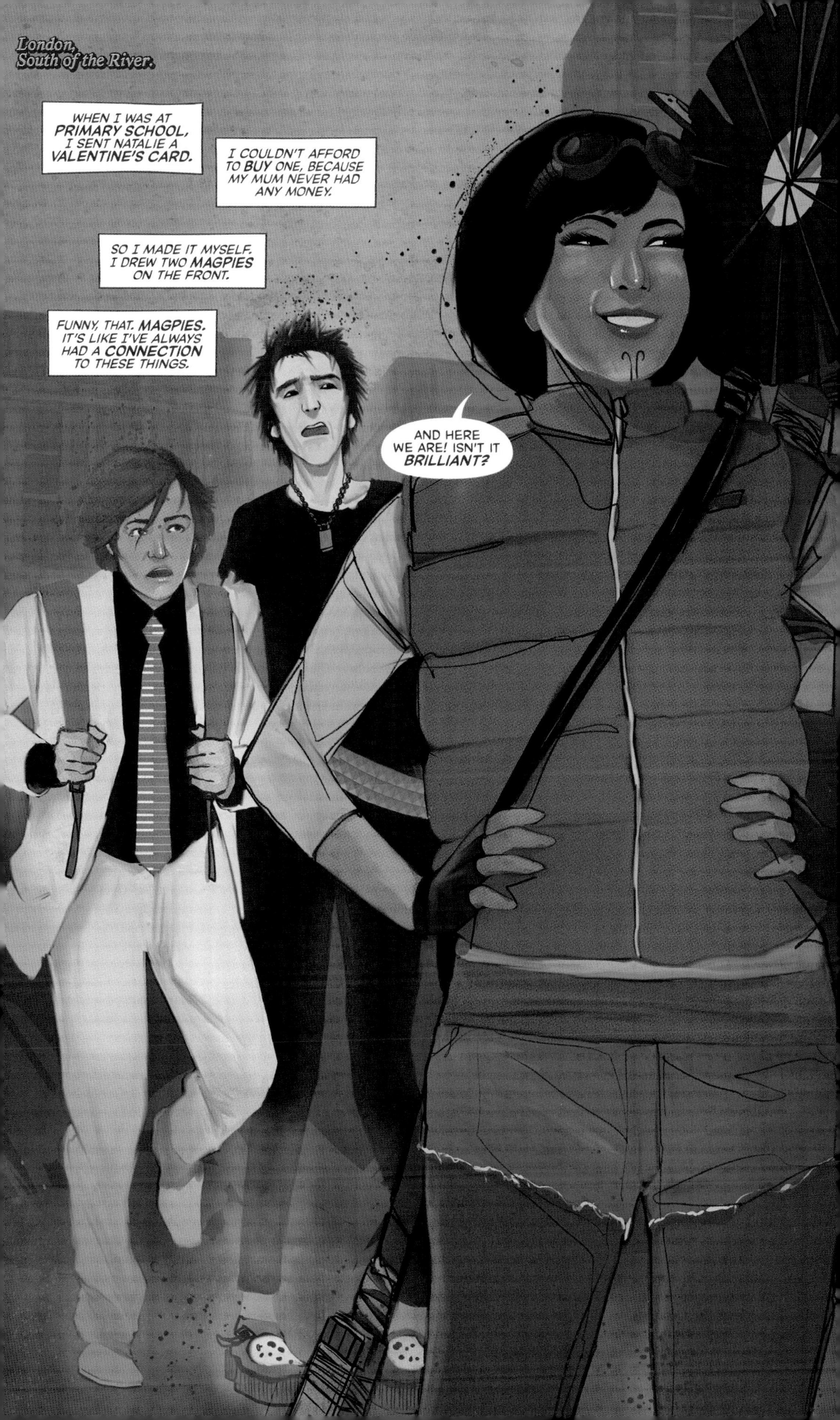
London, South of the River.
WHEN I WAS AT PRIMARY SCHOOL, I SENT NATALIE A VALENTINE'S CARD.
I COULDN'T AFFORD TO BUY ONE, BECAUSE MY MUM NEVER HAD ANY MONEY.
SO I MADE IT MYSELF. I DREW TWO MAGPIES ON THE FRONT.
FUNNY, THAT. MAGPIES. IT'S LIKE I'VE ALWAYS HAD A CONNECTION TO THESE THINGS.
AND HERE WE ARE! ISN'T IT BRILLIANT?

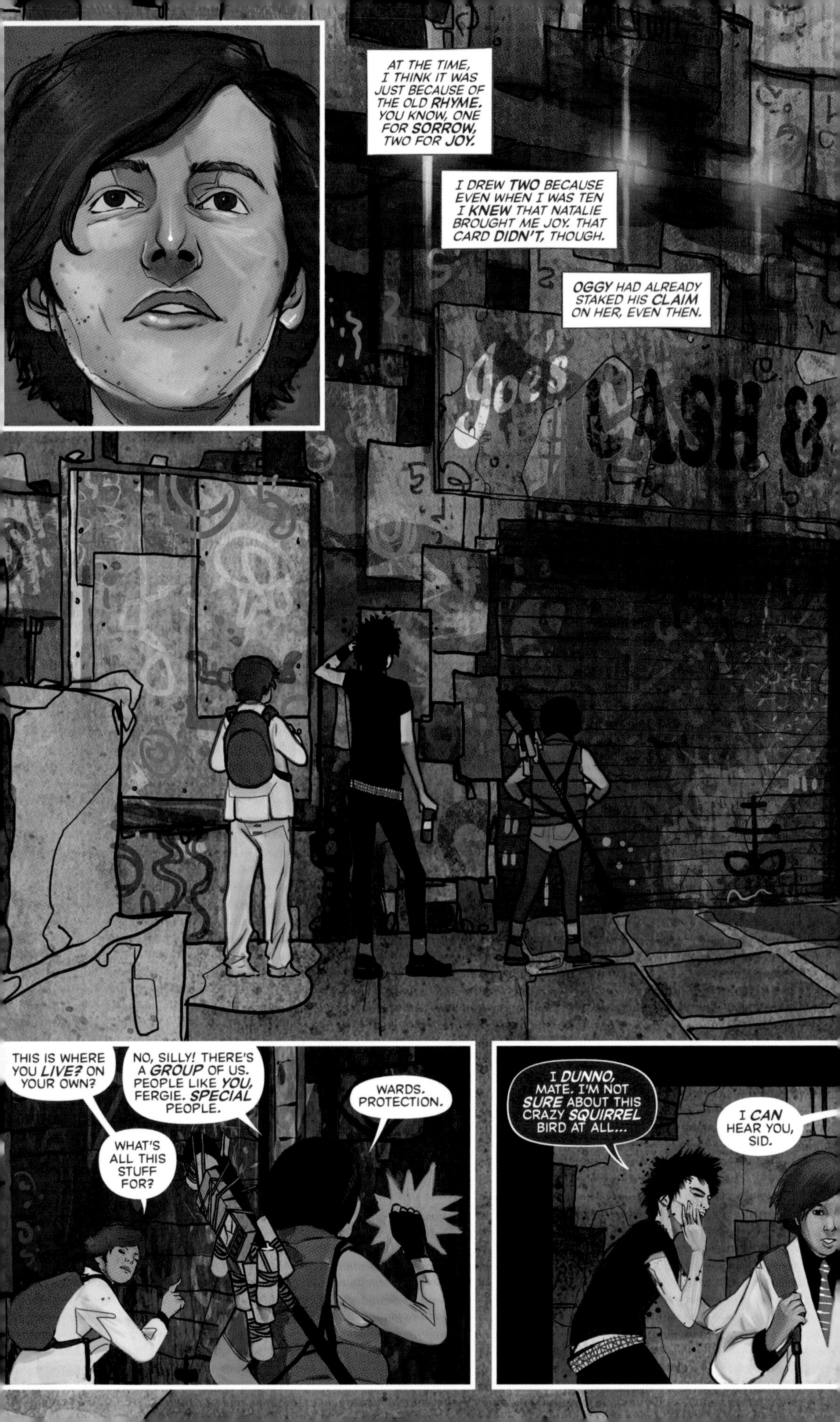
AT THE TIME, I THINK IT WAS JUST BECAUSE OF THE OLD RHYME. YOU KNOW, ONE FOR SORROW, TWO FOR JOY.
I DREW TWO BECAUSE EVEN WHEN I WAS TEN I KNEW THAT NATALIE BROUGHT ME JOY. THAT CARD DIDN'T, THOUGH.
OGGY HAD ALREADY STAKED HIS CLAIM ON HER, EVEN THEN.
Joe's CASH &
THIS IS WHERE YOU LIVE? ON YOUR OWN?
NO, SILLY! THERE'S A GROUP OF US. PEOPLE LIKE YOU, FERGIE. SPECIAL PEOPLE.
WHAT'S ALL THIS STUFF FOR?
WARDS. PROTECTION.
I DUNNO, MATE. I'M NOT SURE ABOUT THIS CRAZY SQUIRREL BIRD AT ALL...
I CAN HEAR YOU, SID.

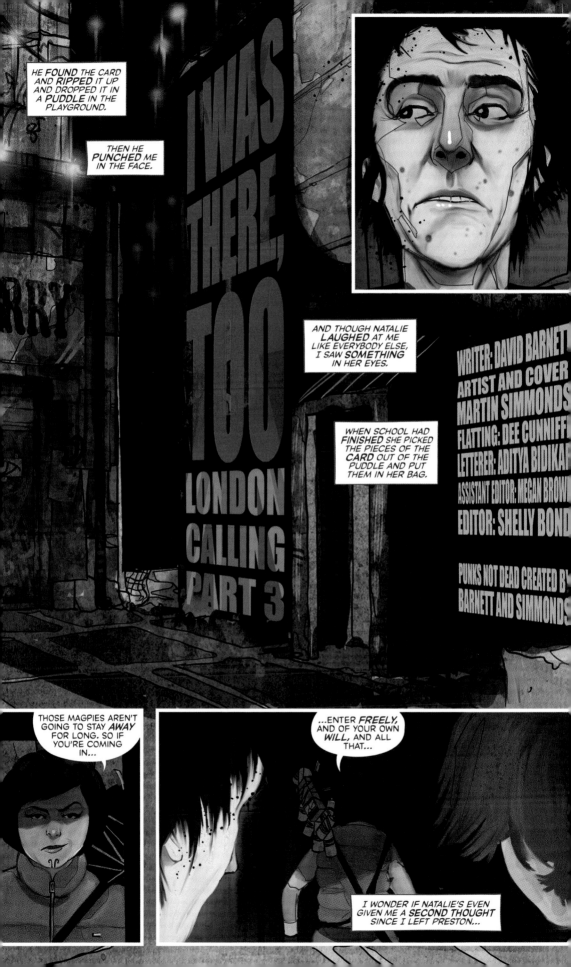

HE FOUND THE CARD AND *RIPPED* IT UP AND DROPPED IT IN A *PUDDLE* IN THE PLAYGROUND.

THEN HE *PUNCHED* ME IN THE FACE.

I WAS THERE, TOO

LONDON CALLING PART 3

AND THOUGH NATALIE *LAUGHED* AT ME LIKE EVERYBODY ELSE, I SAW *SOMETHING* IN HER EYES.

WHEN SCHOOL HAD *FINISHED* SHE PICKED THE PIECES OF THE *CARD* OUT OF THE PUDDLE AND PUT THEM IN HER BAG.

WRITER: DAVID BARNETT
ARTIST AND COVER
MARTIN SIMMONDS
FLATTING: DEE CUNNIFF
LETTERER: ADITYA BIDIKAR
ASSISTANT EDITOR: MEGAN BROW
EDITOR: SHELLY BOND

PUNKS NOT DEAD CREATED B
BARNETT AND SIMMONDS

THOSE MAGPIES AREN'T GOING TO STAY *AWAY* FOR LONG. SO IF YOU'RE COMING IN...

...ENTER *FREELY*, AND OF YOUR OWN *WILL*, AND ALL THAT...

I WONDER IF NATALIE'S EVEN GIVEN ME A *SECOND THOUGHT* SINCE I LEFT PRESTON...

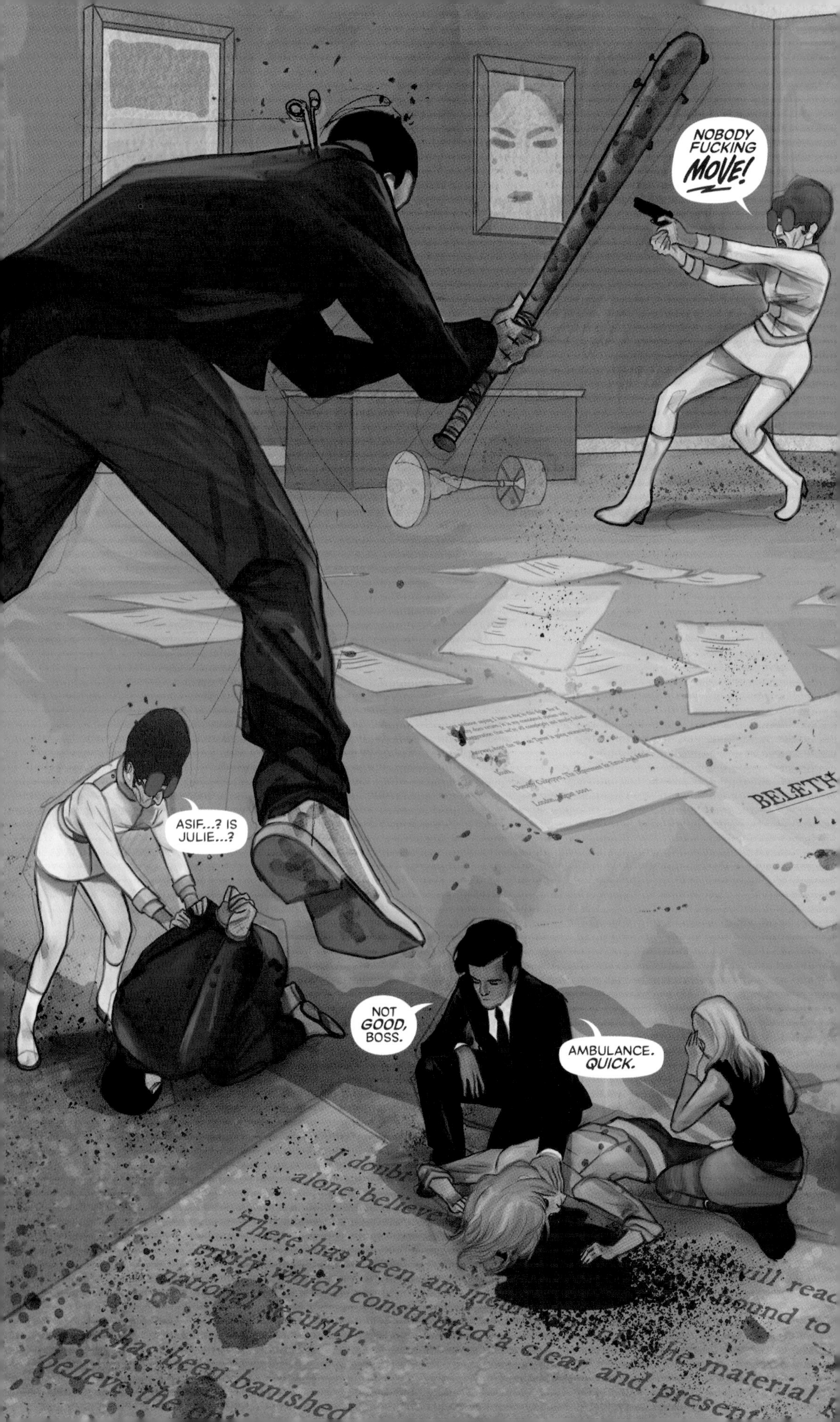
NOBODY FUCKING MOVE!
ASIF...? IS JULIE...?
NOT GOOD, BOSS.
AMBULANCE. QUICK.

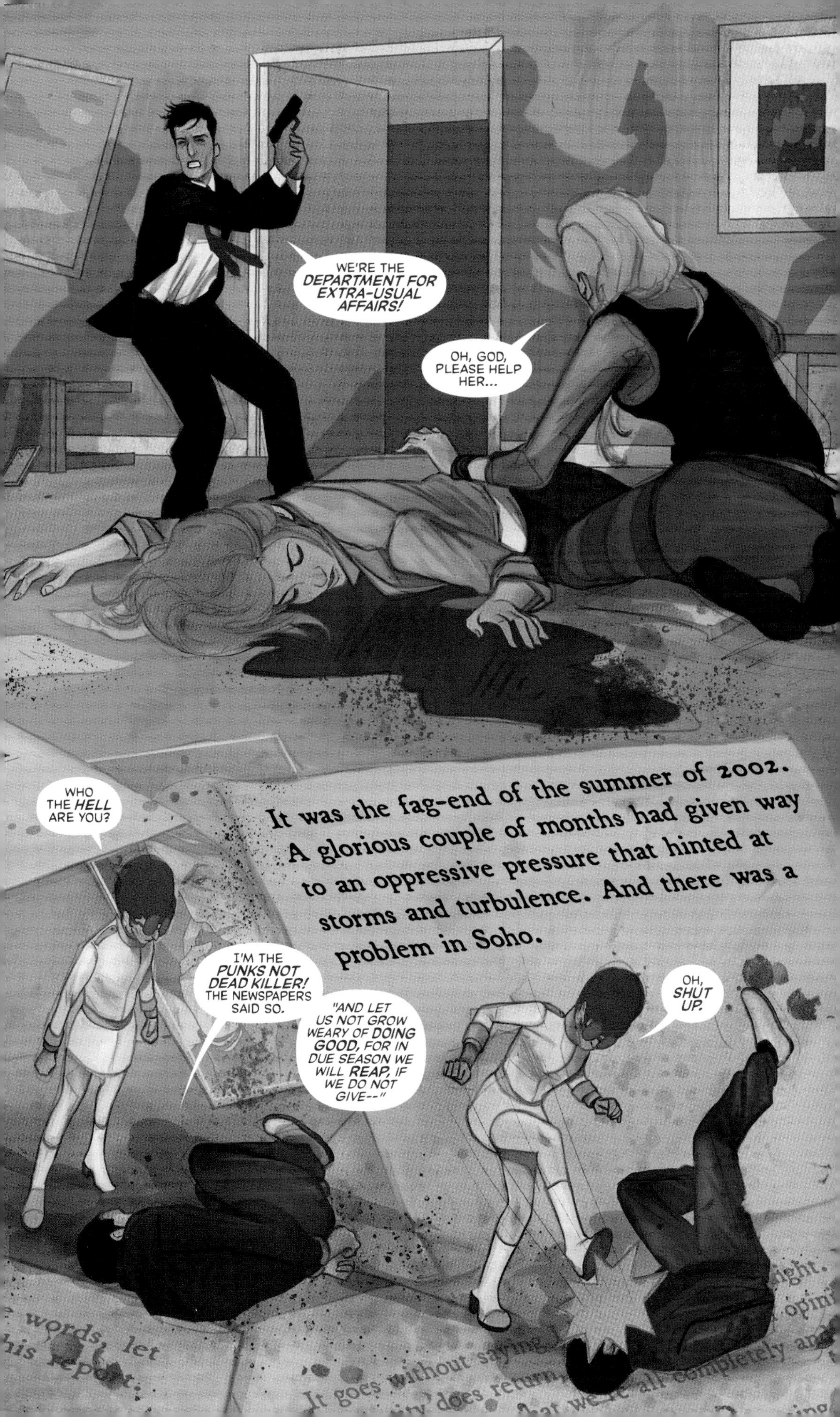
WE'RE THE *DEPARTMENT FOR EXTRA-USUAL AFFAIRS!*
OH, GOD, PLEASE HELP HER...
WHO THE *HELL* ARE YOU?
It was the fag-end of the summer of 2002. A glorious couple of months had given way to an oppressive pressure that hinted at storms and turbulence. And there was a problem in Soho.
I'M THE *PUNKS NOT DEAD KILLER!* THE NEWSPAPERS SAID SO.
"AND LET US NOT GROW WEARY OF **DOING GOOD,** FOR IN DUE SEASON WE WILL **REAP,** IF WE DO NOT GIVE--"
OH, *SHUT UP.*

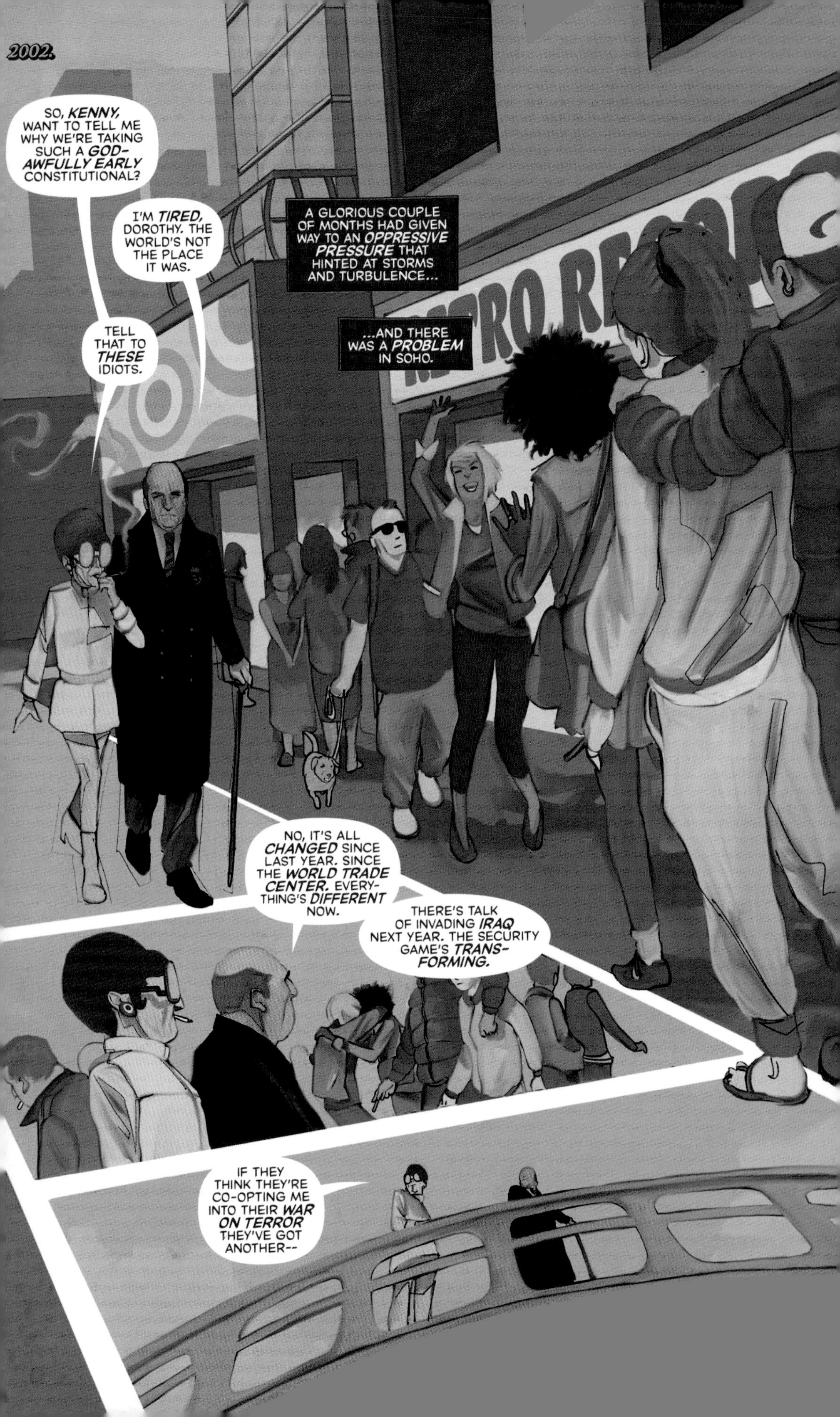
2002.
SO, KENNY, WANT TO TELL ME WHY WE'RE TAKING SUCH A GOD-AWFULLY EARLY CONSTITUTIONAL?
I'M TIRED, DOROTHY. THE WORLD'S NOT THE PLACE IT WAS.
TELL THAT TO THESE IDIOTS.
A GLORIOUS COUPLE OF MONTHS HAD GIVEN WAY TO AN OPPRESSIVE PRESSURE THAT HINTED AT STORMS AND TURBULENCE...
...AND THERE WAS A PROBLEM IN SOHO.
NO, IT'S ALL CHANGED SINCE LAST YEAR. SINCE THE WORLD TRADE CENTER. EVERYTHING'S DIFFERENT NOW.
THERE'S TALK OF INVADING IRAQ NEXT YEAR. THE SECURITY GAME'S TRANSFORMING.
IF THEY THINK THEY'RE CO-OPTING ME INTO THEIR WAR ON TERROR THEY'VE GOT ANOTHER--

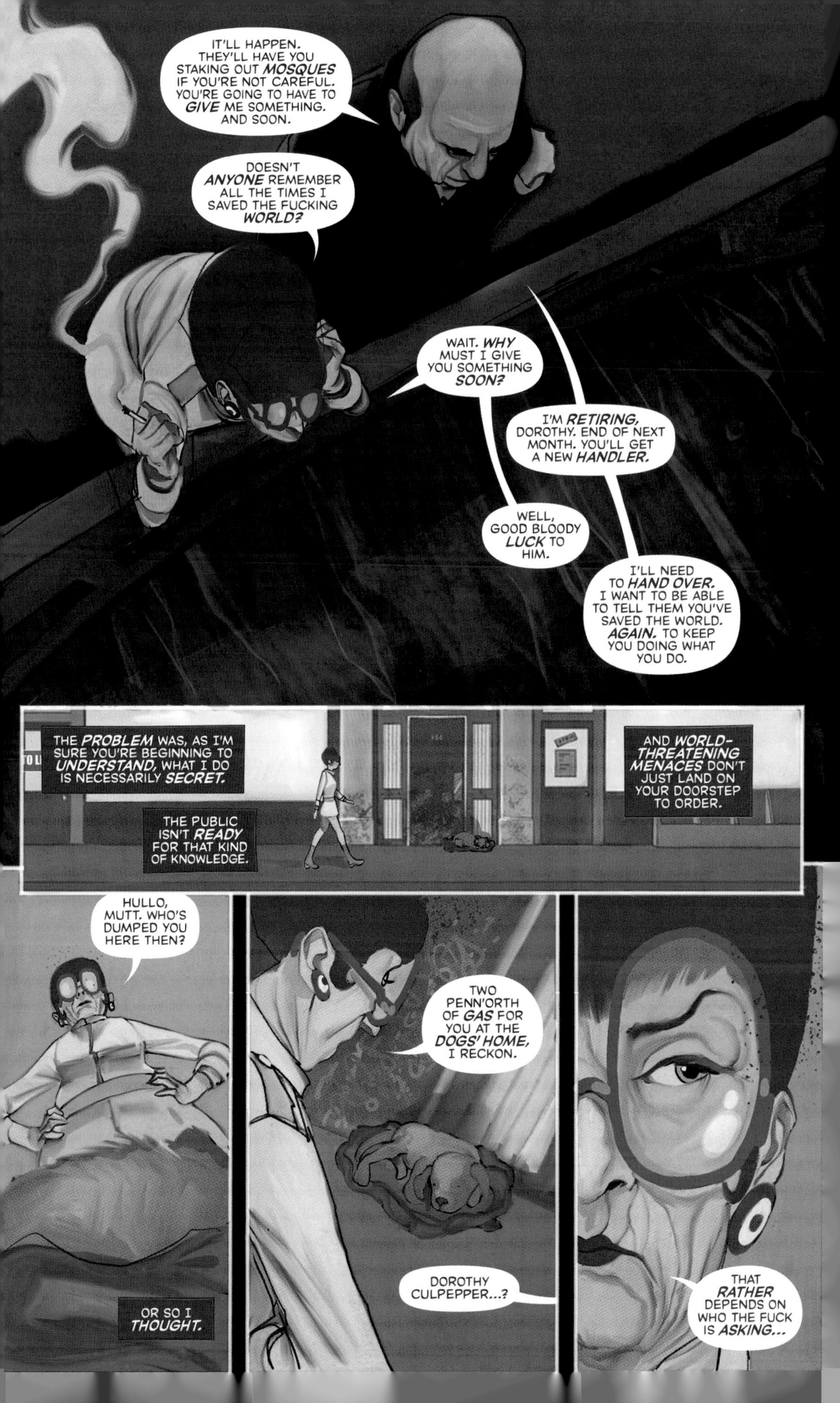
IT'LL HAPPEN. THEY'LL HAVE YOU STAKING OUT MOSQUES IF YOU'RE NOT CAREFUL. YOU'RE GOING TO HAVE TO GIVE ME SOMETHING. AND SOON.
DOESN'T ANYONE REMEMBER ALL THE TIMES I SAVED THE FUCKING WORLD?
WAIT. WHY MUST I GIVE YOU SOMETHING SOON?
I'M RETIRING, DOROTHY. END OF NEXT MONTH. YOU'LL GET A NEW HANDLER.
WELL, GOOD BLOODY LUCK TO HIM.
I'LL NEED TO HAND OVER. I WANT TO BE ABLE TO TELL THEM YOU'VE SAVED THE WORLD. AGAIN. TO KEEP YOU DOING WHAT YOU DO.
THE PROBLEM WAS, AS I'M SURE YOU'RE BEGINNING TO UNDERSTAND, WHAT I DO IS NECESSARILY SECRET.
THE PUBLIC ISN'T READY FOR THAT KIND OF KNOWLEDGE.
AND WORLD-THREATENING MENACES DON'T JUST LAND ON YOUR DOORSTEP TO ORDER.
HULLO, MUTT. WHO'S DUMPED YOU HERE THEN?
OR SO I THOUGHT.
TWO PENN'ORTH OF GAS FOR YOU AT THE DOGS' HOME, I RECKON.
DOROTHY CULPEPPER...?
THAT RATHER DEPENDS ON WHO THE FUCK IS ASKING...

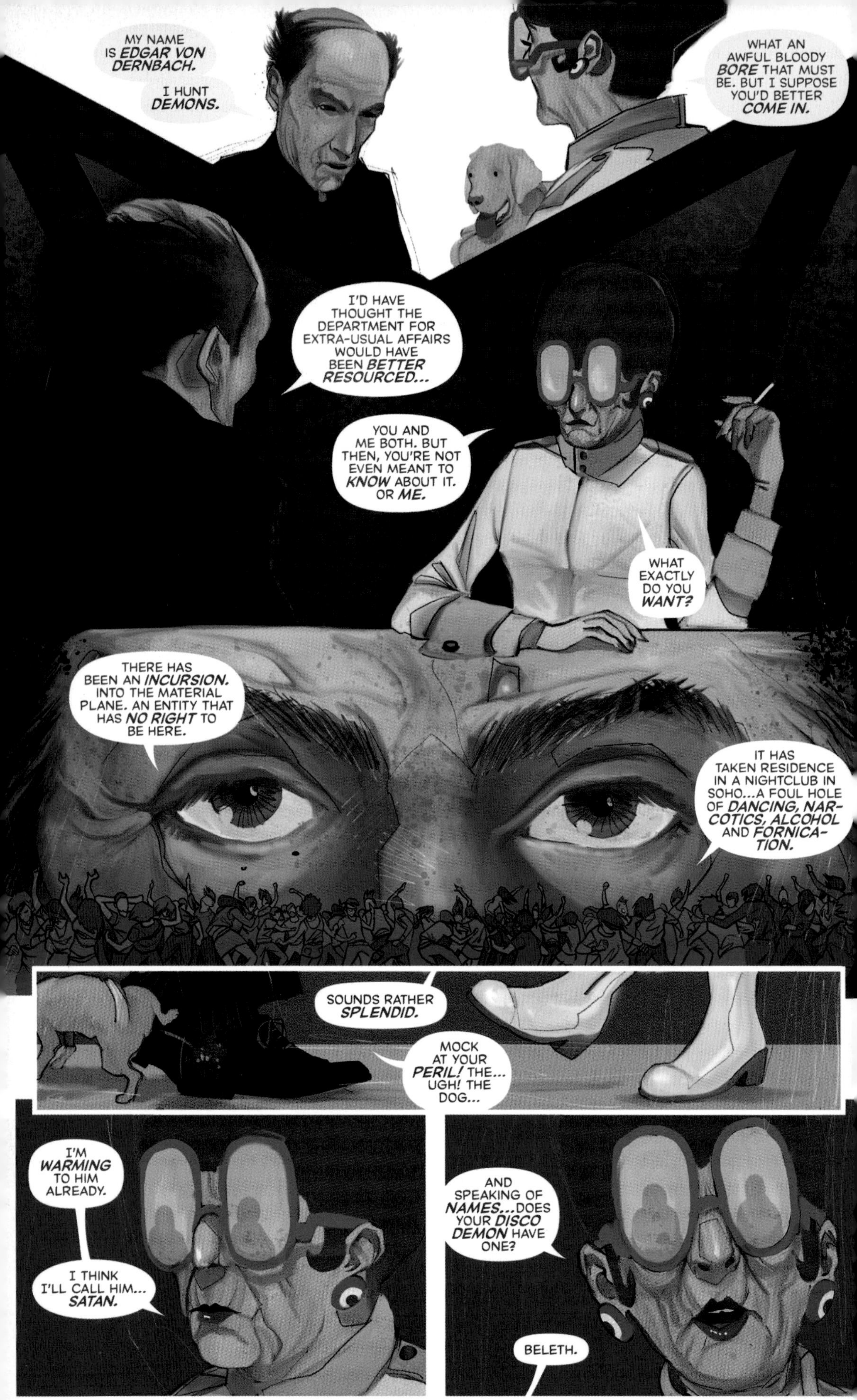
MY NAME IS EDGAR VON DERNBACH.
I HUNT DEMONS.
WHAT AN AWFUL BLOODY BORE THAT MUST BE. BUT I SUPPOSE YOU'D BETTER COME IN.
I'D HAVE THOUGHT THE DEPARTMENT FOR EXTRA-USUAL AFFAIRS WOULD HAVE BEEN BETTER RESOURCED...
YOU AND ME BOTH. BUT THEN, YOU'RE NOT EVEN MEANT TO KNOW ABOUT IT. OR ME.
WHAT EXACTLY DO YOU WANT?
THERE HAS BEEN AN INCURSION. INTO THE MATERIAL PLANE. AN ENTITY THAT HAS NO RIGHT TO BE HERE.
IT HAS TAKEN RESIDENCE IN A NIGHTCLUB IN SOHO...A FOUL HOLE OF DANCING, NARCOTICS, ALCOHOL AND FORNICATION.
SOUNDS RATHER SPLENDID.
MOCK AT YOUR PERIL! THE... UGH! THE DOG...
I'M WARMING TO HIM ALREADY.
I THINK I'LL CALL HIM... SATAN.
AND SPEAKING OF NAMES...DOES YOUR DISCO DEMON HAVE ONE?
BELETH.

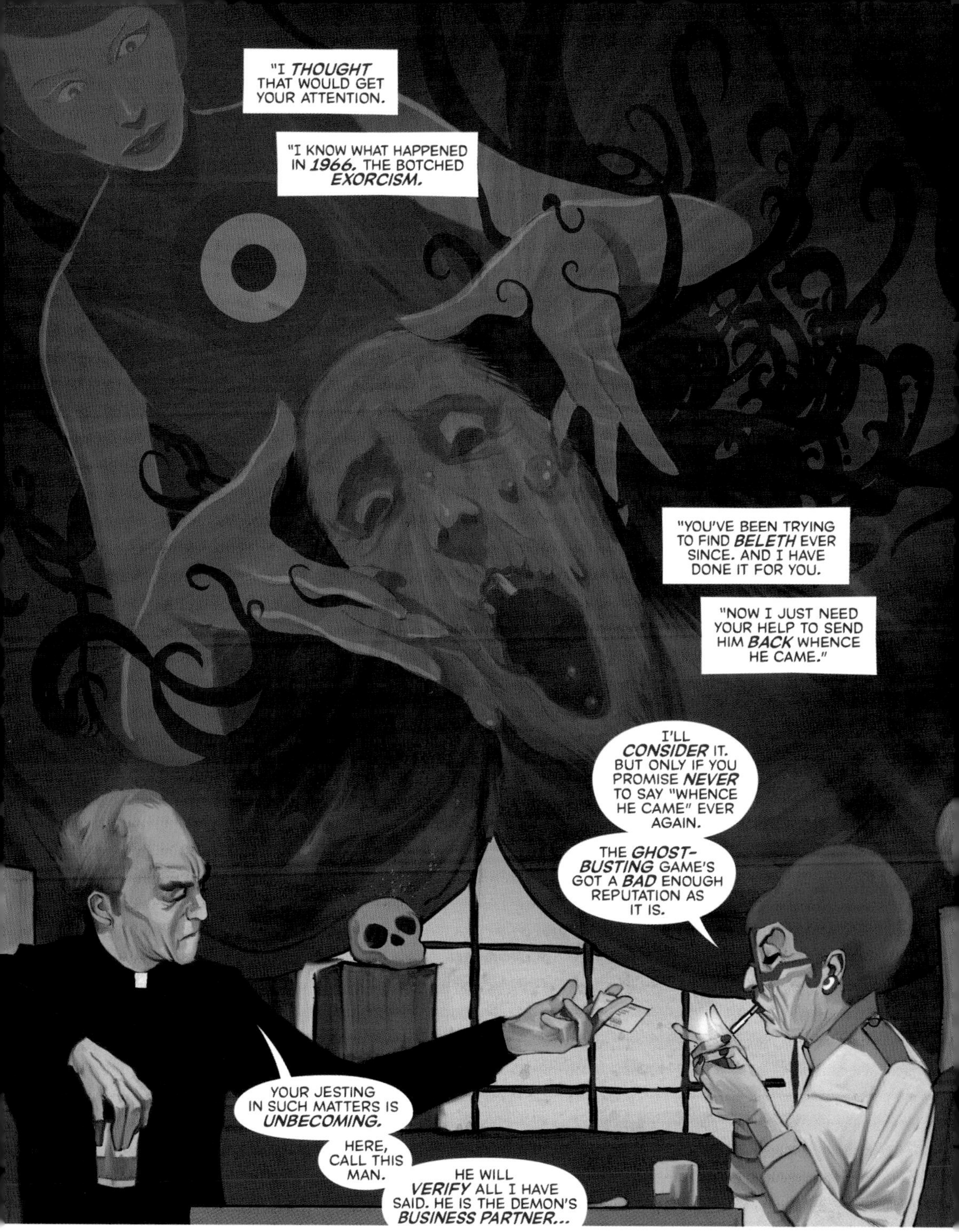
"I THOUGHT THAT WOULD GET YOUR ATTENTION.
"I KNOW WHAT HAPPENED IN 1966. THE BOTCHED EXORCISM.
"YOU'VE BEEN TRYING TO FIND BELETH EVER SINCE. AND I HAVE DONE IT FOR YOU.
"NOW I JUST NEED YOUR HELP TO SEND HIM BACK WHENCE HE CAME."
I'LL CONSIDER IT. BUT ONLY IF YOU PROMISE NEVER TO SAY "WHENCE HE CAME" EVER AGAIN.
THE GHOST-BUSTING GAME'S GOT A BAD ENOUGH REPUTATION AS IT IS.
YOUR JESTING IN SUCH MATTERS IS UNBECOMING.
HERE, CALL THIS MAN.
HE WILL VERIFY ALL I HAVE SAID. HE IS THE DEMON'S BUSINESS PARTNER...

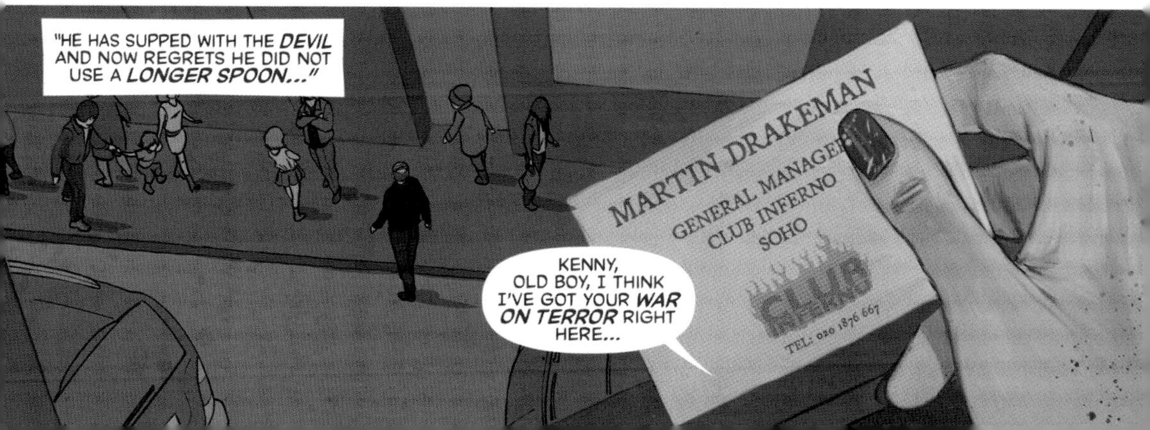
"HE HAS SUPPED WITH THE DEVIL AND NOW REGRETS HE DID NOT USE A LONGER SPOON..."
MARTIN DRAKEMAN
GENERAL MANAGE
CLUB INFERNO
SOHO
TEL: 020 1876 667
KENNY, OLD BOY, I THINK I'VE GOT YOUR WAR ON TERROR RIGHT HERE...

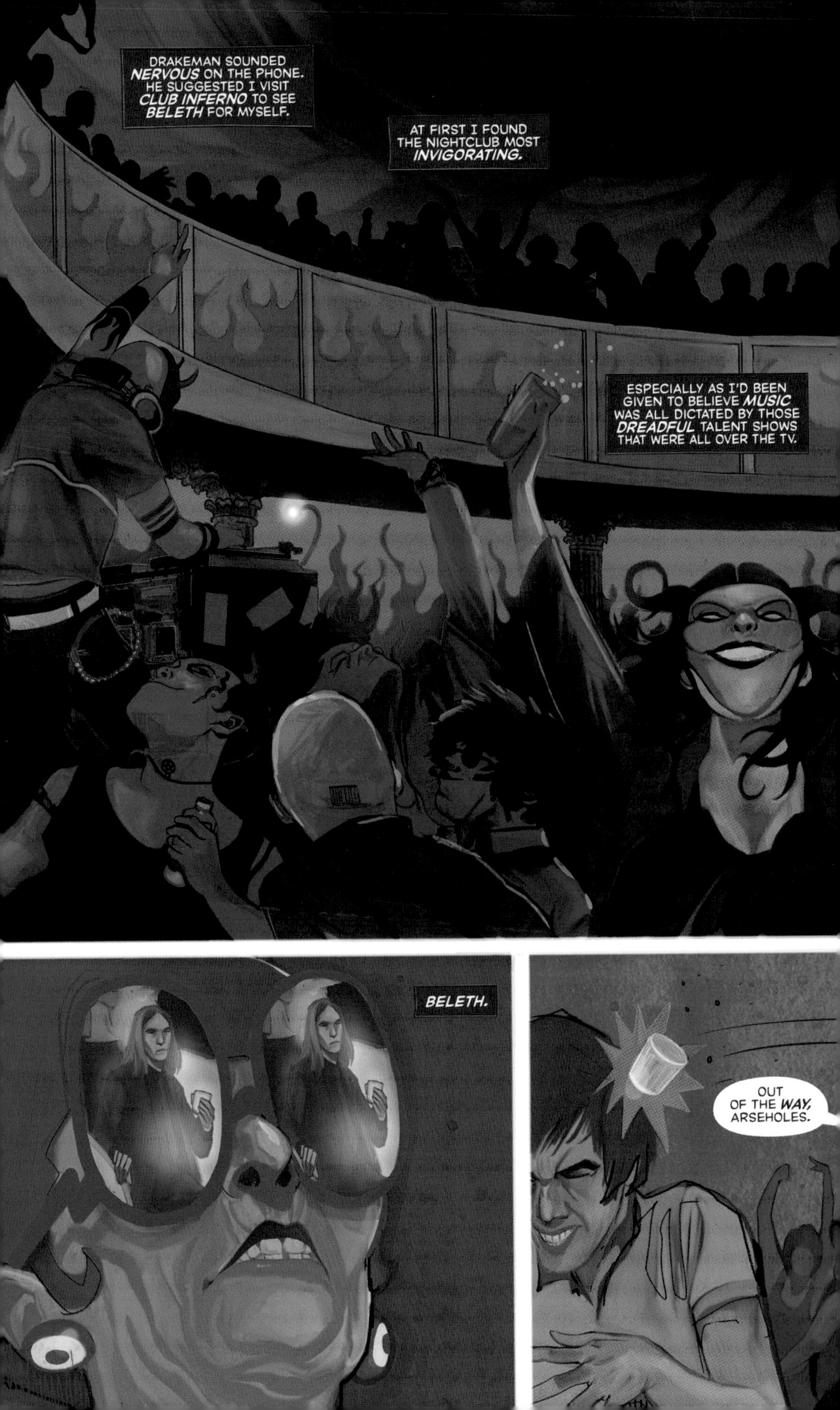
DRAKEMAN SOUNDED NERVOUS ON THE PHONE. HE SUGGESTED I VISIT CLUB INFERNO TO SEE BELETH FOR MYSELF.
AT FIRST I FOUND THE NIGHTCLUB MOST INVIGORATING.
ESPECIALLY AS I'D BEEN GIVEN TO BELIEVE MUSIC WAS ALL DICTATED BY THOSE DREADFUL TALENT SHOWS THAT WERE ALL OVER THE TV.
BELETH.
OUT OF THE WAY, ARSEHOLES.

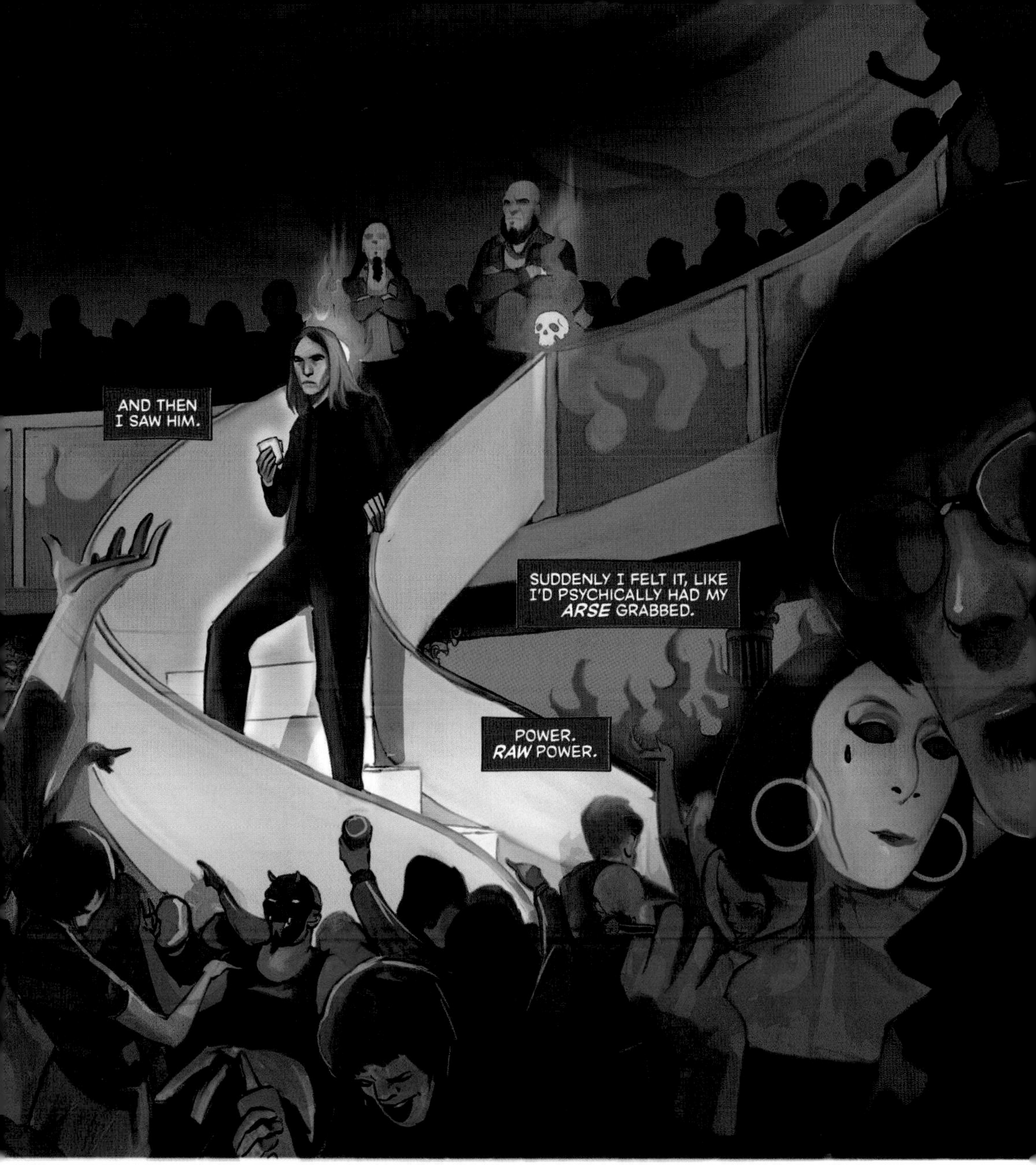
AND THEN I SAW HIM.
SUDDENLY I FELT IT, LIKE I'D PSYCHICALLY HAD MY ARSE GRABBED.
POWER. RAW POWER.

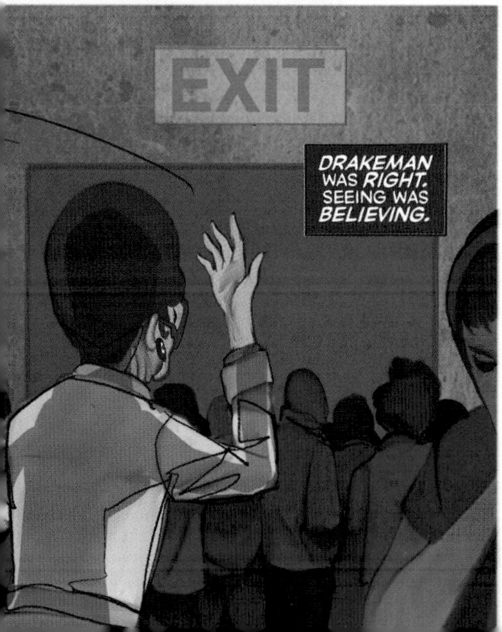
EXIT
DRAKEMAN WAS RIGHT. SEEING WAS BELIEVING.

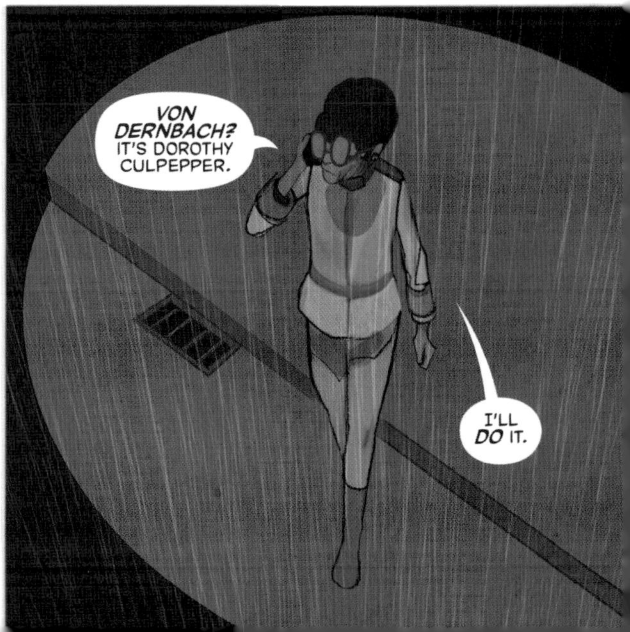
VON DERNBACH? IT'S DOROTHY CULPEPPER.
I'LL DO IT.

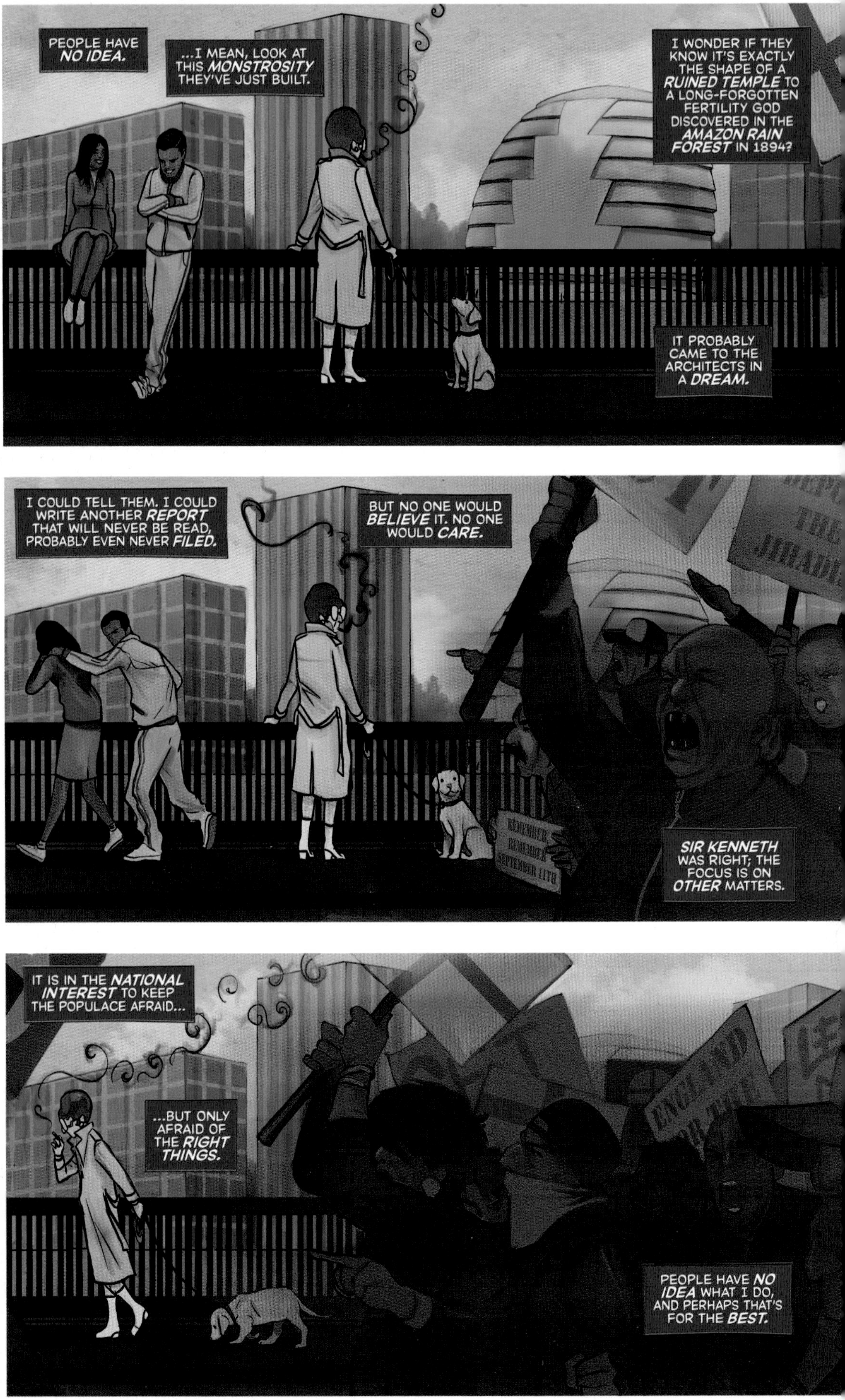
PEOPLE HAVE NO IDEA.
...I MEAN, LOOK AT THIS MONSTROSITY THEY'VE JUST BUILT.
I WONDER IF THEY KNOW IT'S EXACTLY THE SHAPE OF A RUINED TEMPLE TO A LONG-FORGOTTEN FERTILITY GOD DISCOVERED IN THE AMAZON RAIN FOREST IN 1894?
IT PROBABLY CAME TO THE ARCHITECTS IN A DREAM.
I COULD TELL THEM. I COULD WRITE ANOTHER REPORT THAT WILL NEVER BE READ, PROBABLY EVEN NEVER FILED.
BUT NO ONE WOULD BELIEVE IT. NO ONE WOULD CARE.
REMEMBER, REMEMBER SEPTEMBER 11TH
SIR KENNETH WAS RIGHT; THE FOCUS IS ON OTHER MATTERS.
IT IS IN THE NATIONAL INTEREST TO KEEP THE POPULACE AFRAID...
...BUT ONLY AFRAID OF THE RIGHT THINGS.
PEOPLE HAVE NO IDEA WHAT I DO, AND PERHAPS THAT'S FOR THE BEST.

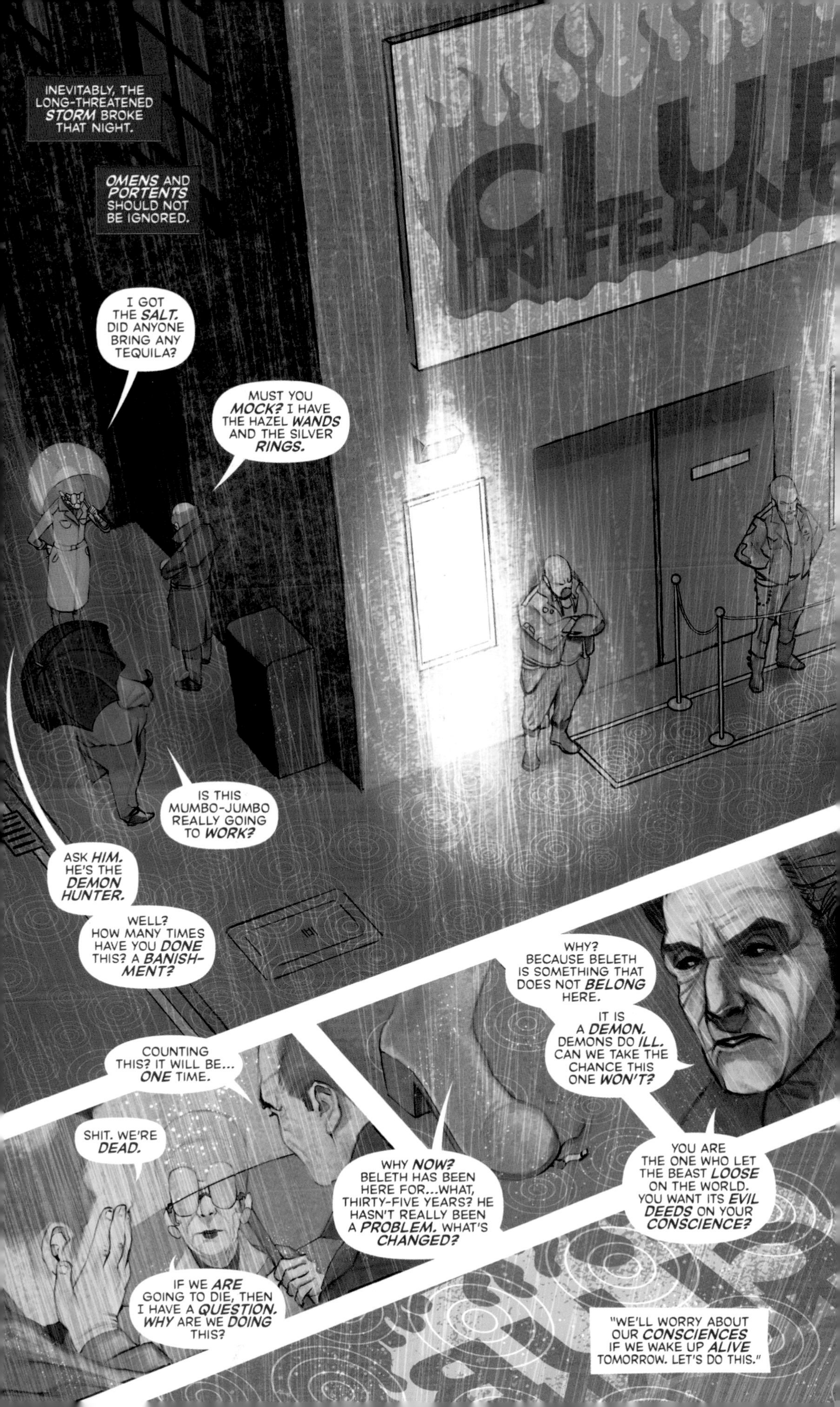
INEVITABLY, THE LONG-THREATENED STORM BROKE THAT NIGHT.
OMENS AND PORTENTS SHOULD NOT BE IGNORED.
CLUB INFERNO
I GOT THE SALT. DID ANYONE BRING ANY TEQUILA?
MUST YOU MOCK? I HAVE THE HAZEL WANDS AND THE SILVER RINGS.
IS THIS MUMBO-JUMBO REALLY GOING TO WORK?
ASK HIM. HE'S THE DEMON HUNTER.
WELL? HOW MANY TIMES HAVE YOU DONE THIS? A BANISHMENT?
COUNTING THIS? IT WILL BE... ONE TIME.
SHIT. WE'RE DEAD.
IF WE ARE GOING TO DIE, THEN I HAVE A QUESTION. WHY ARE WE DOING THIS?
WHY? BECAUSE BELETH IS SOMETHING THAT DOES NOT BELONG HERE.
IT IS A DEMON. DEMONS DO ILL. CAN WE TAKE THE CHANCE THIS ONE WON'T?
WHY NOW? BELETH HAS BEEN HERE FOR...WHAT, THIRTY-FIVE YEARS? HE HASN'T REALLY BEEN A PROBLEM. WHAT'S CHANGED?
YOU ARE THE ONE WHO LET THE BEAST LOOSE ON THE WORLD. YOU WANT ITS EVIL DEEDS ON YOUR CONSCIENCE?
"WE'LL WORRY ABOUT OUR CONSCIENCES IF WE WAKE UP ALIVE TOMORROW. LET'S DO THIS."

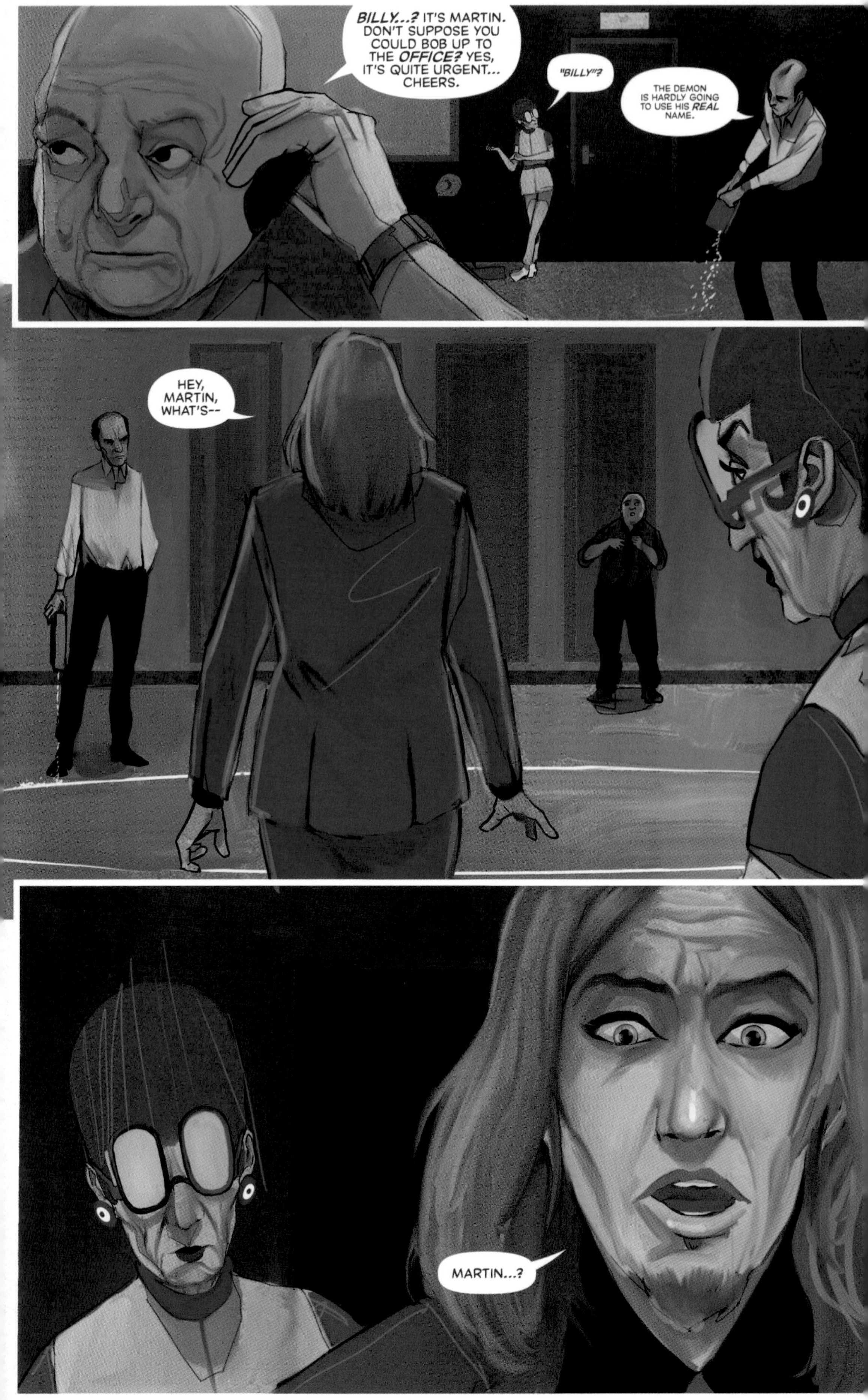
BILLY...? IT'S MARTIN. DON'T SUPPOSE YOU COULD BOB UP TO THE OFFICE? YES, IT'S QUITE URGENT... CHEERS.
"BILLY"?
THE DEMON IS HARDLY GOING TO USE HIS REAL NAME.
HEY, MARTIN, WHAT'S--
MARTIN...?

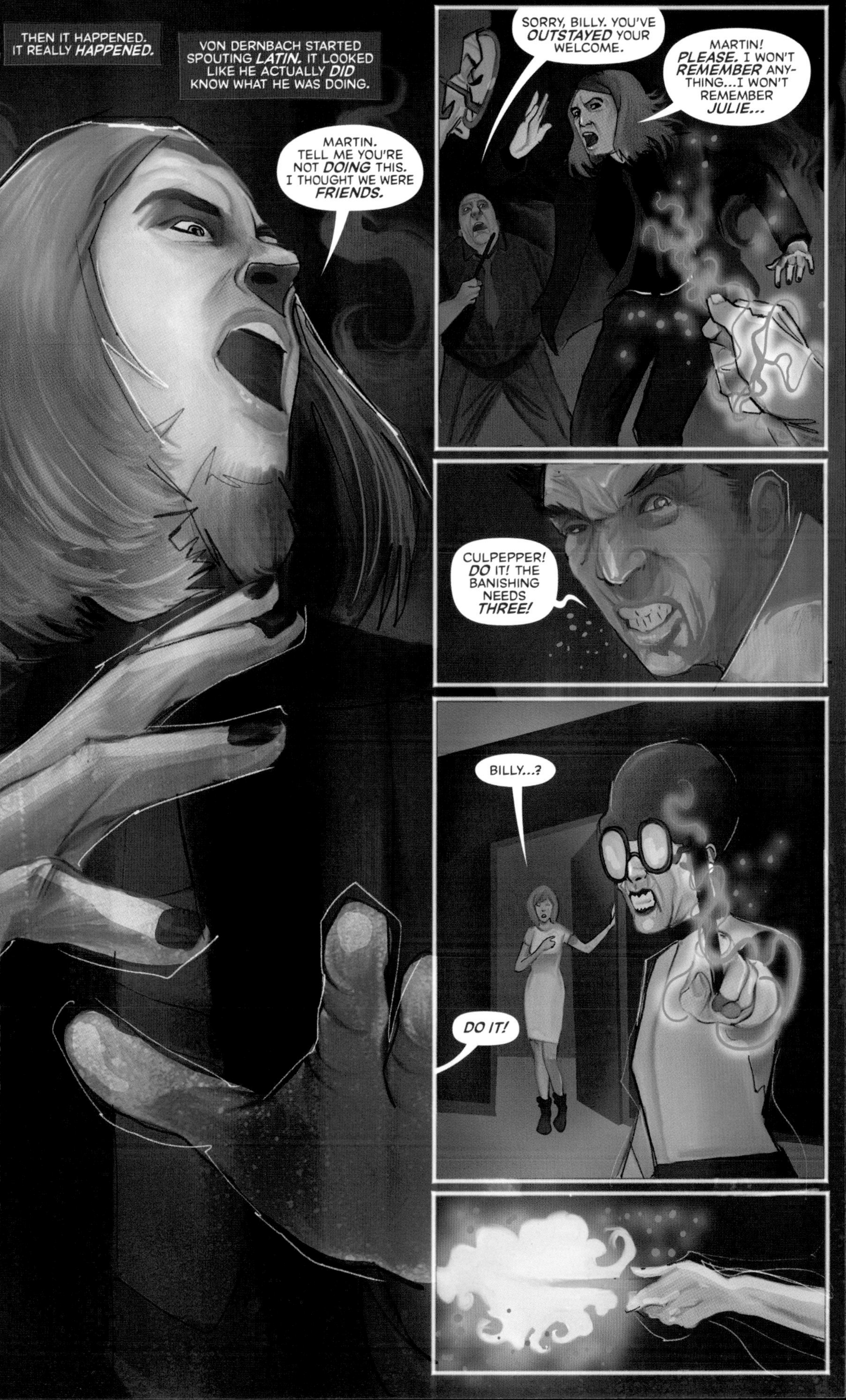
THEN IT HAPPENED. IT REALLY HAPPENED.
VON DERNBACH STARTED SPOUTING LATIN. IT LOOKED LIKE HE ACTUALLY DID KNOW WHAT HE WAS DOING.
MARTIN. TELL ME YOU'RE NOT DOING THIS. I THOUGHT WE WERE FRIENDS.
SORRY, BILLY. YOU'VE OUTSTAYED YOUR WELCOME.
MARTIN! PLEASE. I WON'T REMEMBER ANY-THING...I WON'T REMEMBER JULIE...
CULPEPPER! DO IT! THE BANISHING NEEDS THREE!
BILLY...?
DO IT!

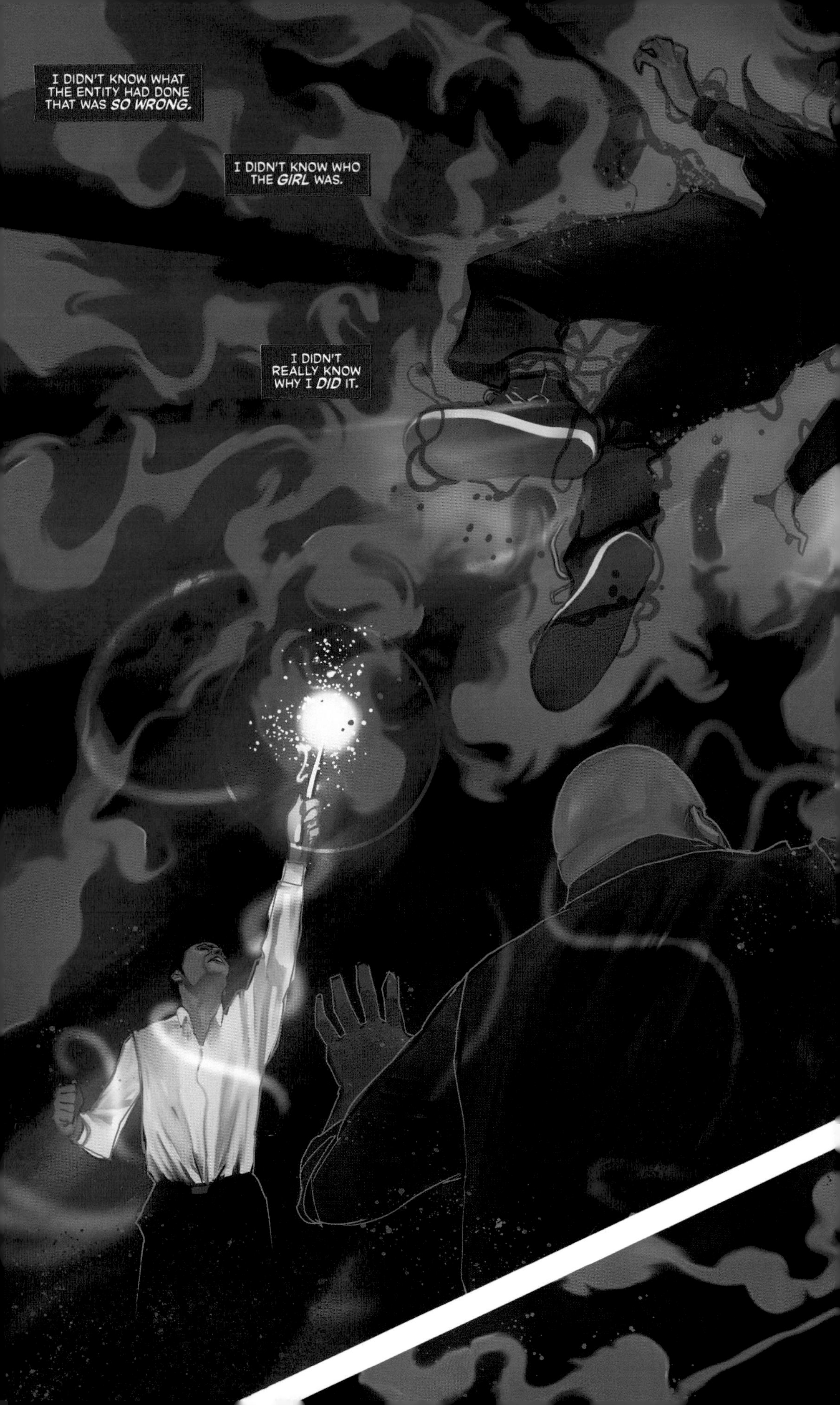
I DIDN'T KNOW WHAT THE ENTITY HAD DONE THAT WAS *SO WRONG.*
I DIDN'T KNOW WHO THE *GIRL* WAS.
I DIDN'T REALLY KNOW WHY I *DID* IT.

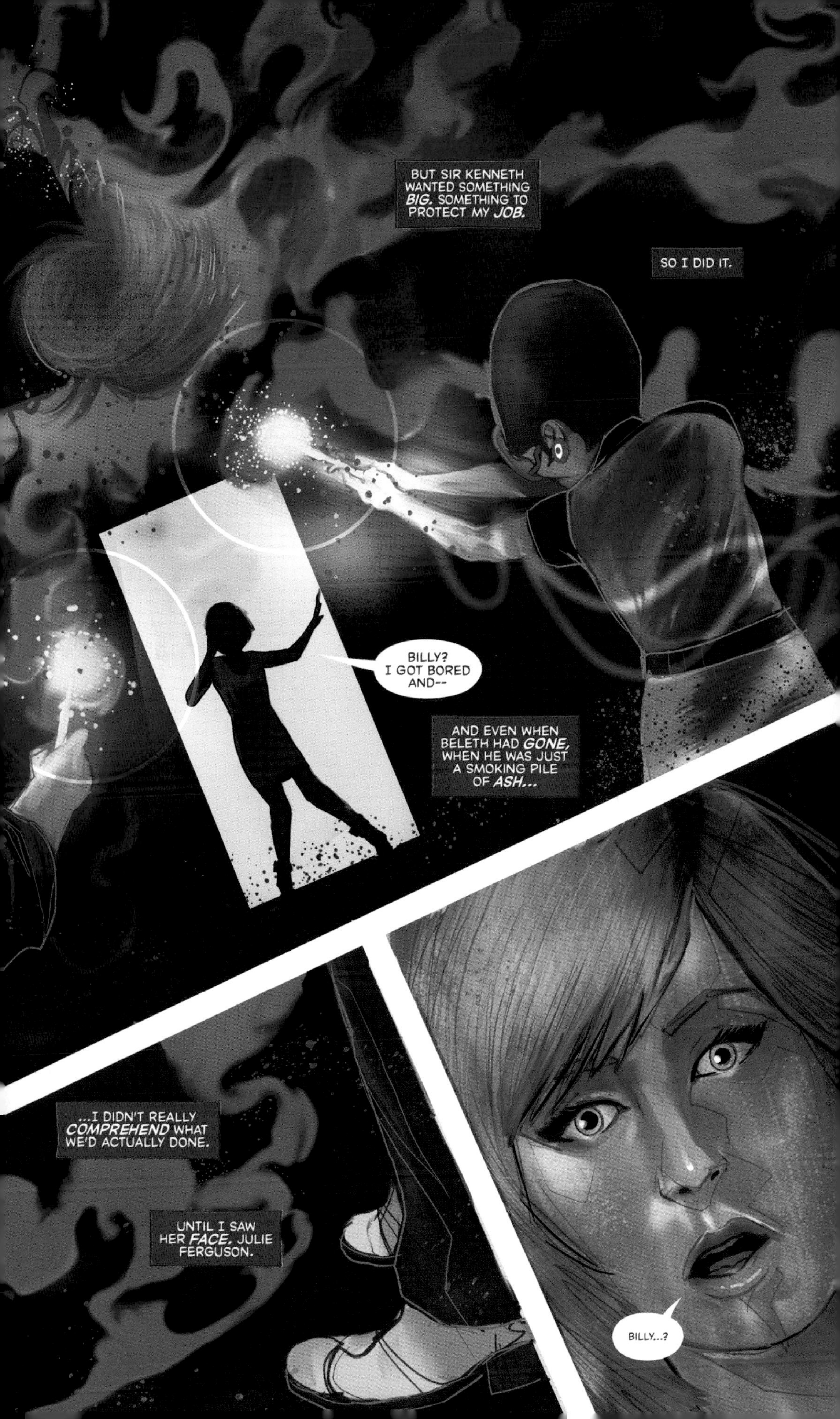
BUT SIR KENNETH WANTED SOMETHING *BIG.* SOMETHING TO PROTECT MY *JOB.*
SO I DID IT.
BILLY? I GOT BORED AND--
AND EVEN WHEN BELETH HAD *GONE,* WHEN HE WAS JUST A SMOKING PILE OF *ASH...*
...I DIDN'T REALLY *COMPREHEND* WHAT WE'D ACTUALLY DONE.
UNTIL I SAW HER *FACE.* JULIE FERGUSON.
BILLY...?

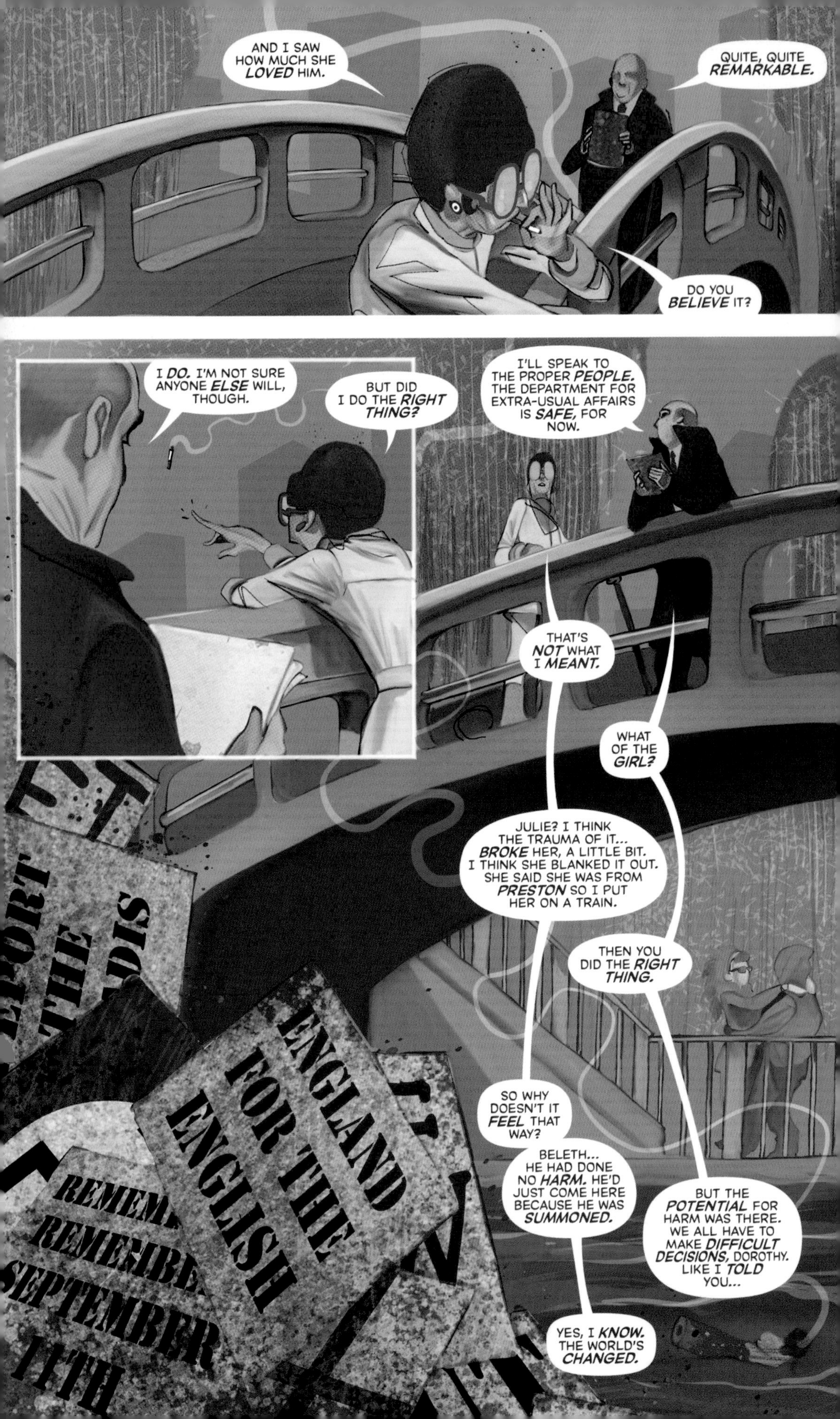
AND I SAW HOW MUCH SHE LOVED HIM.
QUITE, QUITE REMARKABLE.
DO YOU BELIEVE IT?
I DO. I'M NOT SURE ANYONE ELSE WILL, THOUGH.
BUT DID I DO THE RIGHT THING?
I'LL SPEAK TO THE PROPER PEOPLE. THE DEPARTMENT FOR EXTRA-USUAL AFFAIRS IS SAFE, FOR NOW.
THAT'S NOT WHAT I MEANT.
WHAT OF THE GIRL?
JULIE? I THINK THE TRAUMA OF IT... BROKE HER, A LITTLE BIT. I THINK SHE BLANKED IT OUT. SHE SAID SHE WAS FROM PRESTON SO I PUT HER ON A TRAIN.
THEN YOU DID THE RIGHT THING.
SO WHY DOESN'T IT FEEL THAT WAY?
BELETH... HE HAD DONE NO HARM. HE'D JUST COME HERE BECAUSE HE WAS SUMMONED.
BUT THE POTENTIAL FOR HARM WAS THERE. WE ALL HAVE TO MAKE DIFFICULT DECISIONS, DOROTHY. LIKE I TOLD YOU...
YES, I KNOW. THE WORLD'S CHANGED.
ENGLAND FOR THE ENGLISH
REMEMBER SEPTEMBER 11TH

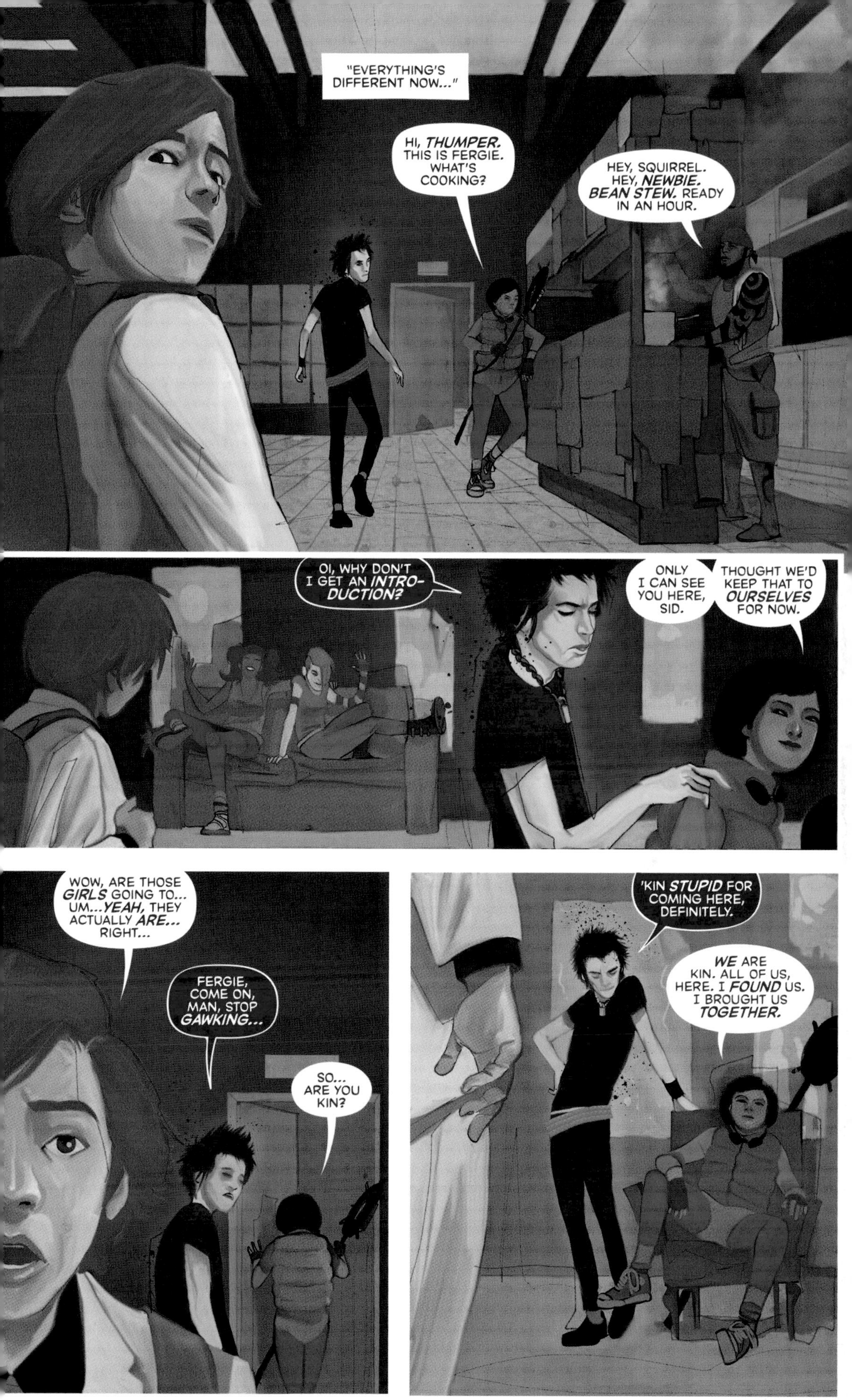
"EVERYTHING'S DIFFERENT NOW..."
HI, *THUMPER.* THIS IS FERGIE. WHAT'S COOKING?
HEY, SQUIRREL. HEY, *NEWBIE. BEAN STEW.* READY IN AN HOUR.
OI, WHY DON'T I GET AN *INTRO-DUCTION?*
ONLY I CAN SEE YOU HERE, SID.
THOUGHT WE'D KEEP THAT TO *OURSELVES* FOR NOW.
WOW, ARE THOSE *GIRLS* GOING TO... UM...*YEAH,* THEY ACTUALLY *ARE...* RIGHT...
FERGIE, COME ON, MAN, STOP *GAWKING...*
SO... ARE YOU KIN?
'KIN *STUPID* FOR COMING HERE, DEFINITELY.
WE ARE KIN. ALL OF US, HERE. I *FOUND* US. I BROUGHT US *TOGETHER.*

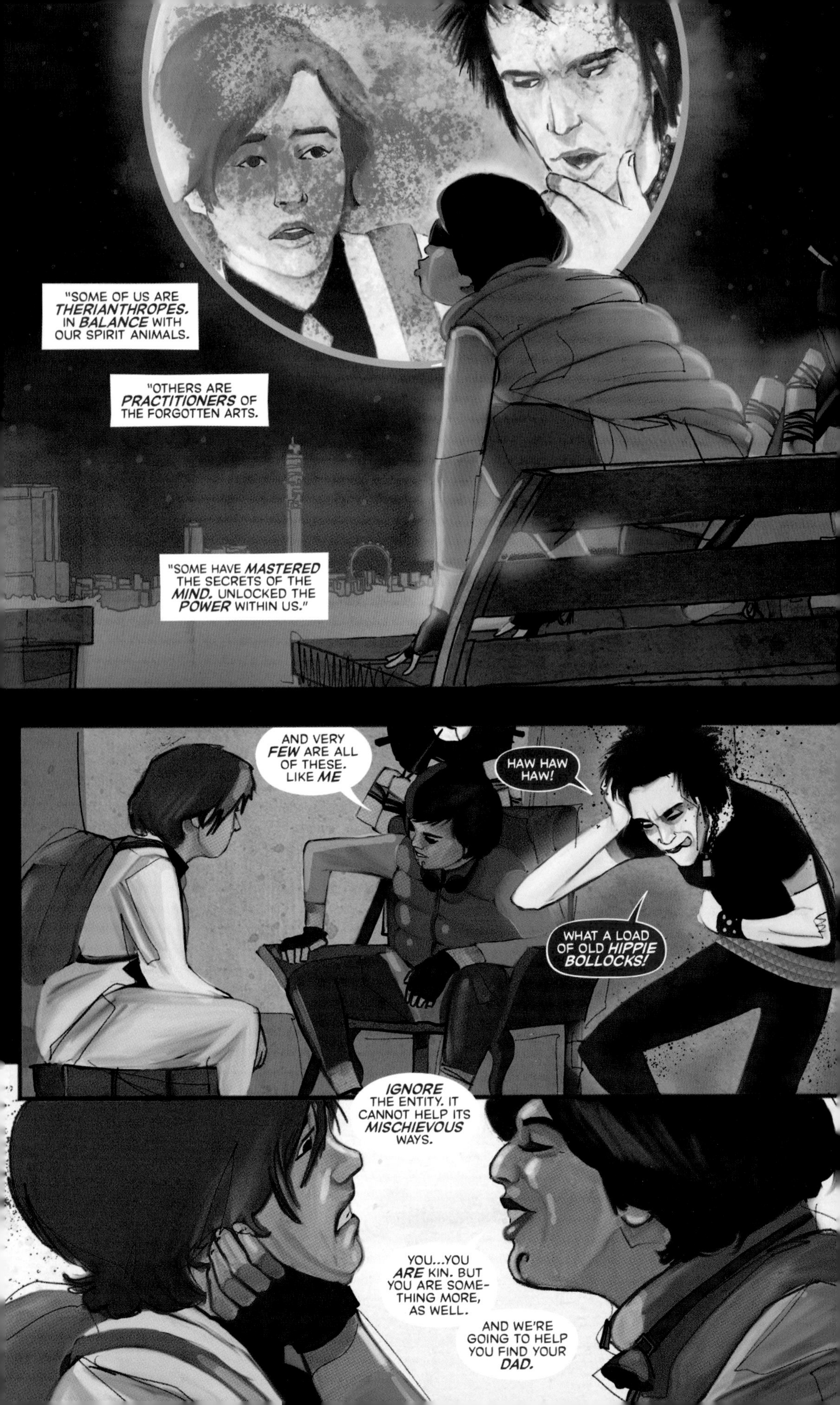
"SOME OF US ARE *THERIANTHROPES.* IN *BALANCE* WITH OUR SPIRIT ANIMALS.
"OTHERS ARE *PRACTITIONERS* OF THE FORGOTTEN ARTS.
"SOME HAVE *MASTERED* THE SECRETS OF THE *MIND.* UNLOCKED THE *POWER* WITHIN US."
AND VERY *FEW* ARE ALL OF THESE. LIKE *ME*
HAW HAW HAW!
WHAT A LOAD OF OLD *HIPPIE BOLLOCKS!*
IGNORE THE ENTITY. IT CANNOT HELP ITS *MISCHIEVOUS* WAYS.
YOU...YOU *ARE* KIN. BUT YOU ARE SOME-THING MORE, AS WELL.
AND WE'RE GOING TO HELP YOU FIND YOUR *DAD.*

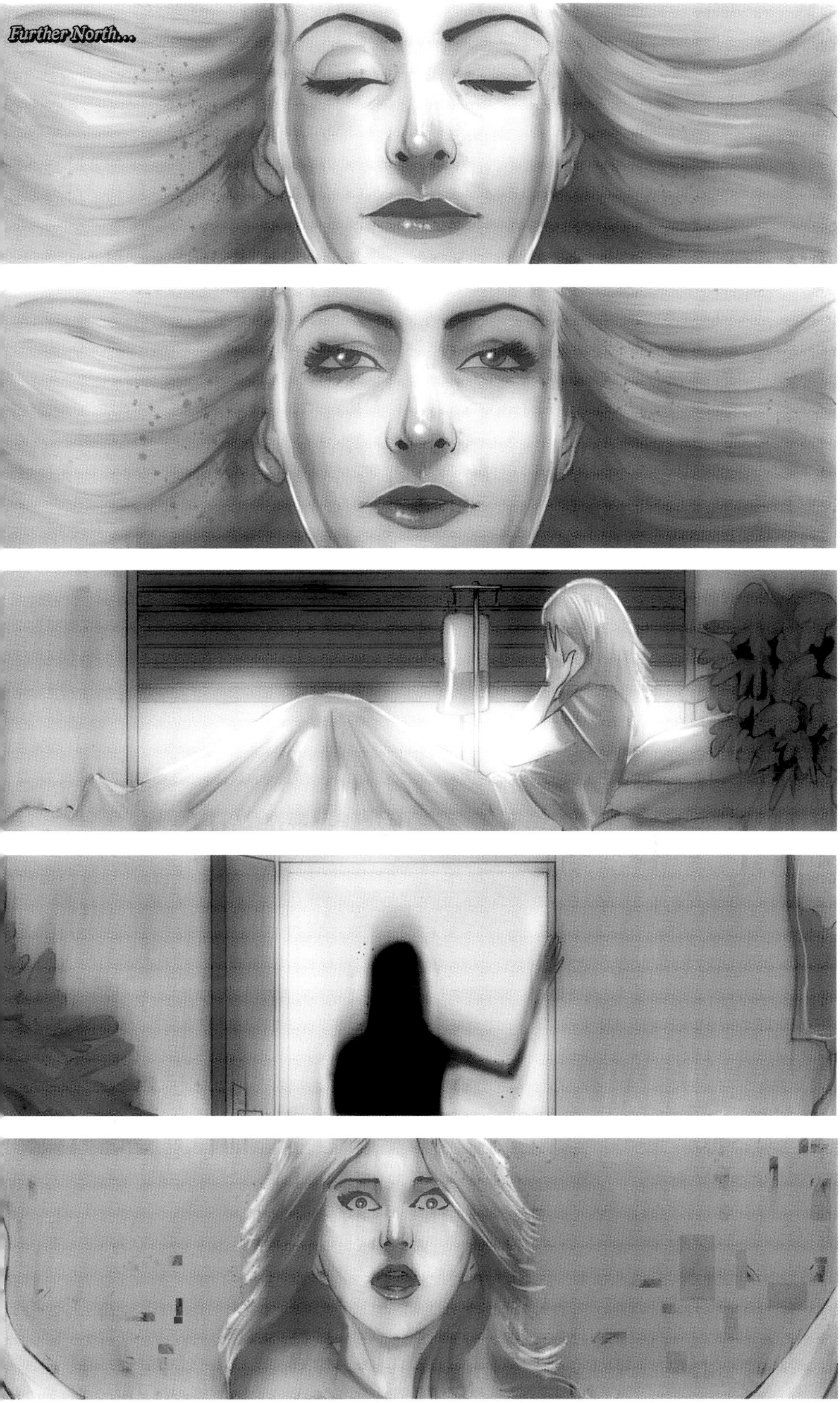
Further North...

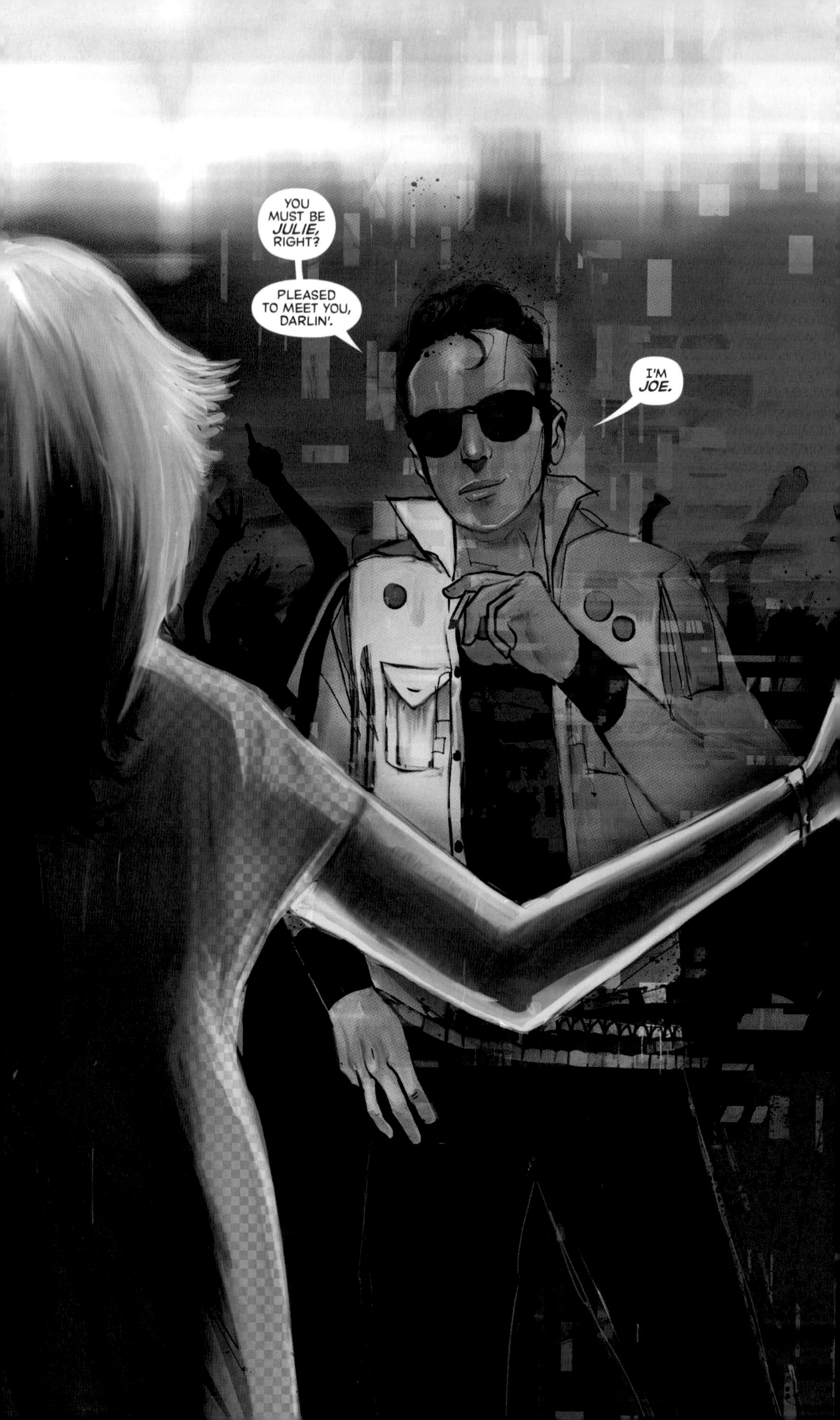
YOU MUST BE JULIE, RIGHT?
PLEASED TO MEET YOU, DARLIN'.
I'M JOE.

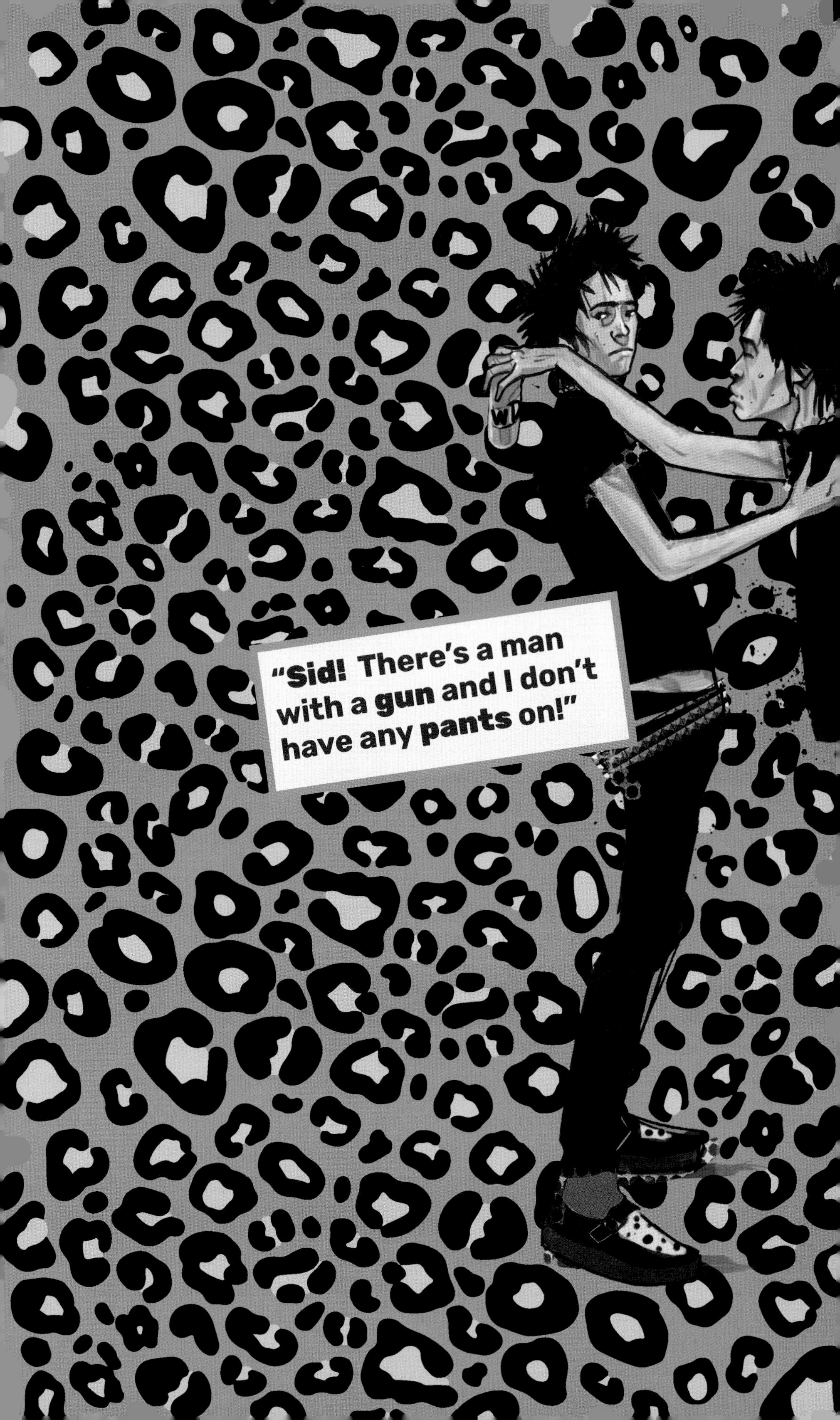
"Sid! There's a man with a gun and I don't have any pants on!"

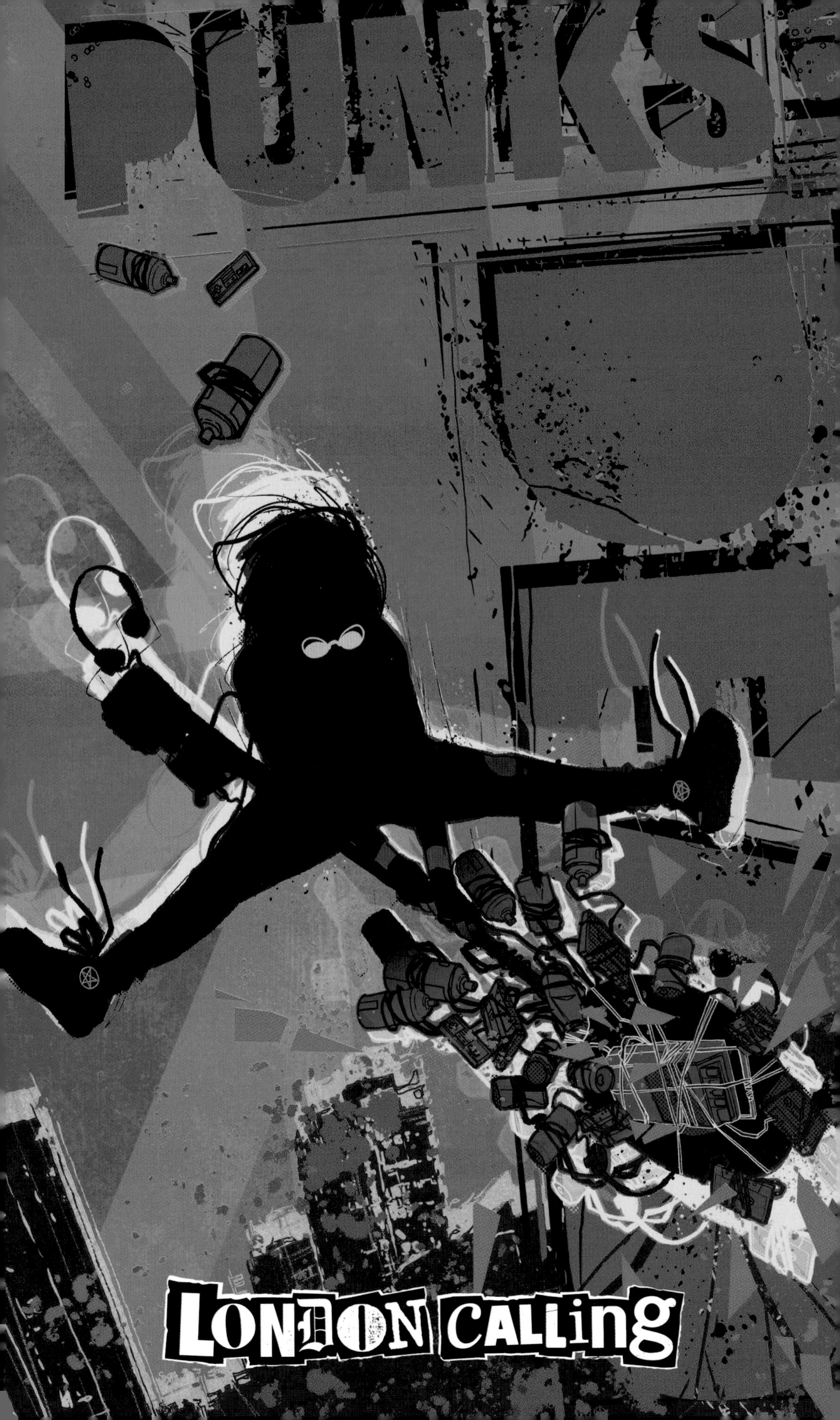
PUNKS
LONDON CALLING

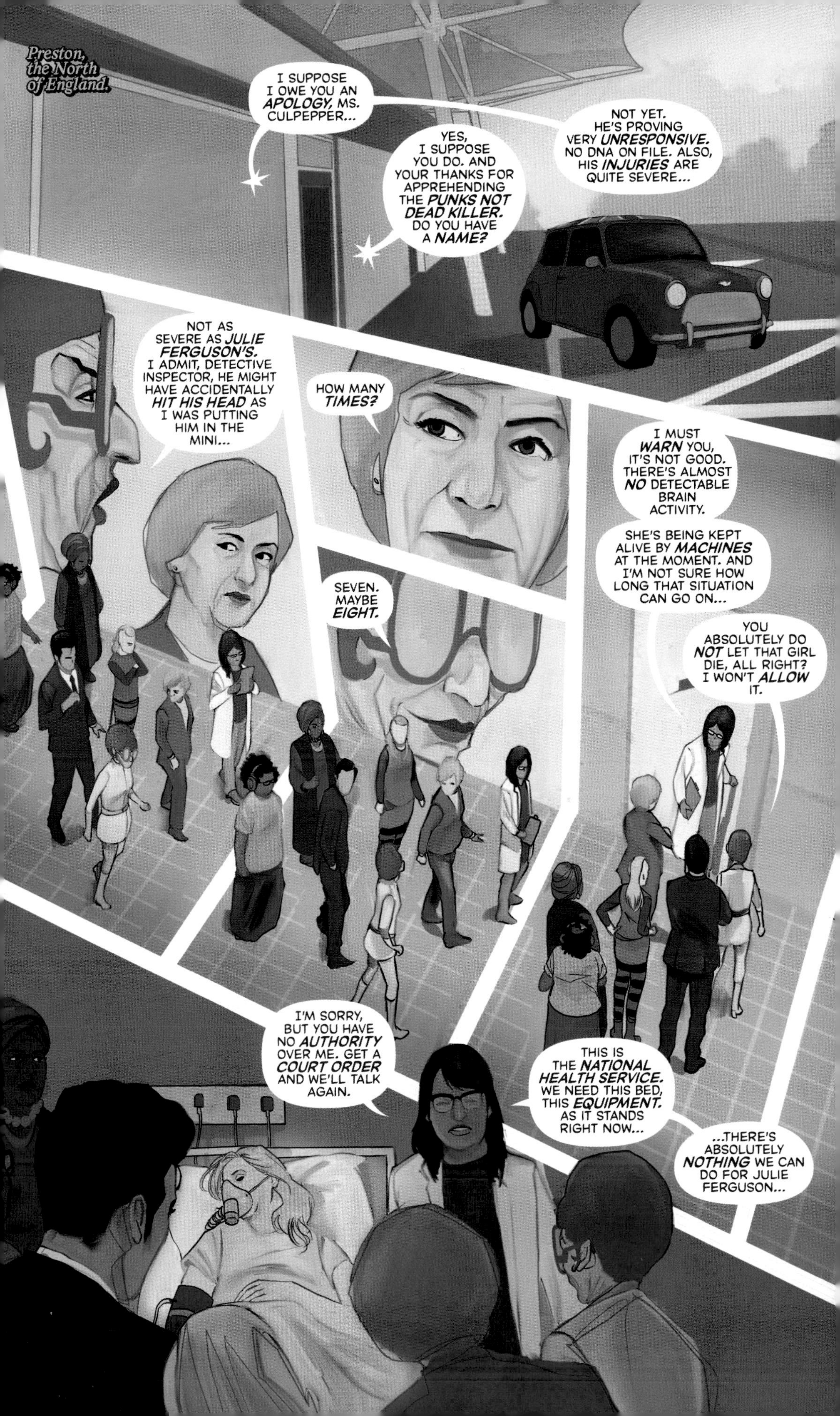
Preston, the North of England.
I SUPPOSE I OWE YOU AN APOLOGY, MS. CULPEPPER...
YES, I SUPPOSE YOU DO. AND YOUR THANKS FOR APPREHENDING THE PUNKS NOT DEAD KILLER. DO YOU HAVE A NAME?
NOT YET. HE'S PROVING VERY UNRESPONSIVE. NO DNA ON FILE. ALSO, HIS INJURIES ARE QUITE SEVERE...
NOT AS SEVERE AS JULIE FERGUSON'S. I ADMIT, DETECTIVE INSPECTOR, HE MIGHT HAVE ACCIDENTALLY HIT HIS HEAD AS I WAS PUTTING HIM IN THE MINI...
HOW MANY TIMES?
SEVEN. MAYBE EIGHT.
I MUST WARN YOU, IT'S NOT GOOD. THERE'S ALMOST NO DETECTABLE BRAIN ACTIVITY.
SHE'S BEING KEPT ALIVE BY MACHINES AT THE MOMENT. AND I'M NOT SURE HOW LONG THAT SITUATION CAN GO ON...
YOU ABSOLUTELY DO NOT LET THAT GIRL DIE, ALL RIGHT? I WON'T ALLOW IT.
I'M SORRY, BUT YOU HAVE NO AUTHORITY OVER ME. GET A COURT ORDER AND WE'LL TALK AGAIN.
THIS IS THE NATIONAL HEALTH SERVICE. WE NEED THIS BED, THIS EQUIPMENT. AS IT STANDS RIGHT NOW...
...THERE'S ABSOLUTELY NOTHING WE CAN DO FOR JULIE FERGUSON...

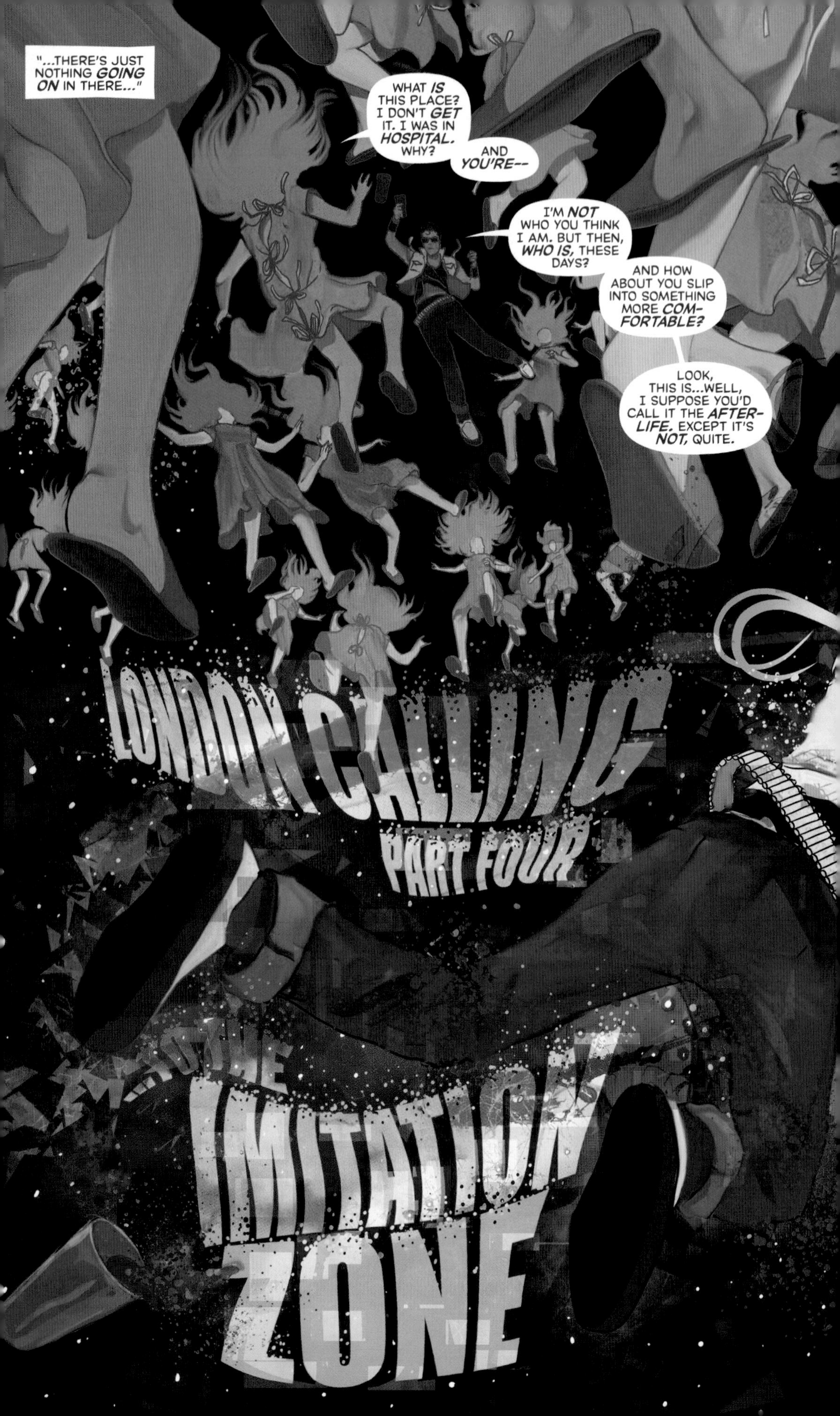
"...THERE'S JUST NOTHING GOING ON IN THERE..."
WHAT IS THIS PLACE? I DON'T GET IT. I WAS IN HOSPITAL. WHY?
AND YOU'RE--
I'M NOT WHO YOU THINK I AM. BUT THEN, WHO IS, THESE DAYS?
AND HOW ABOUT YOU SLIP INTO SOMETHING MORE COM-FORTABLE?
LOOK, THIS IS...WELL, I SUPPOSE YOU'D CALL IT THE AFTER-LIFE. EXCEPT IT'S NOT, QUITE.
LONDON CALLING
PART FOUR
THE IMITATION ZONE

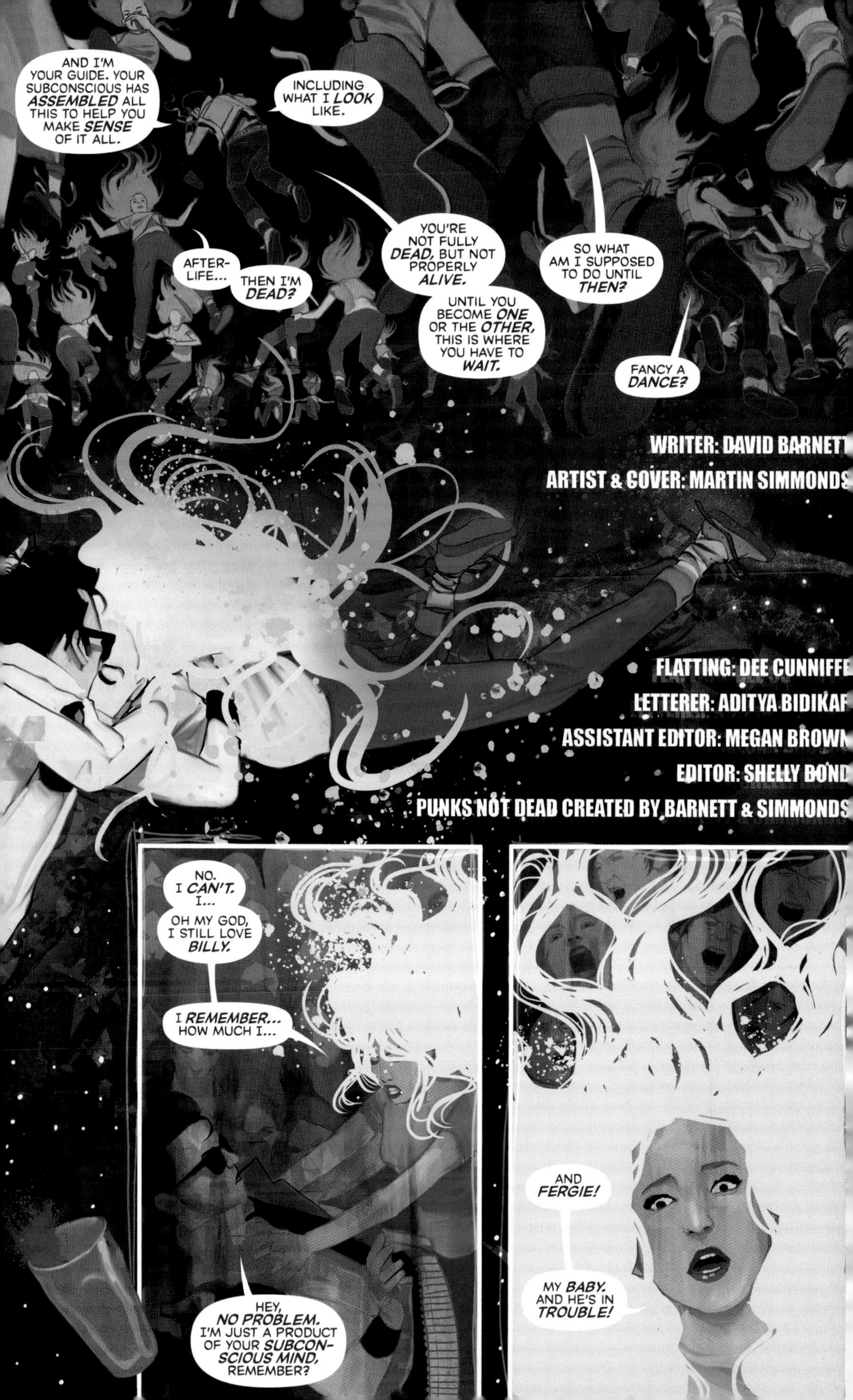
AND I'M YOUR GUIDE. YOUR SUBCONSCIOUS HAS ASSEMBLED ALL THIS TO HELP YOU MAKE SENSE OF IT ALL.
INCLUDING WHAT I LOOK LIKE.
AFTER-LIFE...
THEN I'M DEAD?
YOU'RE NOT FULLY DEAD, BUT NOT PROPERLY ALIVE.
UNTIL YOU BECOME ONE OR THE OTHER, THIS IS WHERE YOU HAVE TO WAIT.
SO WHAT AM I SUPPOSED TO DO UNTIL THEN?
FANCY A DANCE?
WRITER: DAVID BARNETT
ARTIST & COVER: MARTIN SIMMONDS
FLATTING: DEE CUNNIFFE
LETTERER: ADITYA BIDIKAR
ASSISTANT EDITOR: MEGAN BROWN
EDITOR: SHELLY BOND
PUNKS NOT DEAD CREATED BY BARNETT & SIMMONDS
NO. I CAN'T. I...
OH MY GOD, I STILL LOVE BILLY.
I REMEMBER... HOW MUCH I...
HEY, NO PROBLEM. I'M JUST A PRODUCT OF YOUR SUBCON-SCIOUS MIND, REMEMBER?
AND FERGIE!
MY BABY. AND HE'S IN TROUBLE!

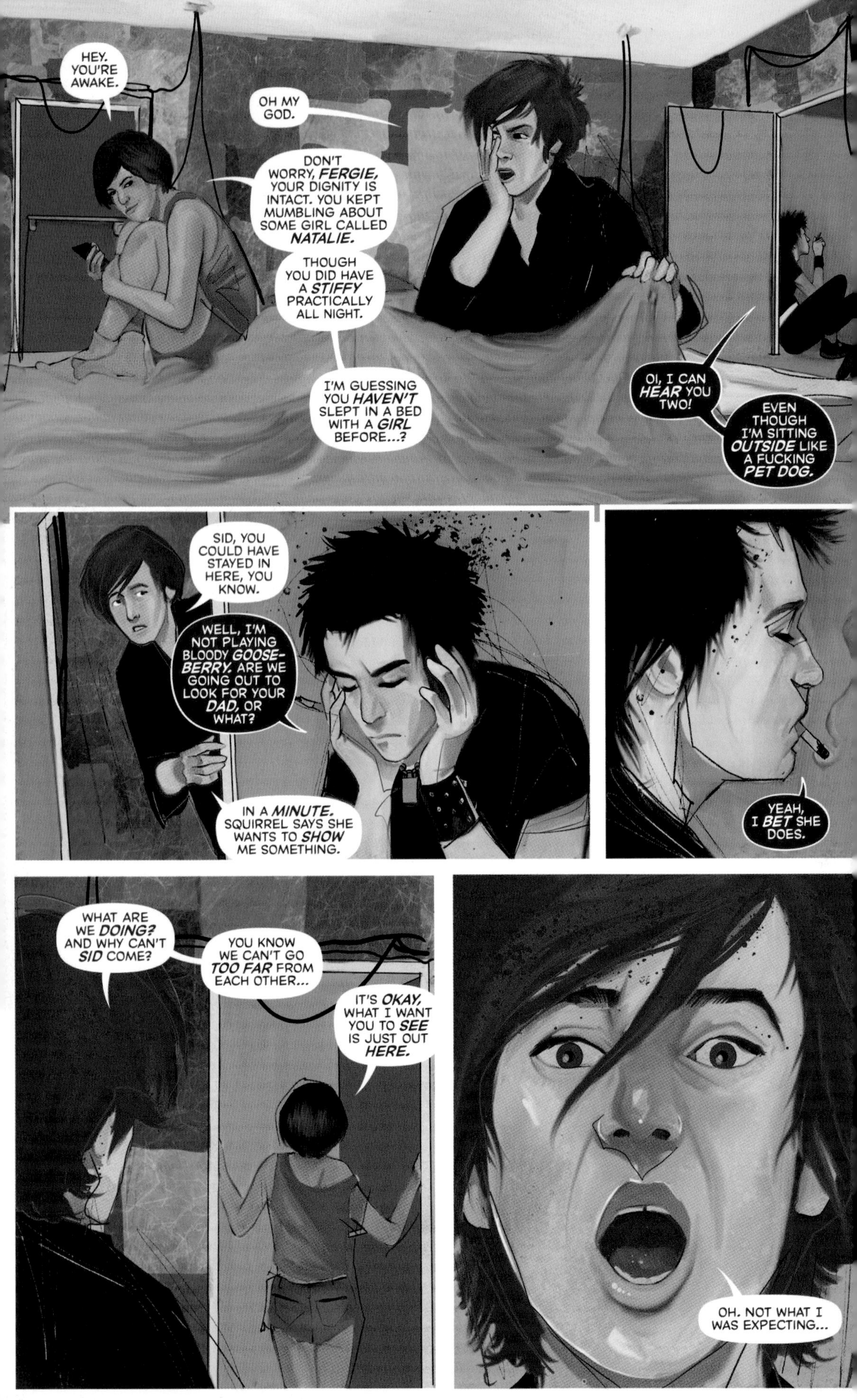
HEY. YOU'RE AWAKE.
OH MY GOD.
DON'T WORRY, FERGIE, YOUR DIGNITY IS INTACT. YOU KEPT MUMBLING ABOUT SOME GIRL CALLED NATALIE.
THOUGH YOU DID HAVE A STIFFY PRACTICALLY ALL NIGHT.
I'M GUESSING YOU HAVEN'T SLEPT IN A BED WITH A GIRL BEFORE...?
OI, I CAN HEAR YOU TWO!
EVEN THOUGH I'M SITTING OUTSIDE LIKE A FUCKING PET DOG.
SID, YOU COULD HAVE STAYED IN HERE, YOU KNOW.
WELL, I'M NOT PLAYING BLOODY GOOSE-BERRY. ARE WE GOING OUT TO LOOK FOR YOUR DAD, OR WHAT?
IN A MINUTE. SQUIRREL SAYS SHE WANTS TO SHOW ME SOMETHING.
YEAH, I BET SHE DOES.
WHAT ARE WE DOING? AND WHY CAN'T SID COME?
YOU KNOW WE CAN'T GO TOO FAR FROM EACH OTHER...
IT'S OKAY, WHAT I WANT YOU TO SEE IS JUST OUT HERE.
OH. NOT WHAT I WAS EXPECTING...

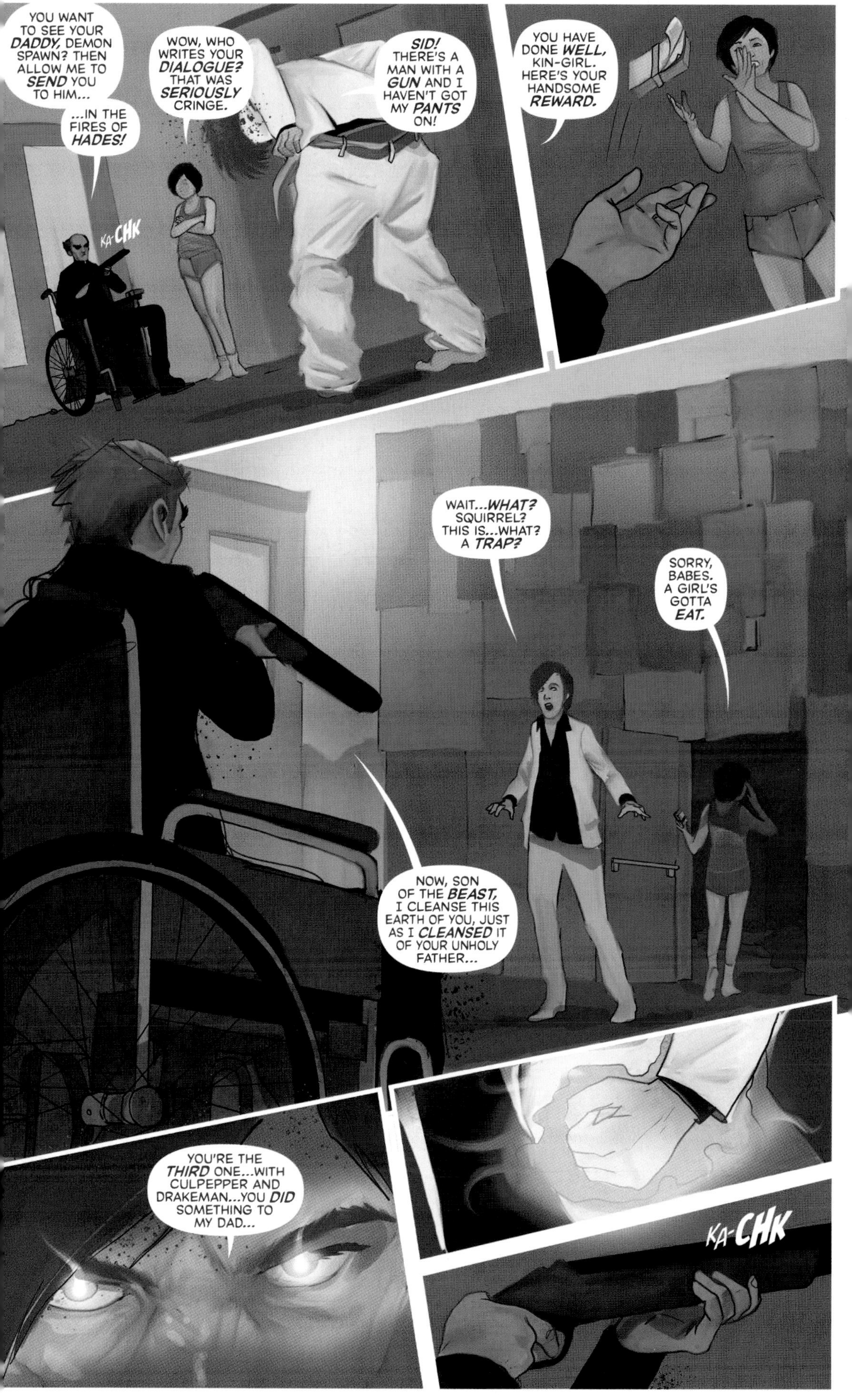
YOU WANT TO SEE YOUR DADDY, DEMON SPAWN? THEN ALLOW ME TO SEND YOU TO HIM...
...IN THE FIRES OF HADES!
KA-CHK
WOW, WHO WRITES YOUR DIALOGUE? THAT WAS SERIOUSLY CRINGE.
SID! THERE'S A MAN WITH A GUN AND I HAVEN'T GOT MY PANTS ON!
YOU HAVE DONE WELL, KIN-GIRL. HERE'S YOUR HANDSOME REWARD.
WAIT...WHAT? SQUIRREL? THIS IS...WHAT? A TRAP?
SORRY, BABES. A GIRL'S GOTTA EAT.
NOW, SON OF THE BEAST, I CLEANSE THIS EARTH OF YOU, JUST AS I CLEANSED IT OF YOUR UNHOLY FATHER...
YOU'RE THE THIRD ONE...WITH CULPEPPER AND DRAKEMAN...YOU DID SOMETHING TO MY DAD...
KA-CHK

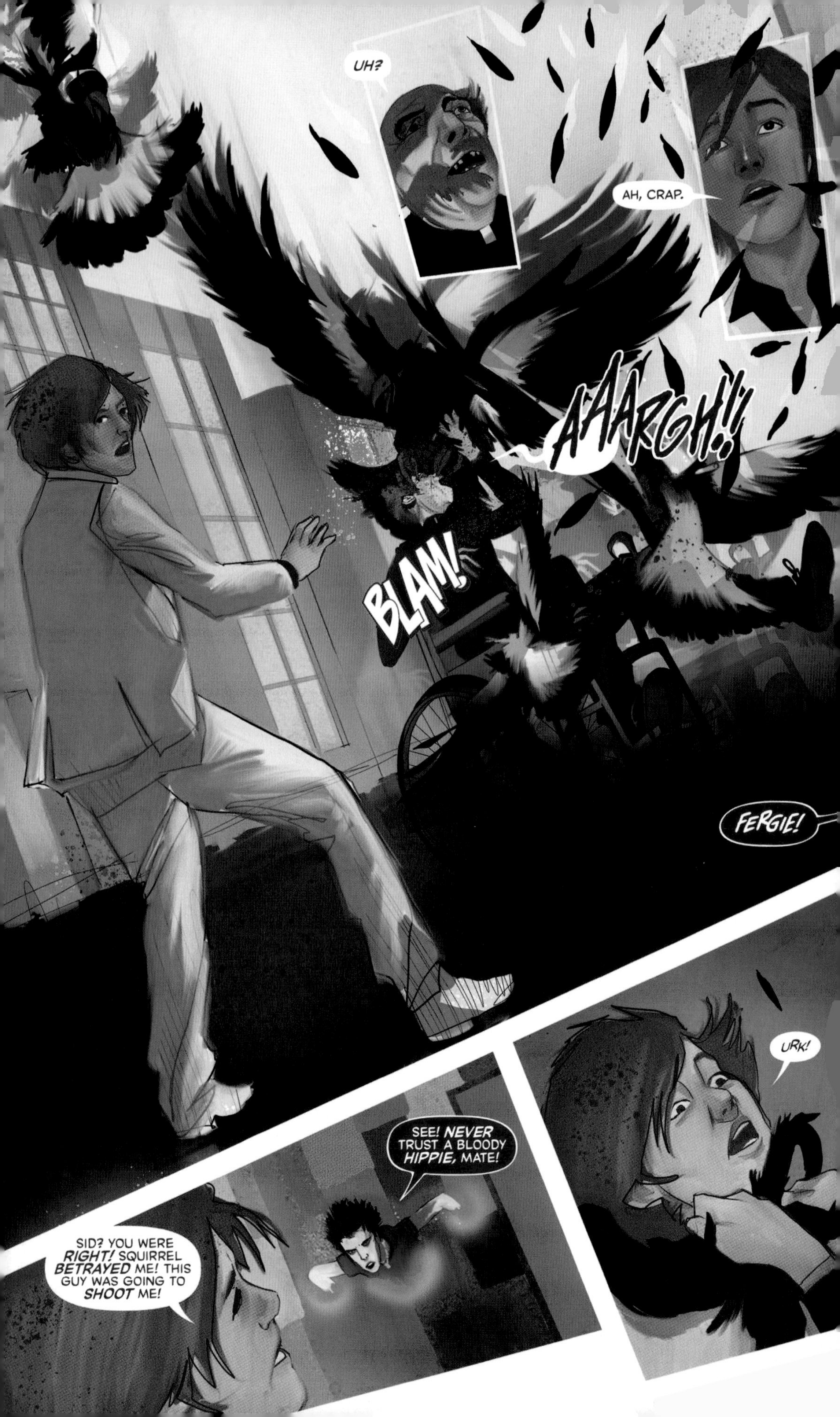
UH?
AH, CRAP.
AAARGH!!
BLAM!
FERGIE!
SID? YOU WERE RIGHT! SQUIRREL BETRAYED ME! THIS GUY WAS GOING TO SHOOT ME!
SEE! NEVER TRUST A BLOODY HIPPIE, MATE!
URK!

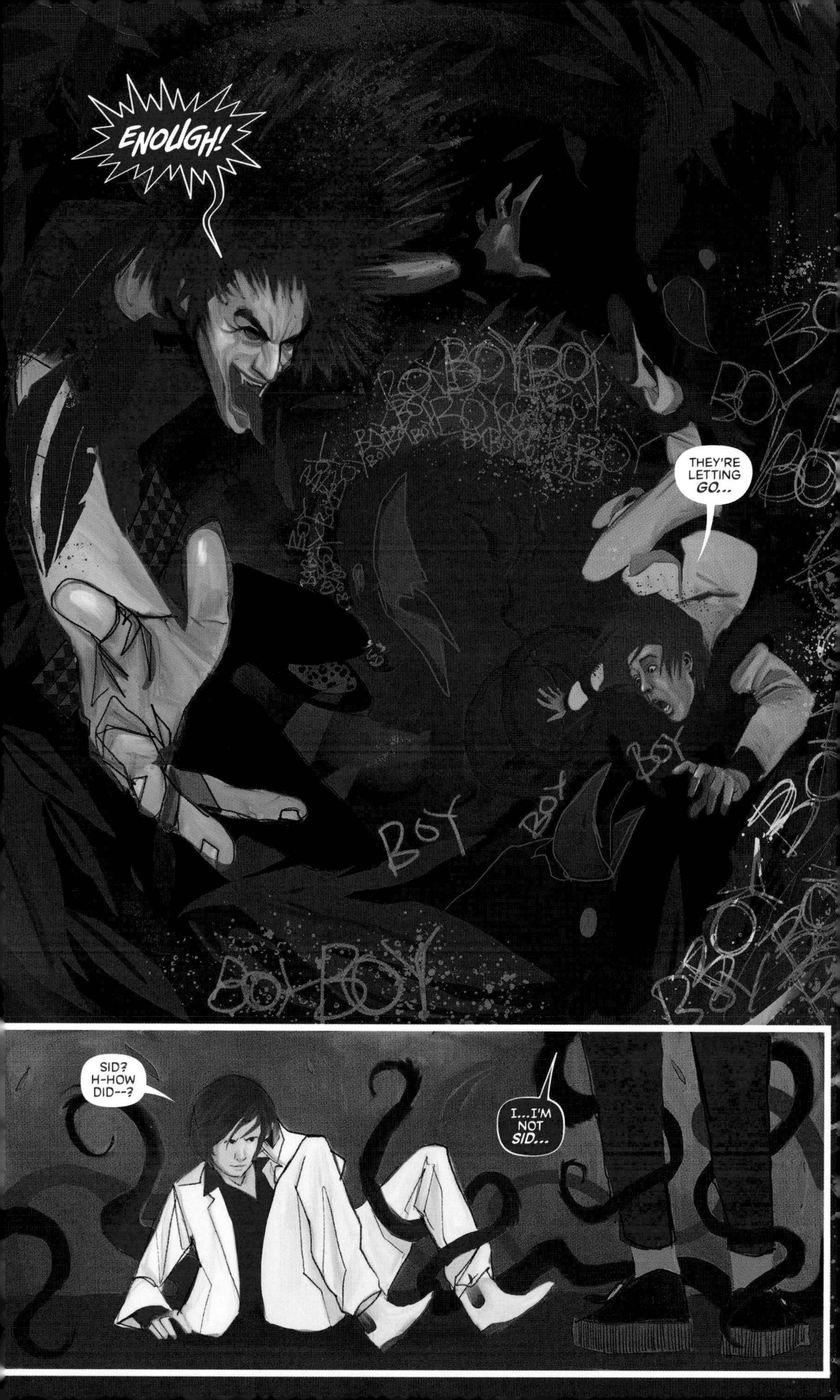
ENOUGH!
THEY'RE LETTING GO...
BOY
BOY
BOY
BOY BOY
SID? H-HOW DID--?
I...I'M NOT SID...

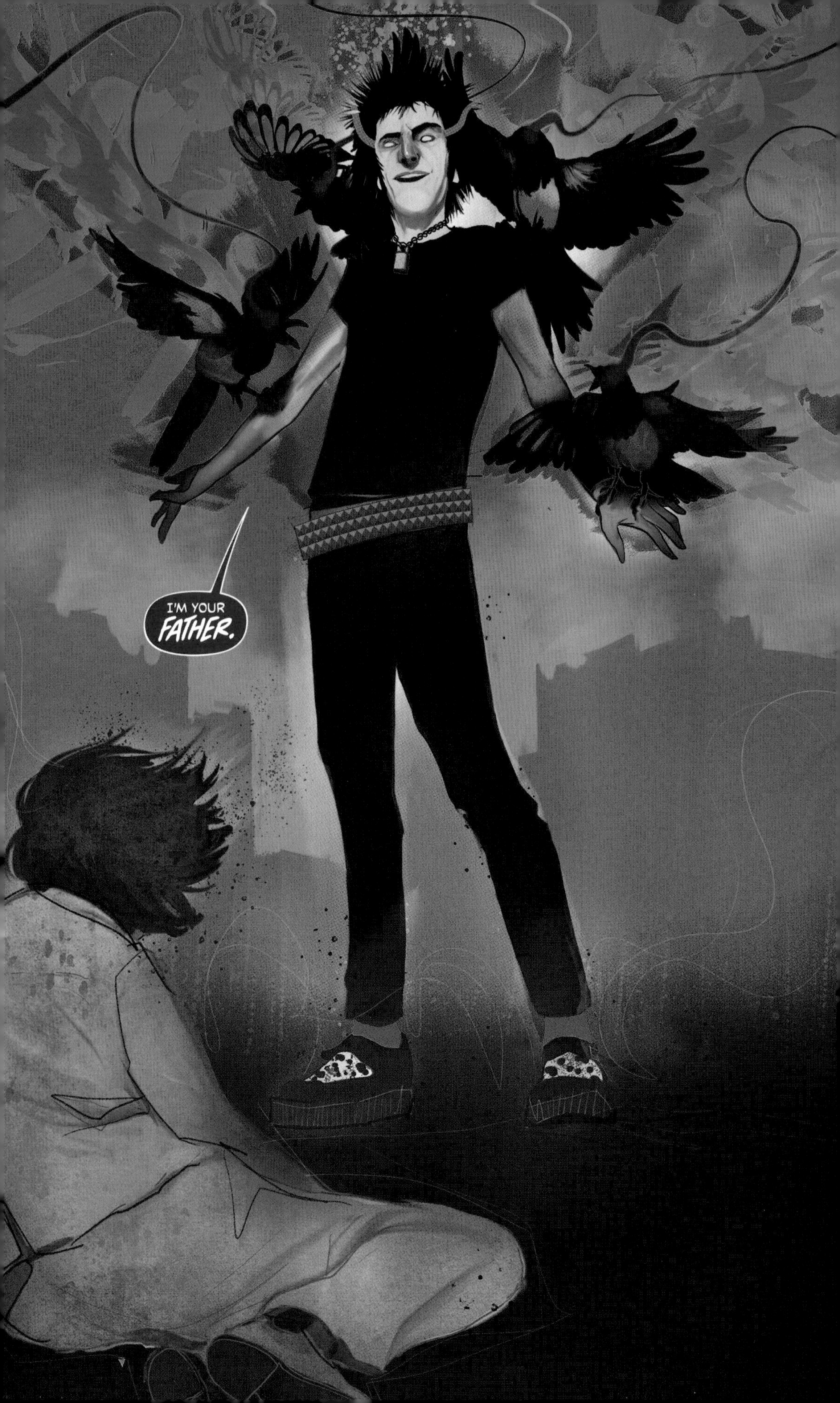
I'M YOUR FATHER.

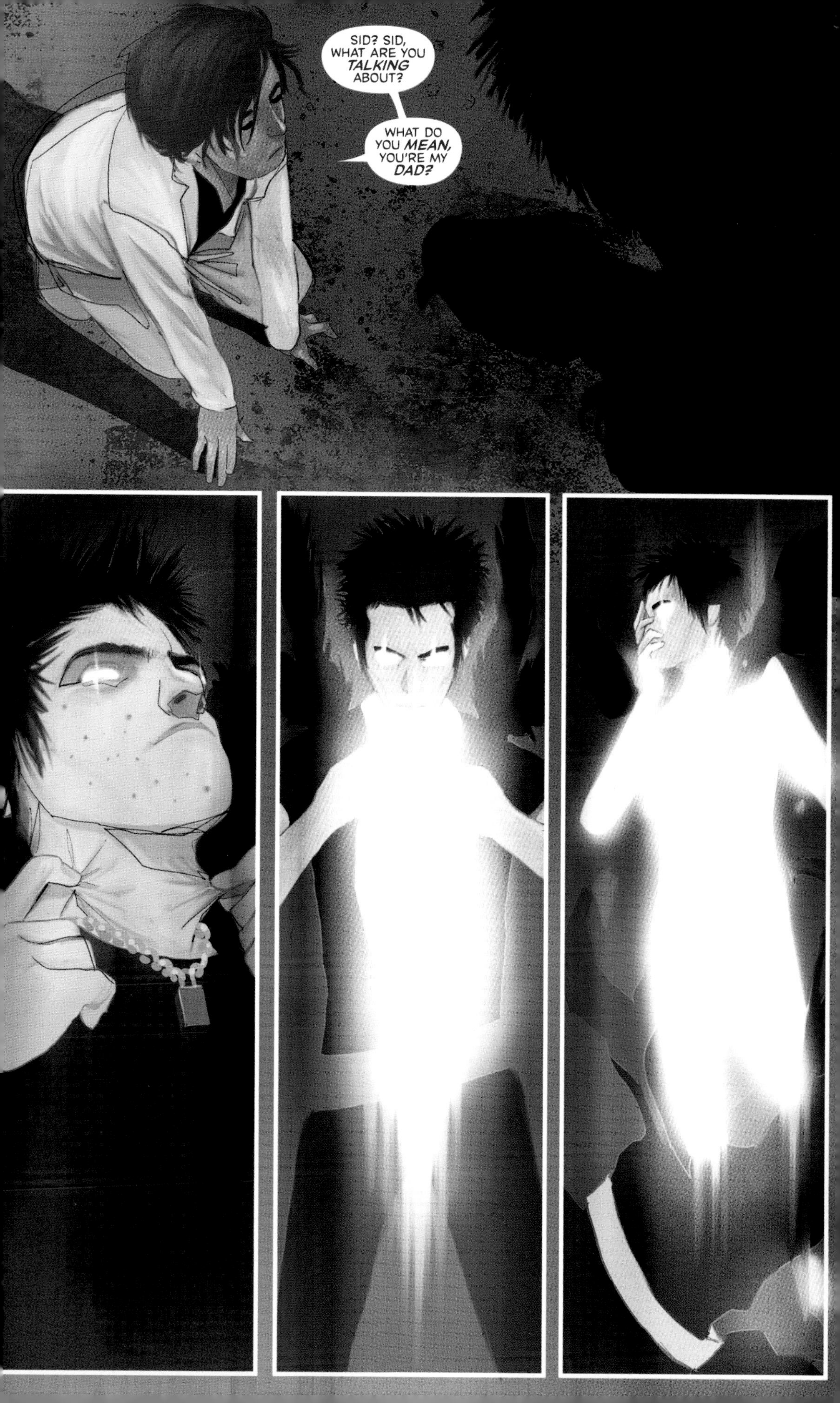
SID? SID, WHAT ARE YOU *TALKING* ABOUT?
WHAT DO YOU *MEAN,* YOU'RE MY *DAD?*

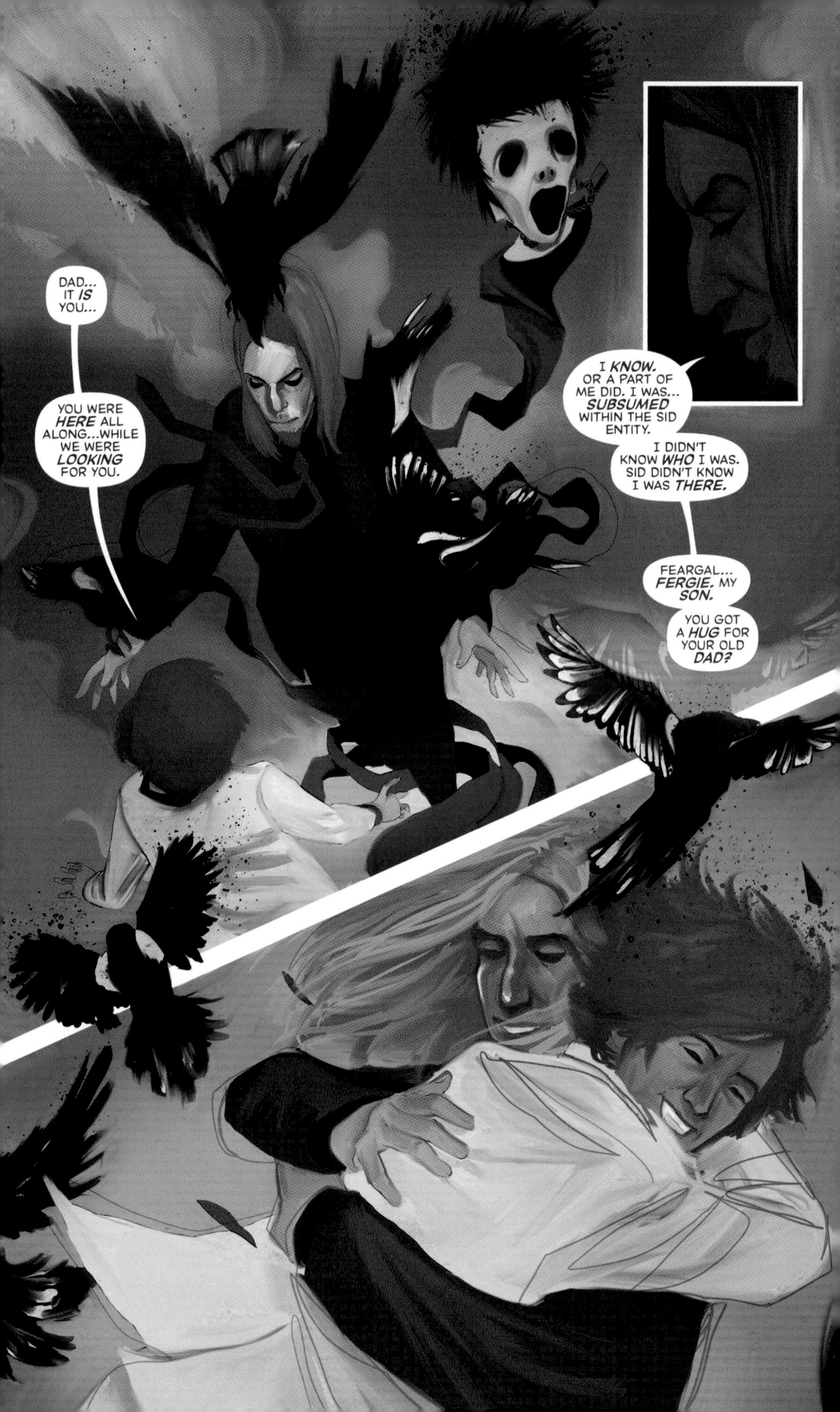
DAD... IT IS YOU...
YOU WERE HERE ALL ALONG...WHILE WE WERE LOOKING FOR YOU.
I KNOW. OR A PART OF ME DID. I WAS... SUBSUMED WITHIN THE SID ENTITY.
I DIDN'T KNOW WHO I WAS. SID DIDN'T KNOW I WAS THERE.
FEARGAL... FERGIE. MY SON.
YOU GOT A HUG FOR YOUR OLD DAD?

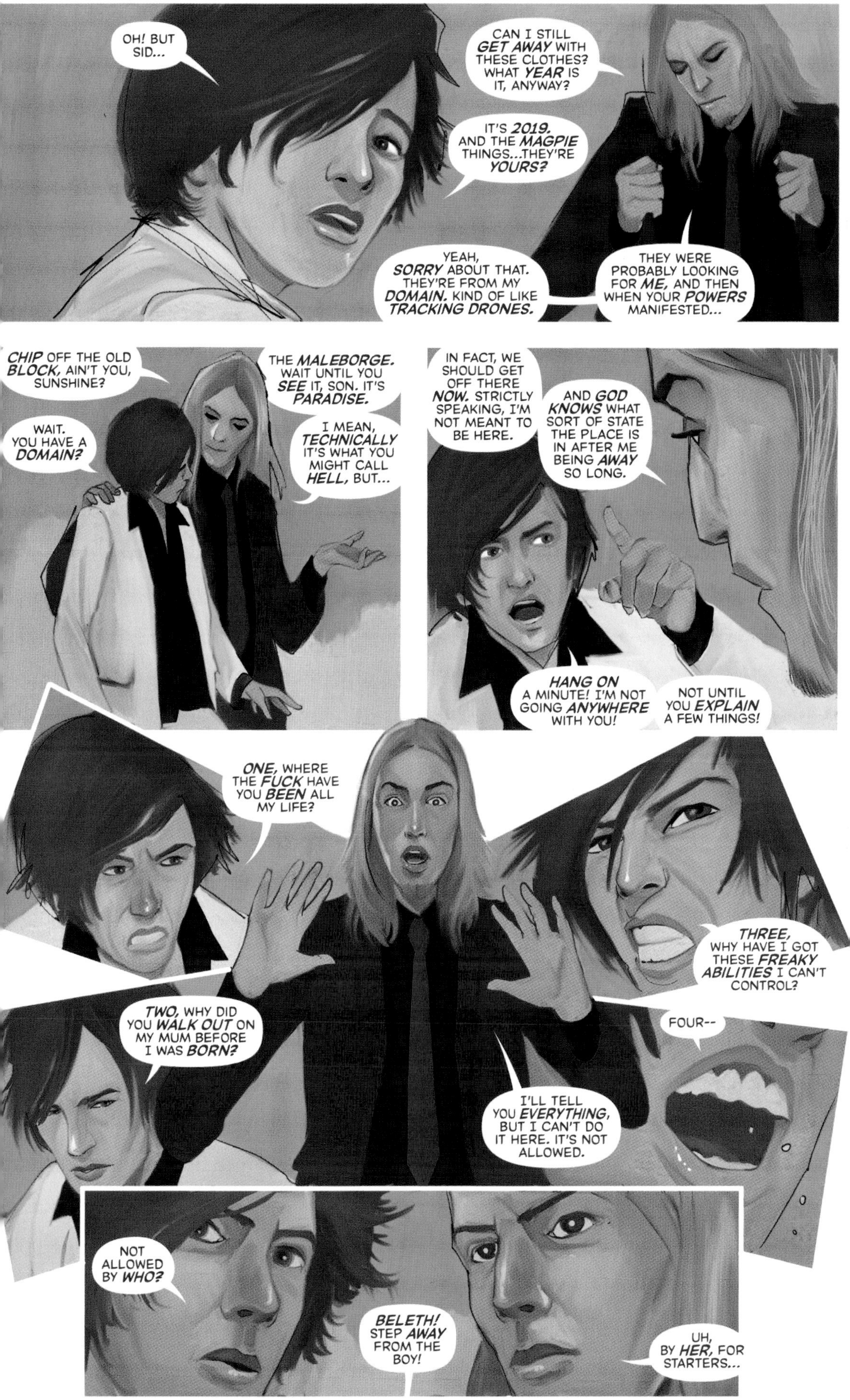
OH! BUT SID...
CAN I STILL GET AWAY WITH THESE CLOTHES? WHAT YEAR IS IT, ANYWAY?
IT'S 2019. AND THE MAGPIE THINGS...THEY'RE YOURS?
YEAH, SORRY ABOUT THAT. THEY'RE FROM MY DOMAIN. KIND OF LIKE TRACKING DRONES.
THEY WERE PROBABLY LOOKING FOR ME, AND THEN WHEN YOUR POWERS MANIFESTED...
CHIP OFF THE OLD BLOCK, AIN'T YOU, SUNSHINE?
WAIT. YOU HAVE A DOMAIN?
THE MALEBORGE. WAIT UNTIL YOU SEE IT, SON. IT'S PARADISE.
I MEAN, TECHNICALLY IT'S WHAT YOU MIGHT CALL HELL, BUT...
IN FACT, WE SHOULD GET OFF THERE NOW. STRICTLY SPEAKING, I'M NOT MEANT TO BE HERE.
AND GOD KNOWS WHAT SORT OF STATE THE PLACE IS IN AFTER ME BEING AWAY SO LONG.
HANG ON A MINUTE! I'M NOT GOING ANYWHERE WITH YOU!
NOT UNTIL YOU EXPLAIN A FEW THINGS!
ONE, WHERE THE FUCK HAVE YOU BEEN ALL MY LIFE?
TWO, WHY DID YOU WALK OUT ON MY MUM BEFORE I WAS BORN?
THREE, WHY HAVE I GOT THESE FREAKY ABILITIES I CAN'T CONTROL?
FOUR--
I'LL TELL YOU EVERYTHING, BUT I CAN'T DO IT HERE. IT'S NOT ALLOWED.
NOT ALLOWED BY WHO?
UH, BY HER, FOR STARTERS...
BELETH! STEP AWAY FROM THE BOY!

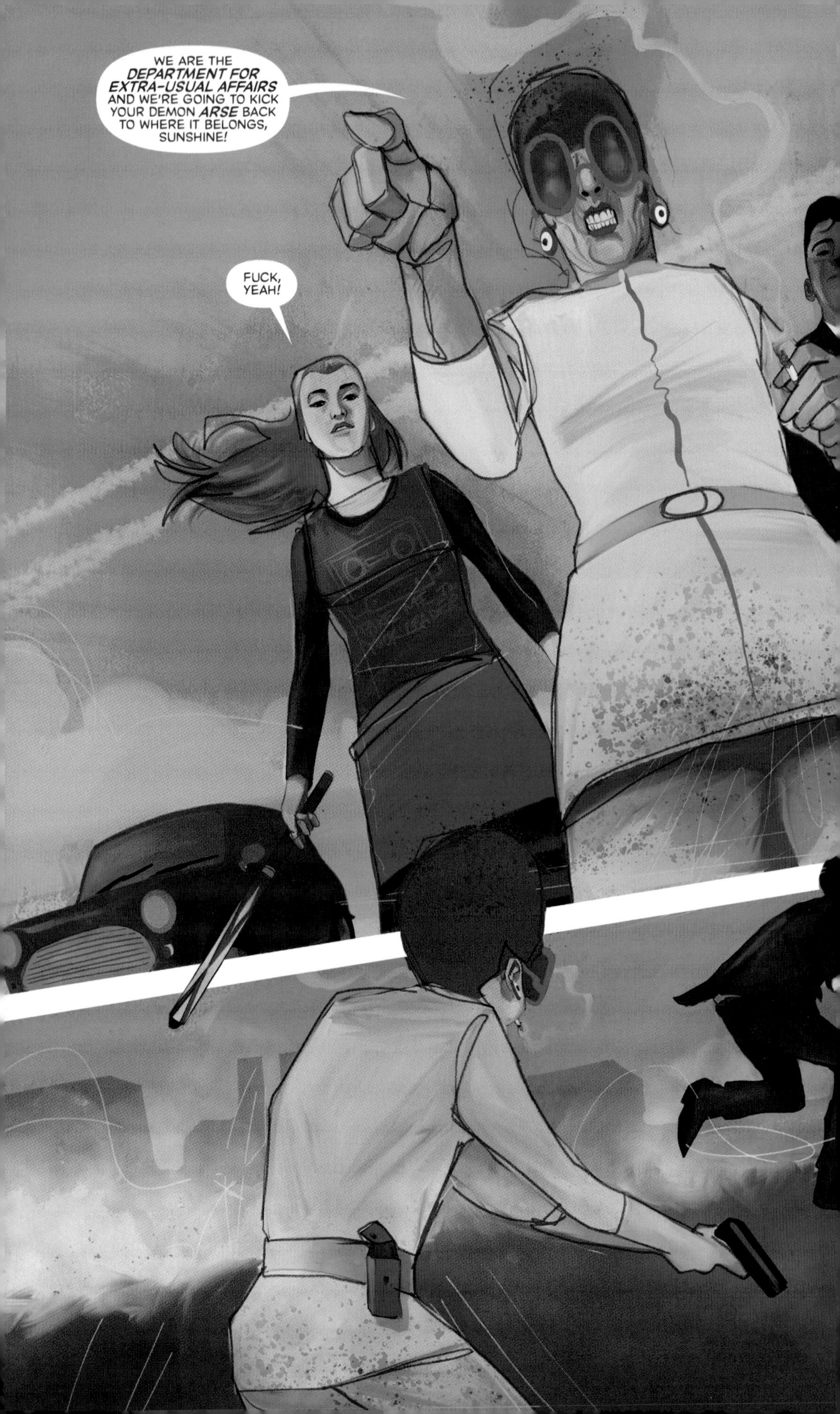
WE ARE THE *DEPARTMENT FOR EXTRA-USUAL AFFAIRS* AND WE'RE GOING TO KICK YOUR DEMON *ARSE* BACK TO WHERE IT BELONGS, SUNSHINE!
FUCK, YEAH!

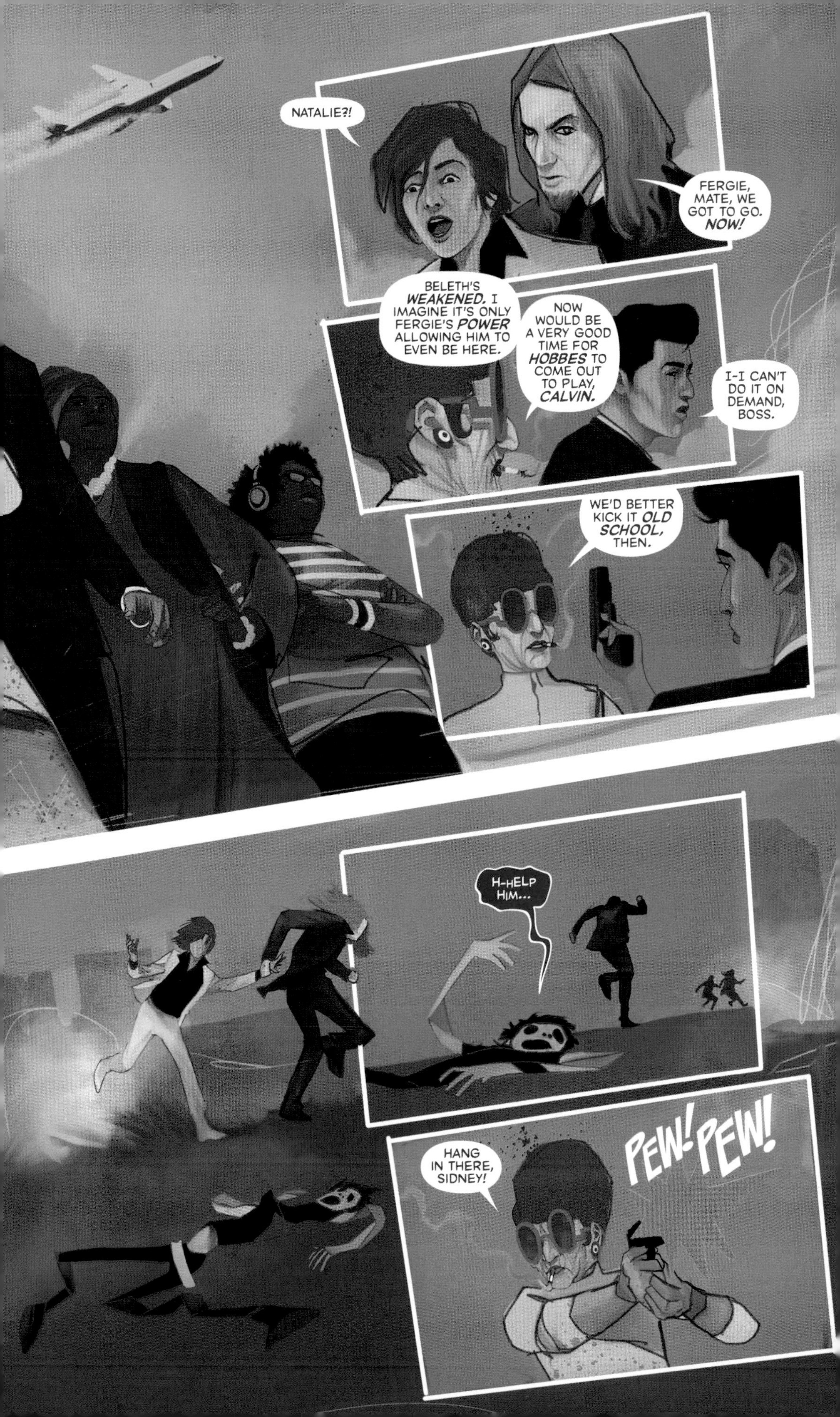
NATALIE?!
FERGIE, MATE, WE GOT TO GO. NOW!
BELETH'S WEAKENED. I IMAGINE IT'S ONLY FERGIE'S POWER ALLOWING HIM TO EVEN BE HERE.
NOW WOULD BE A VERY GOOD TIME FOR HOBBES TO COME OUT TO PLAY, CALVIN.
I-I CAN'T DO IT ON DEMAND, BOSS.
WE'D BETTER KICK IT OLD SCHOOL, THEN.
H-HELP HIM...
HANG IN THERE, SIDNEY!
PEW! PEW!

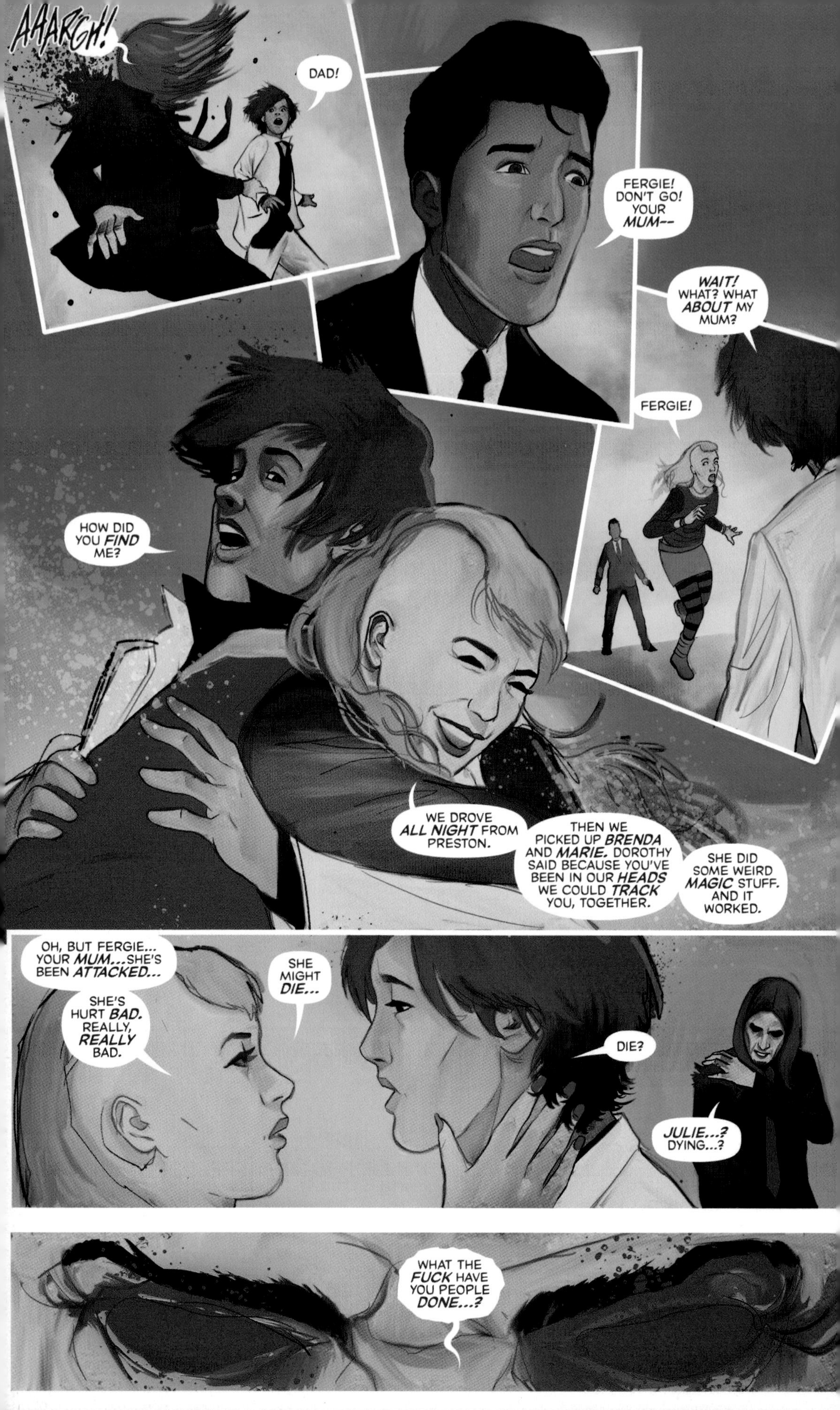

AAARGH!
DAD!
FERGIE! DON'T GO! YOUR MUM--
WAIT! WHAT? WHAT ABOUT MY MUM?
FERGIE!
HOW DID YOU FIND ME?
WE DROVE ALL NIGHT FROM PRESTON.
THEN WE PICKED UP BRENDA AND MARIE. DOROTHY SAID BECAUSE YOU'VE BEEN IN OUR HEADS WE COULD TRACK YOU, TOGETHER.
SHE DID SOME WEIRD MAGIC STUFF. AND IT WORKED.
OH, BUT FERGIE... YOUR MUM...SHE'S BEEN ATTACKED...
SHE'S HURT BAD. REALLY, REALLY BAD.
SHE MIGHT DIE...
DIE?
JULIE...? DYING...?
WHAT THE FUCK HAVE YOU PEOPLE DONE...?

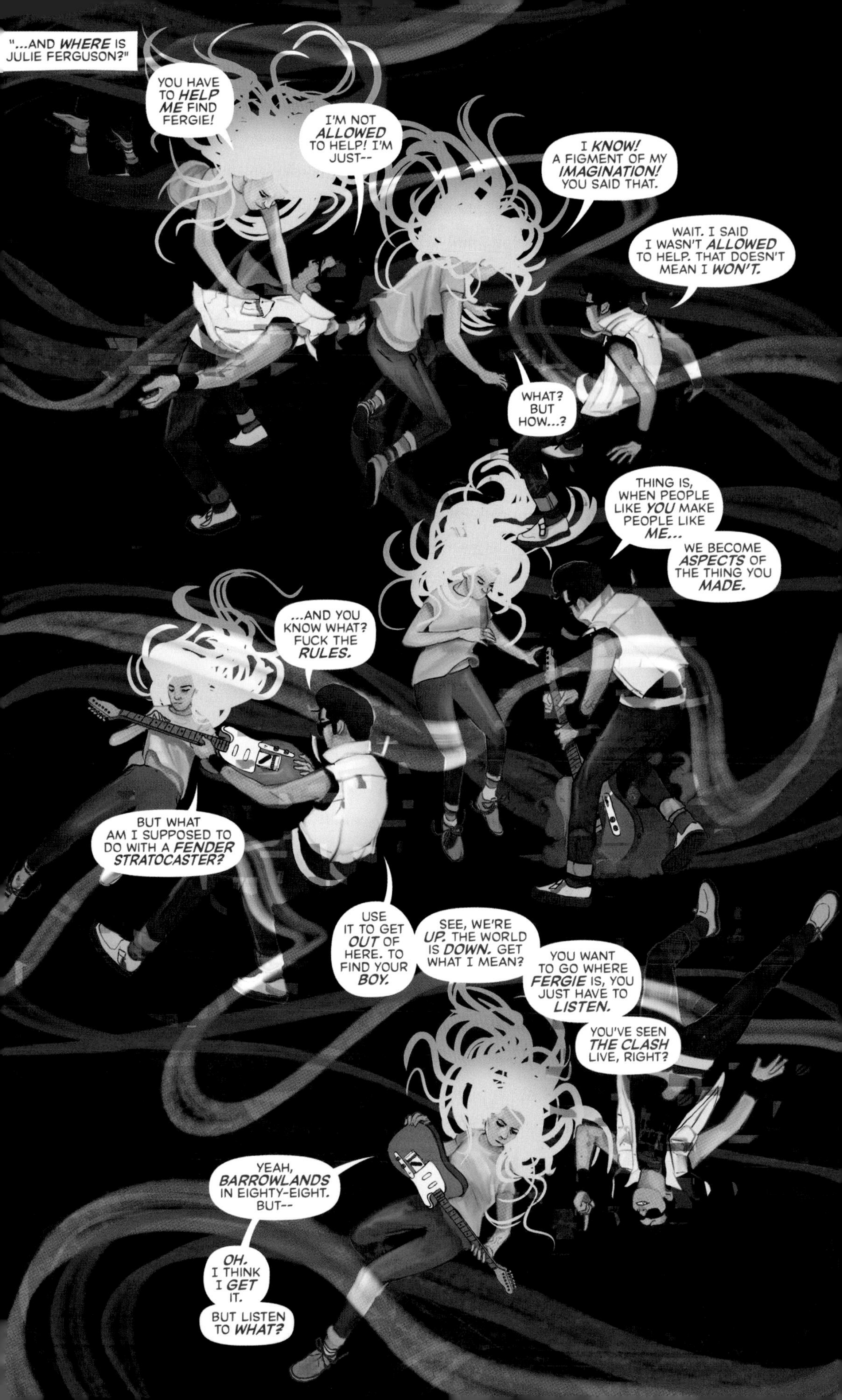

"...AND *WHERE* IS JULIE FERGUSON?"
YOU HAVE TO *HELP ME* FIND FERGIE!
I'M NOT *ALLOWED* TO HELP! I'M JUST--
I *KNOW!* A FIGMENT OF MY *IMAGINATION!* YOU SAID THAT.
WAIT. I SAID I WASN'T *ALLOWED* TO HELP. THAT DOESN'T MEAN I *WON'T.*
WHAT? BUT HOW...?
THING IS, WHEN PEOPLE LIKE *YOU* MAKE PEOPLE LIKE *ME...*
WE BECOME *ASPECTS* OF THE THING YOU *MADE.*
...AND YOU KNOW WHAT? FUCK THE *RULES.*
BUT WHAT AM I SUPPOSED TO DO WITH A *FENDER STRATOCASTER?*
USE IT TO GET *OUT* OF HERE. TO FIND YOUR *BOY.*
SEE, WE'RE *UP.* THE WORLD IS *DOWN.* GET WHAT I MEAN?
YOU WANT TO GO WHERE *FERGIE* IS, YOU JUST HAVE TO *LISTEN.*
YOU'VE SEEN *THE CLASH* LIVE, RIGHT?
YEAH, *BARROWLANDS* IN EIGHTY-EIGHT. BUT--
OH. I THINK I *GET* IT.
BUT LISTEN TO *WHAT?*

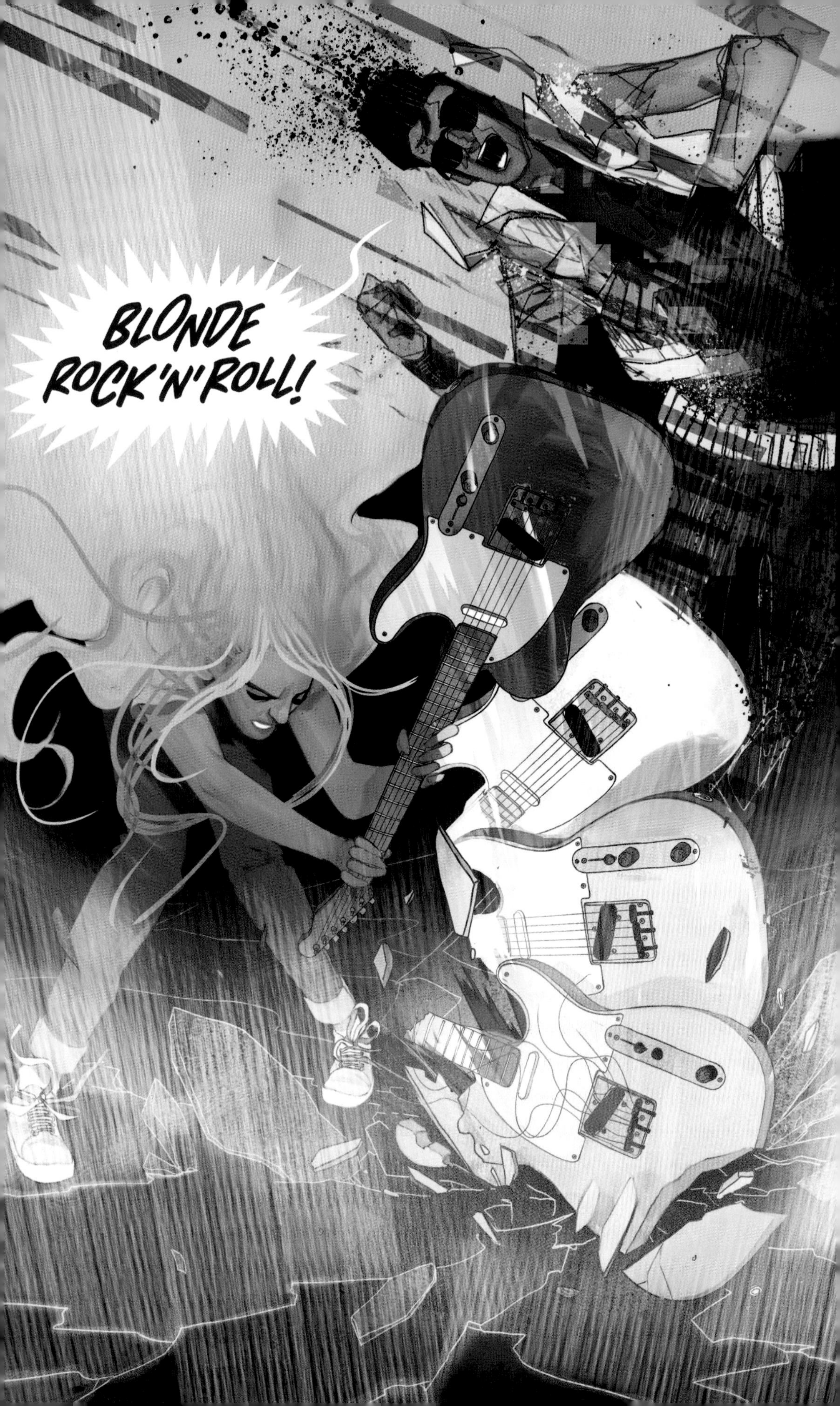
BLONDE ROCK'N'ROLL!

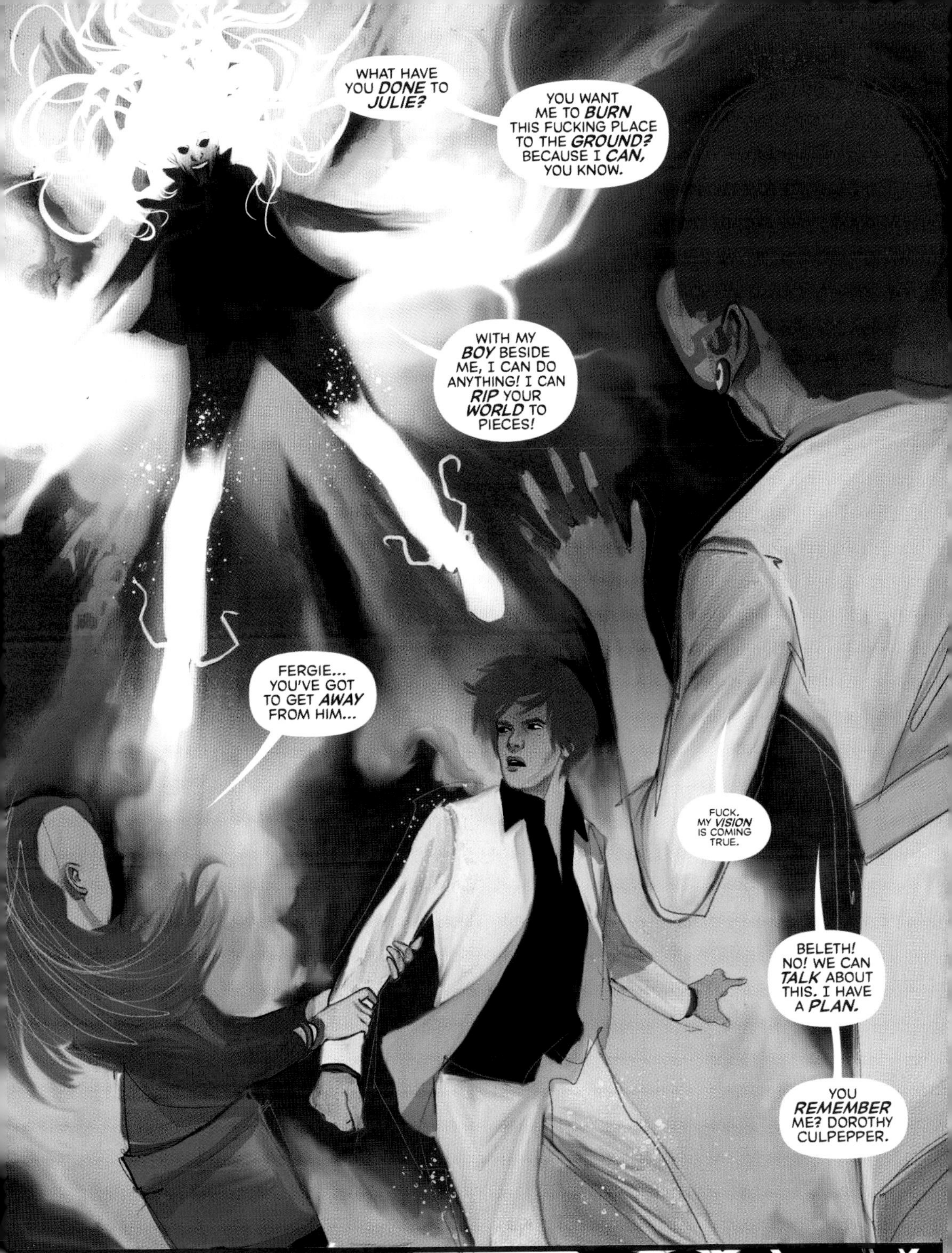
WHAT HAVE YOU DONE TO JULIE?
YOU WANT ME TO BURN THIS FUCKING PLACE TO THE GROUND? BECAUSE I CAN, YOU KNOW.
WITH MY BOY BESIDE ME, I CAN DO ANYTHING! I CAN RIP YOUR WORLD TO PIECES!
FERGIE... YOU'VE GOT TO GET AWAY FROM HIM...
FUCK. MY VISION IS COMING TRUE.
BELETH! NO! WE CAN TALK ABOUT THIS. I HAVE A PLAN.
YOU REMEMBER ME? DOROTHY CULPEPPER.
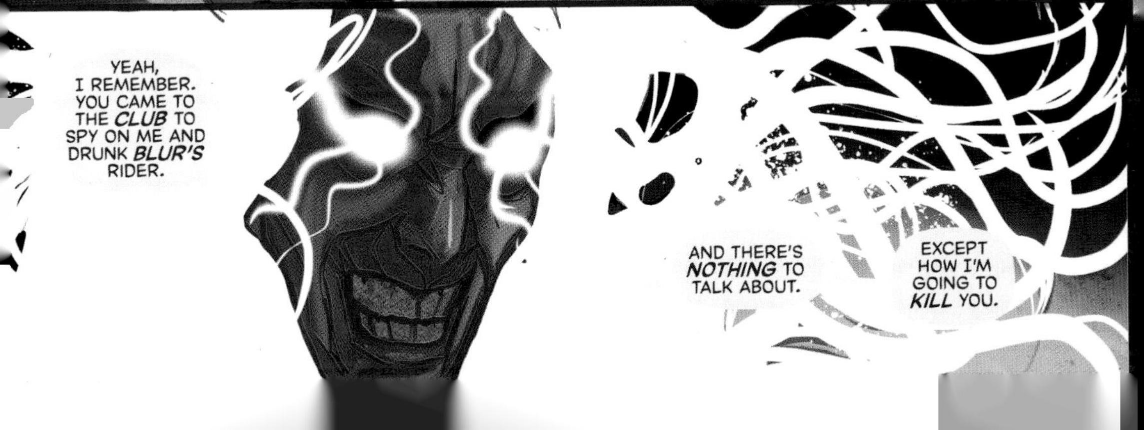
YEAH, I REMEMBER. YOU CAME TO THE CLUB TO SPY ON ME AND DRUNK BLUR'S RIDER.
AND THERE'S NOTHING TO TALK ABOUT.
EXCEPT HOW I'M GOING TO KILL YOU.

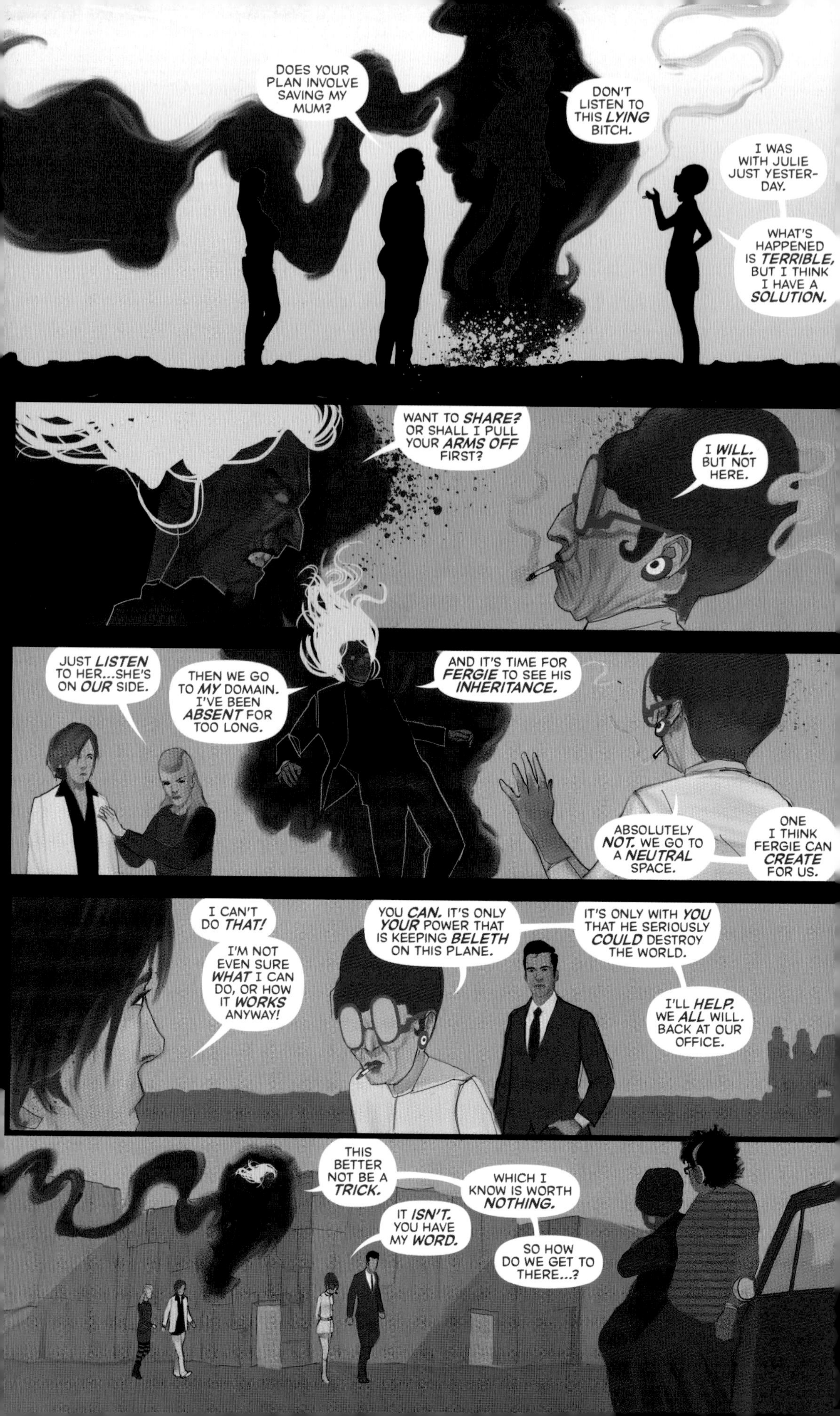
DOES YOUR PLAN INVOLVE SAVING MY MUM?
DON'T LISTEN TO THIS *LYING* BITCH.
I WAS WITH JULIE JUST YESTER-DAY.
WHAT'S HAPPENED IS *TERRIBLE,* BUT I THINK I HAVE A *SOLUTION.*
WANT TO *SHARE?* OR SHALL I PULL YOUR *ARMS OFF* FIRST?
I *WILL.* BUT NOT HERE.
JUST *LISTEN* TO HER...SHE'S ON *OUR* SIDE.
THEN WE GO TO *MY* DOMAIN. I'VE BEEN *ABSENT* FOR TOO LONG.
AND IT'S TIME FOR *FERGIE* TO SEE HIS *INHERITANCE.*
ABSOLUTELY *NOT.* WE GO TO A *NEUTRAL* SPACE.
ONE I THINK FERGIE CAN *CREATE* FOR US.
I CAN'T DO *THAT!*
I'M NOT EVEN SURE *WHAT* I CAN DO, OR HOW IT *WORKS* ANYWAY!
YOU *CAN.* IT'S ONLY *YOUR* POWER THAT IS KEEPING *BELETH* ON THIS PLANE.
IT'S ONLY WITH *YOU* THAT HE SERIOUSLY *COULD* DESTROY THE WORLD.
I'LL *HELP.* WE *ALL* WILL. BACK AT OUR OFFICE.
THIS BETTER NOT BE A *TRICK.*
WHICH I KNOW IS WORTH *NOTHING.*
IT *ISN'T.* YOU HAVE MY *WORD.*
SO HOW DO WE GET TO THERE...?

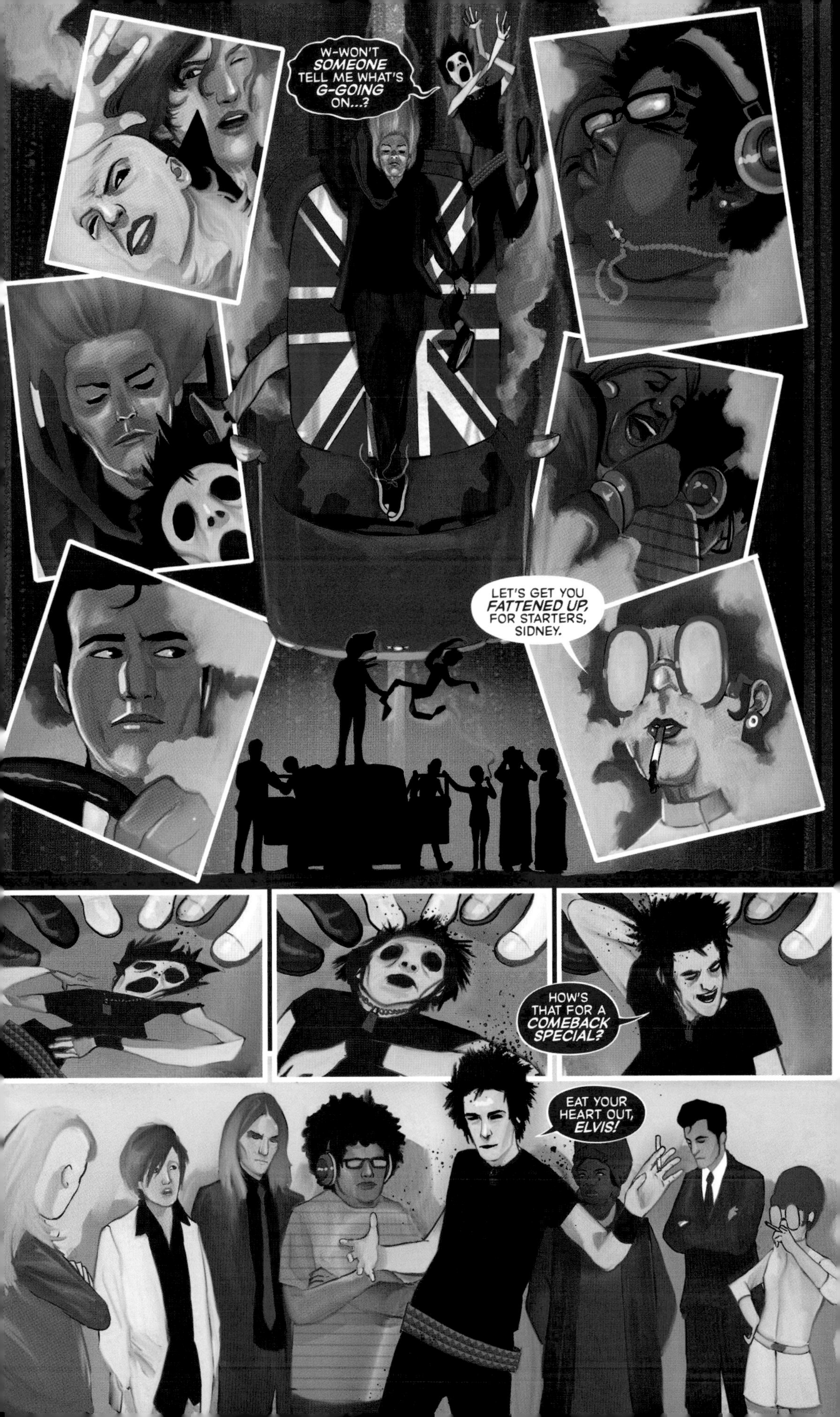
W-WON'T *SOMEONE* TELL ME WHAT'S *G-GOING* ON...?
LET'S GET YOU *FATTENED UP,* FOR STARTERS, SIDNEY.
HOW'S THAT FOR A *COMEBACK SPECIAL?*
EAT YOUR HEART OUT, *ELVIS!*

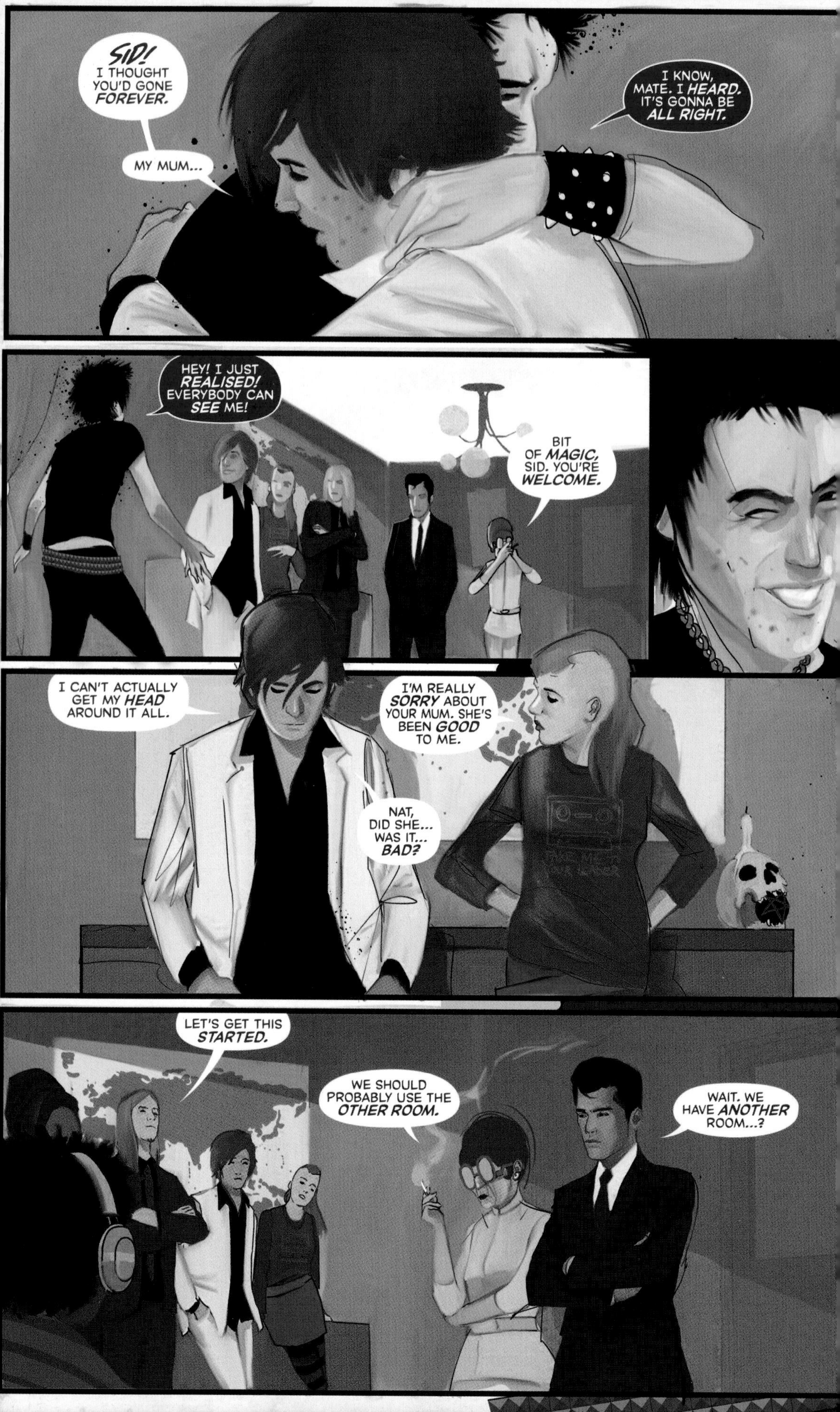
SID! I THOUGHT YOU'D GONE FOREVER.
MY MUM...
I KNOW, MATE. I HEARD. IT'S GONNA BE ALL RIGHT.
HEY! I JUST REALISED! EVERYBODY CAN SEE ME!
BIT OF MAGIC, SID. YOU'RE WELCOME.
I CAN'T ACTUALLY GET MY HEAD AROUND IT ALL.
I'M REALLY SORRY ABOUT YOUR MUM. SHE'S BEEN GOOD TO ME.
NAT, DID SHE... WAS IT... BAD?
LET'S GET THIS STARTED.
WE SHOULD PROBABLY USE THE OTHER ROOM.
WAIT. WE HAVE ANOTHER ROOM...?

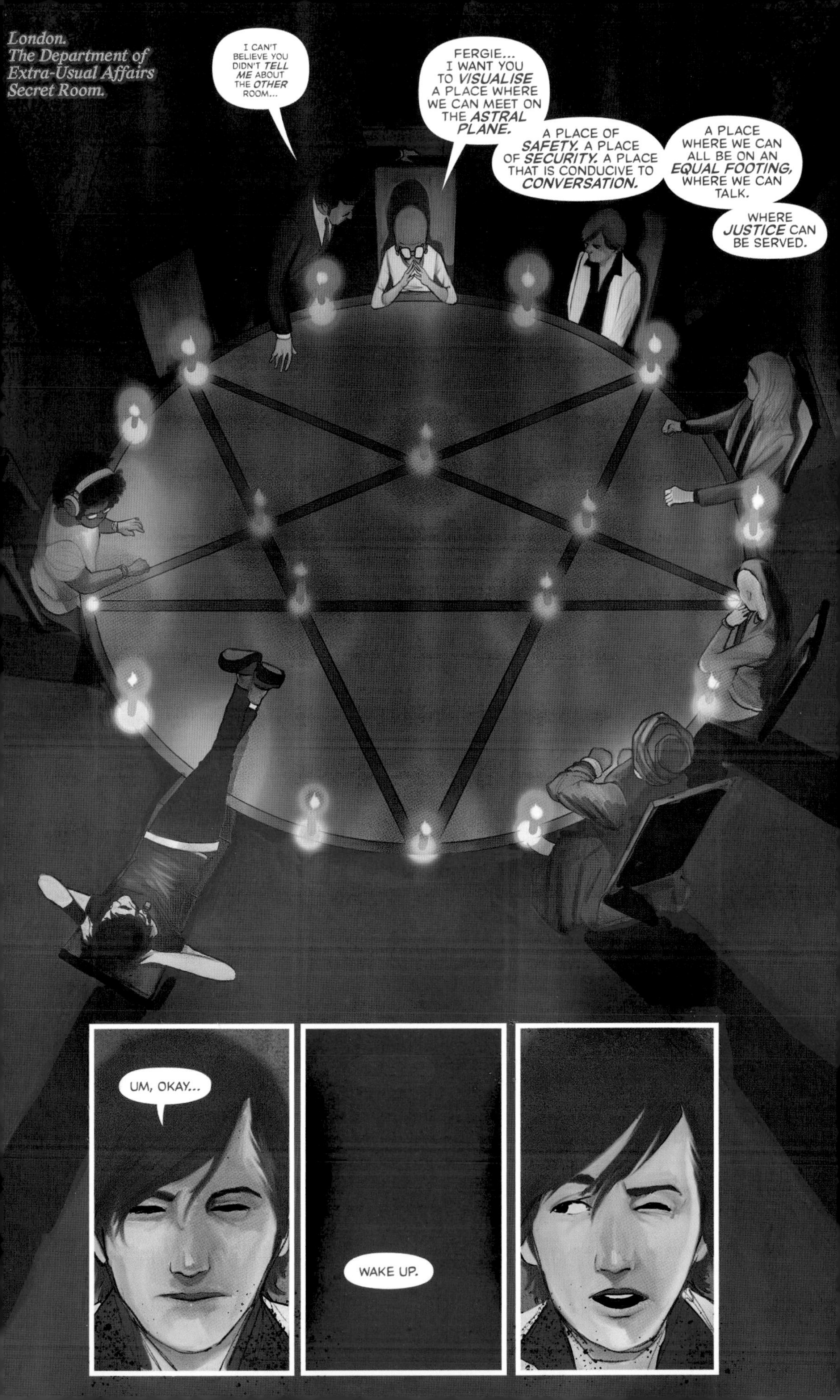
London.
The Department of
Extra-Usual Affairs
Secret Room.
I CAN'T BELIEVE YOU DIDN'T TELL ME ABOUT THE OTHER ROOM...
FERGIE... I WANT YOU TO VISUALISE A PLACE WHERE WE CAN MEET ON THE ASTRAL PLANE.
A PLACE OF SAFETY. A PLACE OF SECURITY. A PLACE THAT IS CONDUCIVE TO CONVERSATION.
A PLACE WHERE WE CAN ALL BE ON AN EQUAL FOOTING, WHERE WE CAN TALK.
WHERE JUSTICE CAN BE SERVED.
UM, OKAY...
WAKE UP.

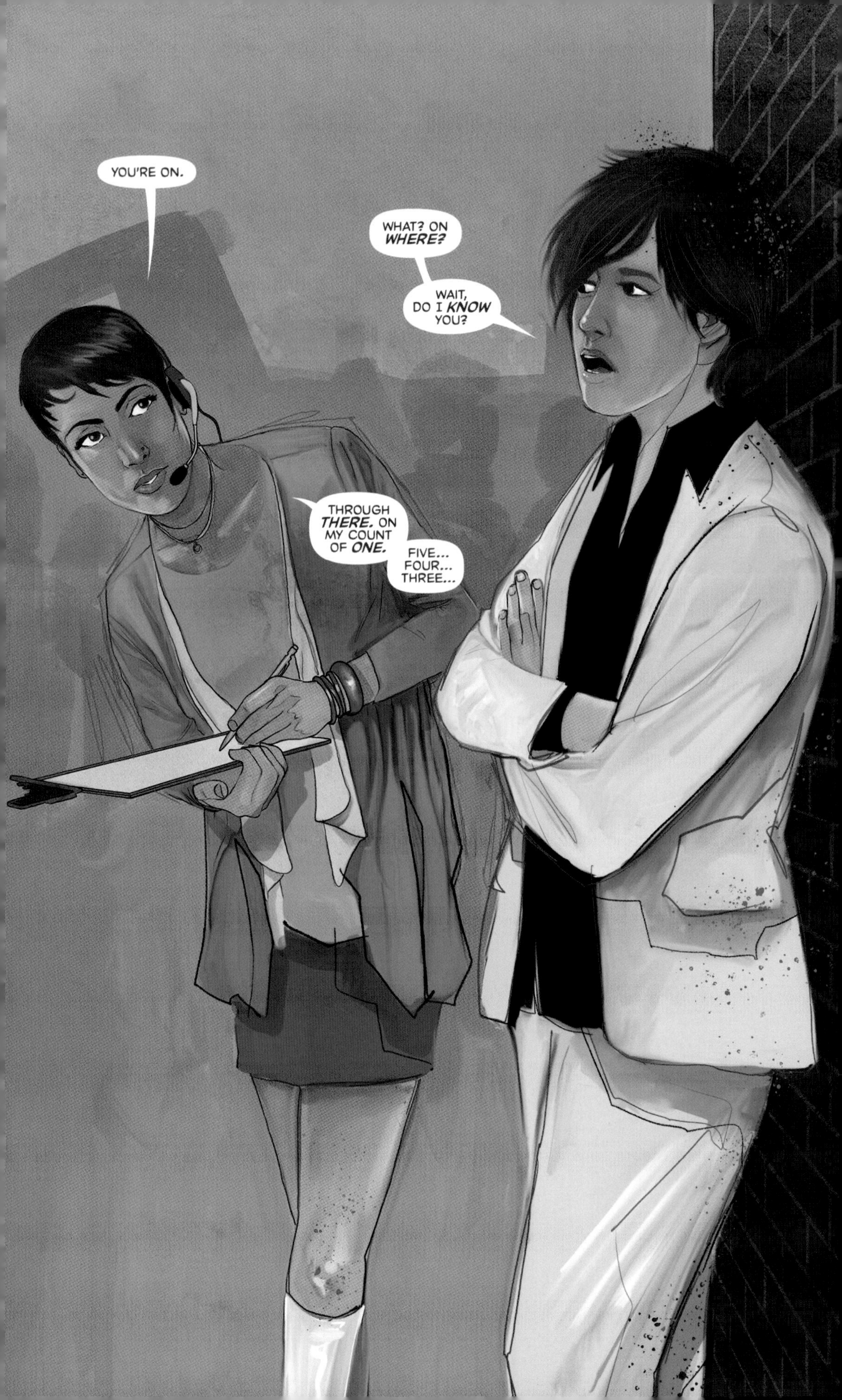
YOU'RE ON.
WHAT? ON WHERE?
WAIT, DO I KNOW YOU?
THROUGH THERE. ON MY COUNT OF ONE.
FIVE... FOUR... THREE...

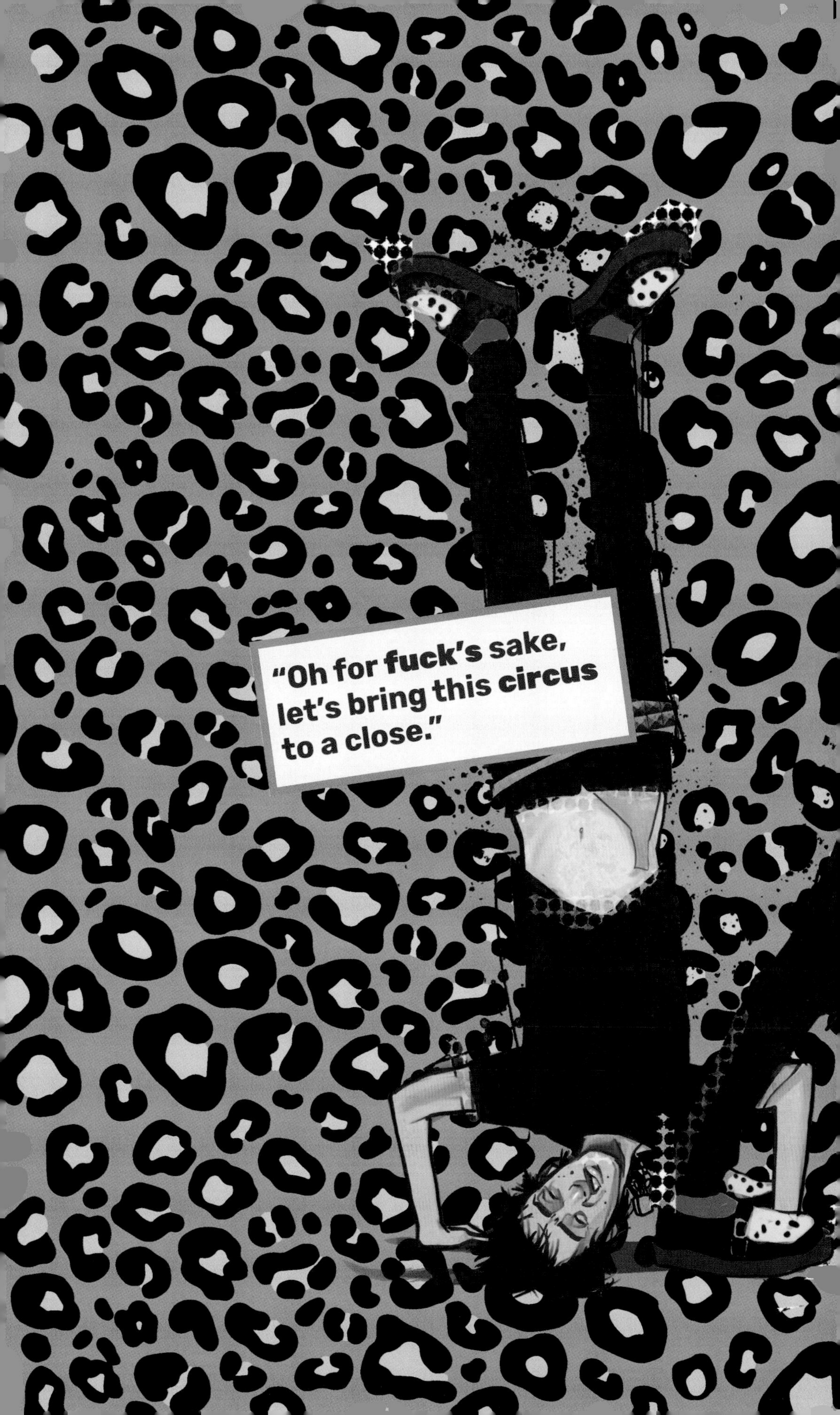
"Oh for fuck's sake, let's bring this circus to a close."

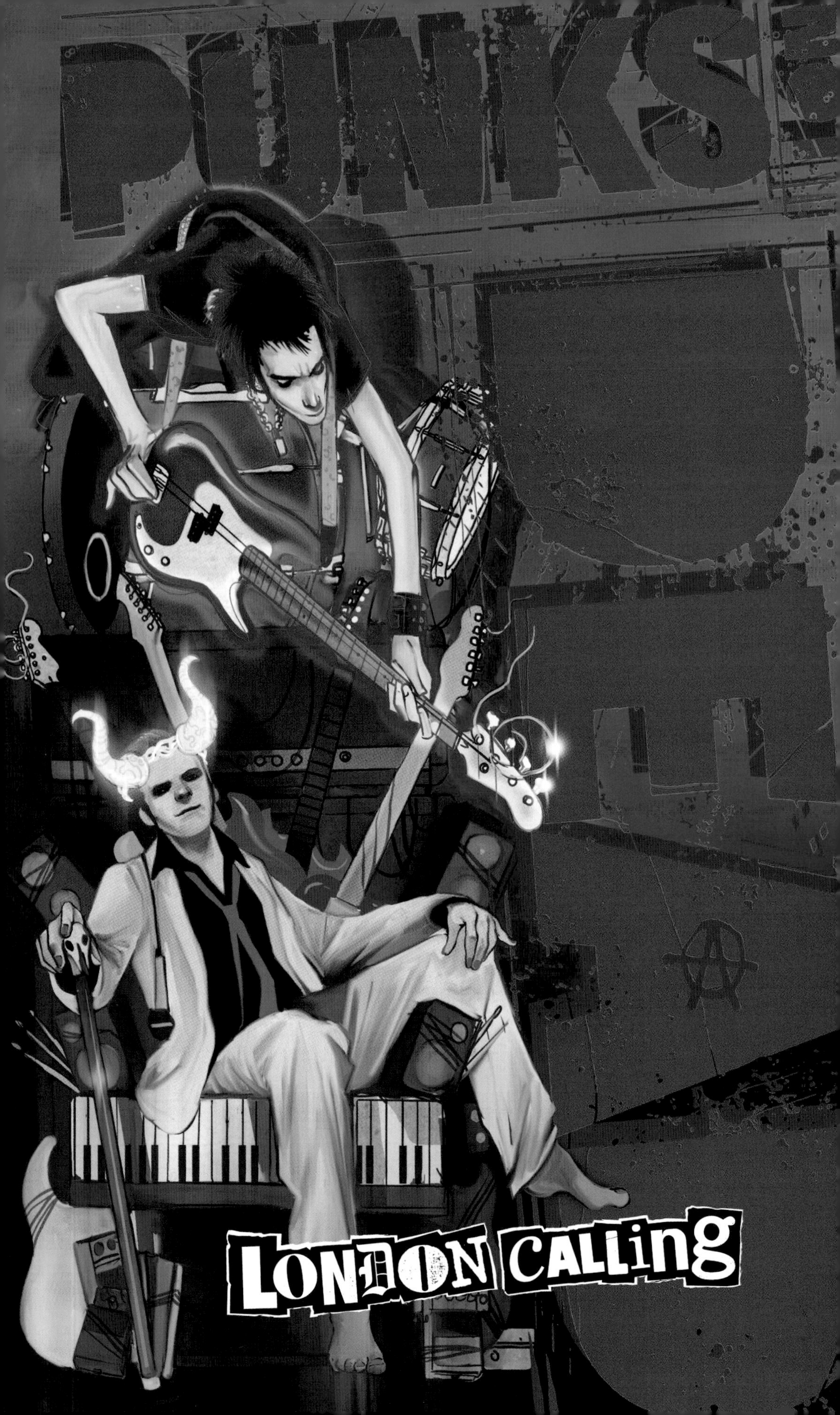
PUNKS
LONDON CALLING

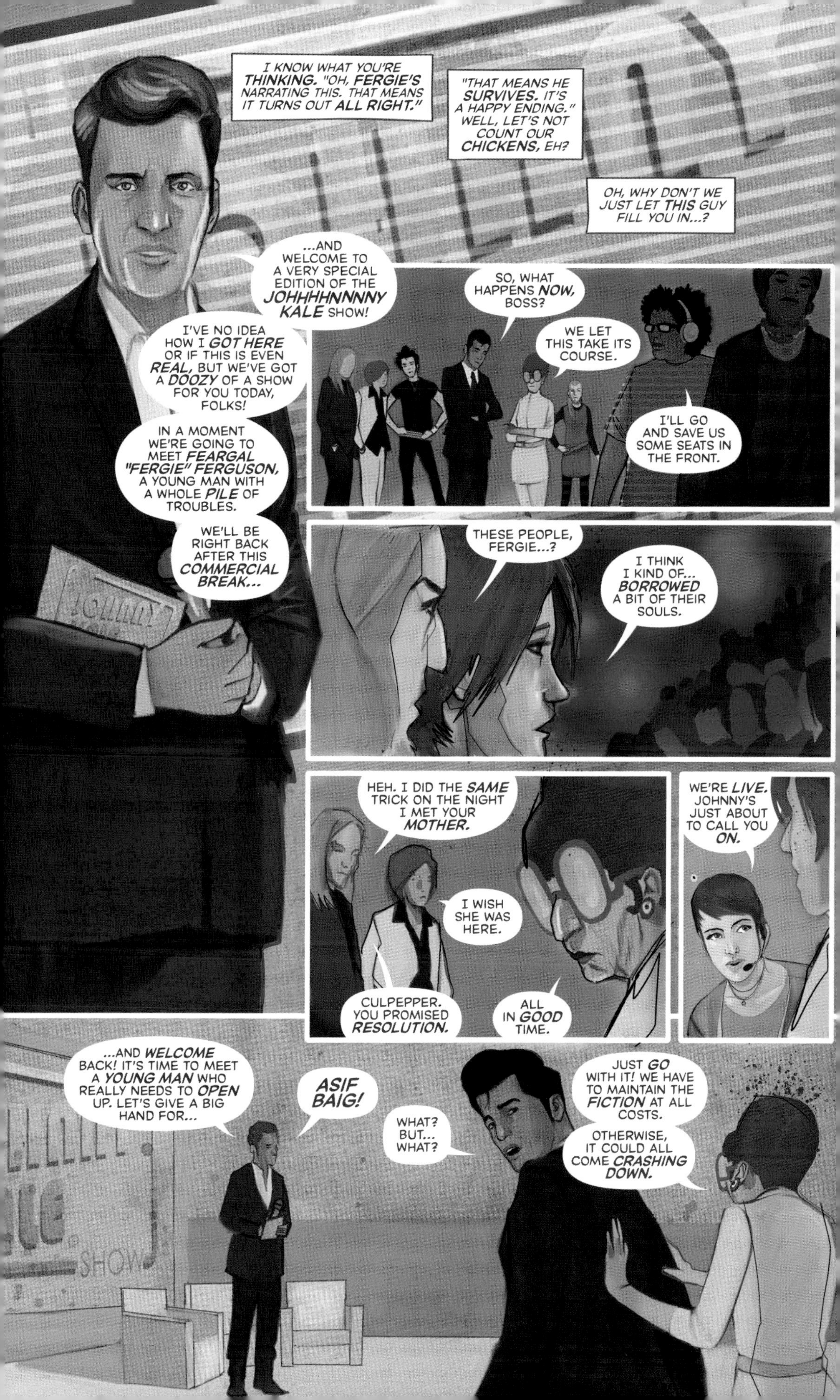
I KNOW WHAT YOU'RE THINKING. "OH, FERGIE'S NARRATING THIS. THAT MEANS IT TURNS OUT ALL RIGHT."
"THAT MEANS HE SURVIVES. IT'S A HAPPY ENDING." WELL, LET'S NOT COUNT OUR CHICKENS, EH?
OH, WHY DON'T WE JUST LET THIS GUY FILL YOU IN...?
...AND WELCOME TO A VERY SPECIAL EDITION OF THE JOHHHHNNNNY KALE SHOW!
I'VE NO IDEA HOW I GOT HERE OR IF THIS IS EVEN REAL, BUT WE'VE GOT A DOOZY OF A SHOW FOR YOU TODAY, FOLKS!
IN A MOMENT WE'RE GOING TO MEET FEARGAL "FERGIE" FERGUSON, A YOUNG MAN WITH A WHOLE PILE OF TROUBLES.
WE'LL BE RIGHT BACK AFTER THIS COMMERCIAL BREAK...
SO, WHAT HAPPENS NOW, BOSS?
WE LET THIS TAKE ITS COURSE.
I'LL GO AND SAVE US SOME SEATS IN THE FRONT.
THESE PEOPLE, FERGIE...?
I THINK I KIND OF... BORROWED A BIT OF THEIR SOULS.
HEH. I DID THE SAME TRICK ON THE NIGHT I MET YOUR MOTHER.
I WISH SHE WAS HERE.
CULPEPPER. YOU PROMISED RESOLUTION.
ALL IN GOOD TIME.
WE'RE LIVE. JOHNNY'S JUST ABOUT TO CALL YOU ON.
...AND WELCOME BACK! IT'S TIME TO MEET A YOUNG MAN WHO REALLY NEEDS TO OPEN UP. LET'S GIVE A BIG HAND FOR...
ASIF BAIG!
WHAT? BUT... WHAT?
JUST GO WITH IT! WE HAVE TO MAINTAIN THE FICTION AT ALL COSTS.
OTHERWISE, IT COULD ALL COME CRASHING DOWN.
SHOW

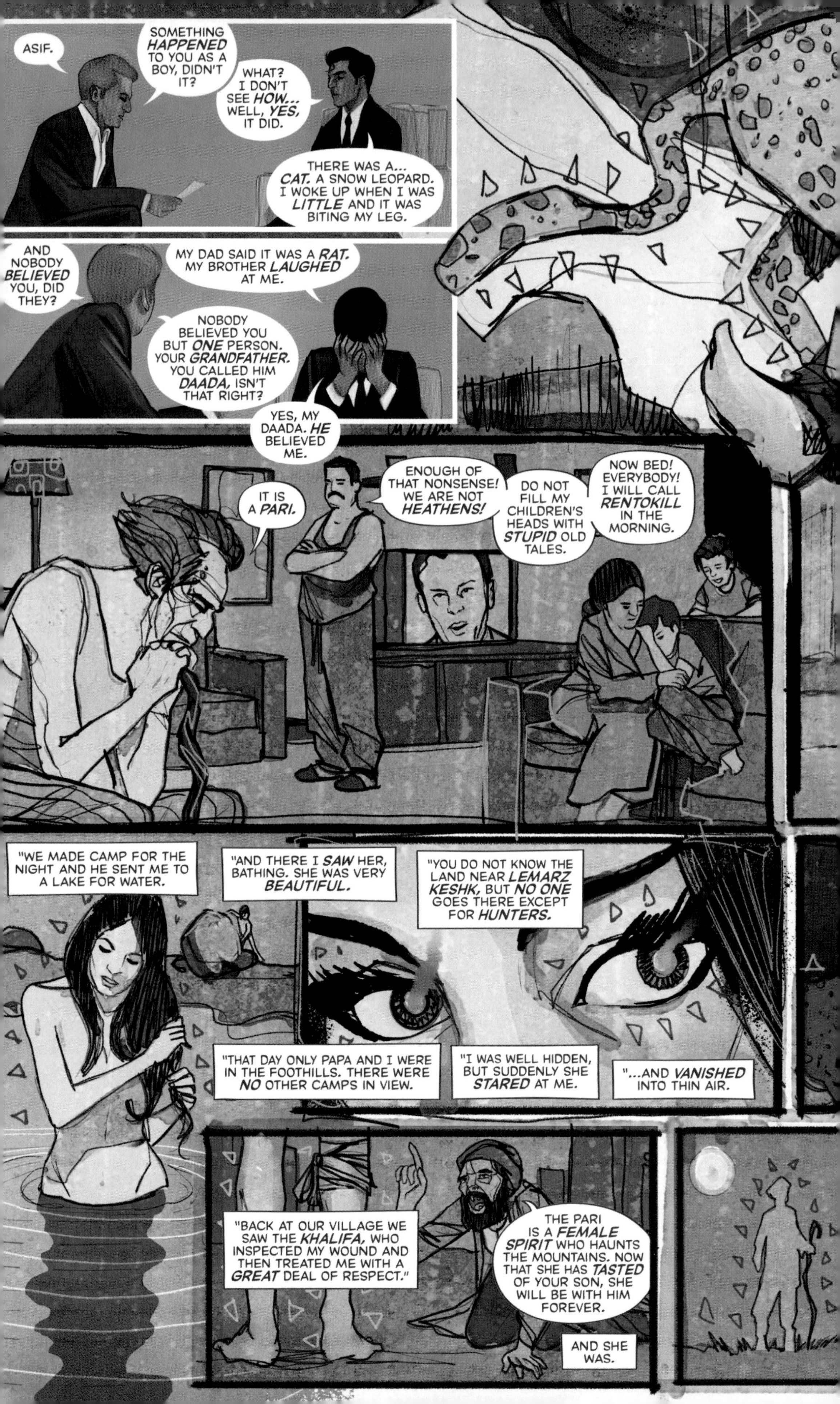
ASIF.
SOMETHING HAPPENED TO YOU AS A BOY, DIDN'T IT?
WHAT? I DON'T SEE HOW... WELL, YES, IT DID.
THERE WAS A... CAT. A SNOW LEOPARD. I WOKE UP WHEN I WAS LITTLE AND IT WAS BITING MY LEG.
AND NOBODY BELIEVED YOU, DID THEY?
MY DAD SAID IT WAS A RAT. MY BROTHER LAUGHED AT ME.
NOBODY BELIEVED YOU BUT ONE PERSON. YOUR GRANDFATHER. YOU CALLED HIM DAADA, ISN'T THAT RIGHT?
YES, MY DAADA. HE BELIEVED ME.
IT IS A PARI.
ENOUGH OF THAT NONSENSE! WE ARE NOT HEATHENS!
DO NOT FILL MY CHILDREN'S HEADS WITH STUPID OLD TALES.
NOW BED! EVERYBODY! I WILL CALL RENTOKILL IN THE MORNING.
"WE MADE CAMP FOR THE NIGHT AND HE SENT ME TO A LAKE FOR WATER.
"AND THERE I SAW HER, BATHING. SHE WAS VERY BEAUTIFUL.
"YOU DO NOT KNOW THE LAND NEAR LEMARZ KESHK, BUT NO ONE GOES THERE EXCEPT FOR HUNTERS.
"THAT DAY ONLY PAPA AND I WERE IN THE FOOTHILLS. THERE WERE NO OTHER CAMPS IN VIEW.
"I WAS WELL HIDDEN, BUT SUDDENLY SHE STARED AT ME.
"...AND VANISHED INTO THIN AIR.
"BACK AT OUR VILLAGE WE SAW THE KHALIFA, WHO INSPECTED MY WOUND AND THEN TREATED ME WITH A GREAT DEAL OF RESPECT."
THE PARI IS A FEMALE SPIRIT WHO HAUNTS THE MOUNTAINS. NOW THAT SHE HAS TASTED OF YOUR SON, SHE WILL BE WITH HIM FOREVER.
AND SHE WAS.

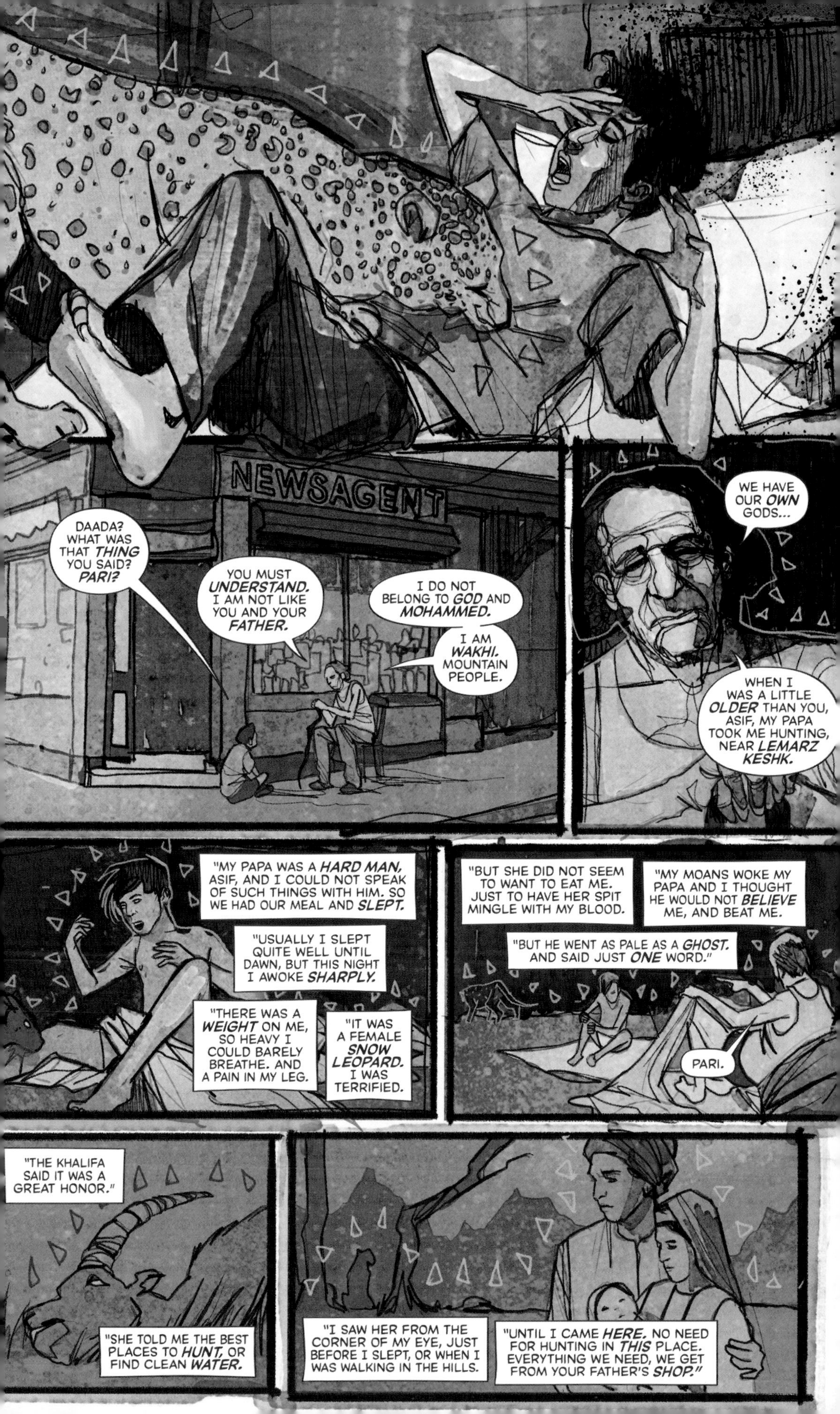
NEWSAGENT
DAADA? WHAT WAS THAT THING YOU SAID? PARI?
YOU MUST UNDERSTAND. I AM NOT LIKE YOU AND YOUR FATHER.
I DO NOT BELONG TO GOD AND MOHAMMED.
I AM WAKHI. MOUNTAIN PEOPLE.
WE HAVE OUR OWN GODS...
WHEN I WAS A LITTLE OLDER THAN YOU, ASIF, MY PAPA TOOK ME HUNTING, NEAR LEMARZ KESHK.
"MY PAPA WAS A HARD MAN, ASIF, AND I COULD NOT SPEAK OF SUCH THINGS WITH HIM. SO WE HAD OUR MEAL AND SLEPT.
"USUALLY I SLEPT QUITE WELL UNTIL DAWN, BUT THIS NIGHT I AWOKE SHARPLY.
"THERE WAS A WEIGHT ON ME, SO HEAVY I COULD BARELY BREATHE. AND A PAIN IN MY LEG.
"IT WAS A FEMALE SNOW LEOPARD. I WAS TERRIFIED.
"BUT SHE DID NOT SEEM TO WANT TO EAT ME. JUST TO HAVE HER SPIT MINGLE WITH MY BLOOD.
"MY MOANS WOKE MY PAPA AND I THOUGHT HE WOULD NOT BELIEVE ME, AND BEAT ME.
"BUT HE WENT AS PALE AS A GHOST. AND SAID JUST ONE WORD."
PARI.
"THE KHALIFA SAID IT WAS A GREAT HONOR."
"SHE TOLD ME THE BEST PLACES TO HUNT, OR FIND CLEAN WATER.
"I SAW HER FROM THE CORNER OF MY EYE, JUST BEFORE I SLEPT, OR WHEN I WAS WALKING IN THE HILLS.
"UNTIL I CAME HERE. NO NEED FOR HUNTING IN THIS PLACE. EVERYTHING WE NEED, WE GET FROM YOUR FATHER'S SHOP."

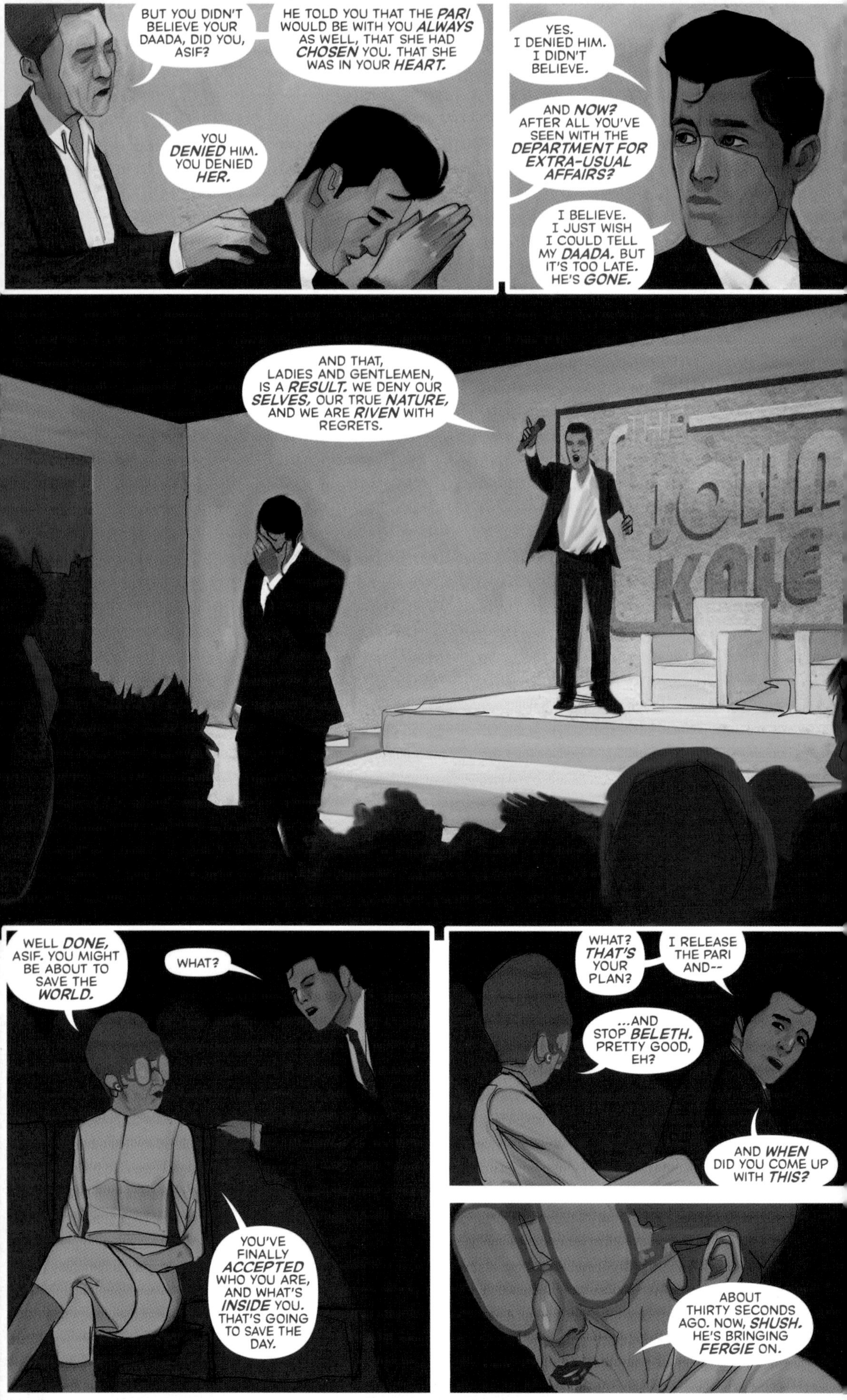
BUT YOU DIDN'T BELIEVE YOUR DAADA, DID YOU, ASIF?
HE TOLD YOU THAT THE PARI WOULD BE WITH YOU ALWAYS AS WELL, THAT SHE HAD CHOSEN YOU. THAT SHE WAS IN YOUR HEART.
YOU DENIED HIM. YOU DENIED HER.
YES. I DENIED HIM. I DIDN'T BELIEVE.
AND NOW? AFTER ALL YOU'VE SEEN WITH THE DEPARTMENT FOR EXTRA-USUAL AFFAIRS?
I BELIEVE. I JUST WISH I COULD TELL MY DAADA. BUT IT'S TOO LATE. HE'S GONE.
AND THAT, LADIES AND GENTLEMEN, IS A RESULT. WE DENY OUR SELVES, OUR TRUE NATURE, AND WE ARE RIVEN WITH REGRETS.
WELL DONE, ASIF. YOU MIGHT BE ABOUT TO SAVE THE WORLD.
WHAT?
YOU'VE FINALLY ACCEPTED WHO YOU ARE, AND WHAT'S INSIDE YOU. THAT'S GOING TO SAVE THE DAY.
WHAT? THAT'S YOUR PLAN?
I RELEASE THE PARI AND--
...AND STOP BELETH. PRETTY GOOD, EH?
AND WHEN DID YOU COME UP WITH THIS?
ABOUT THIRTY SECONDS AGO. NOW, SHUSH. HE'S BRINGING FERGIE ON.

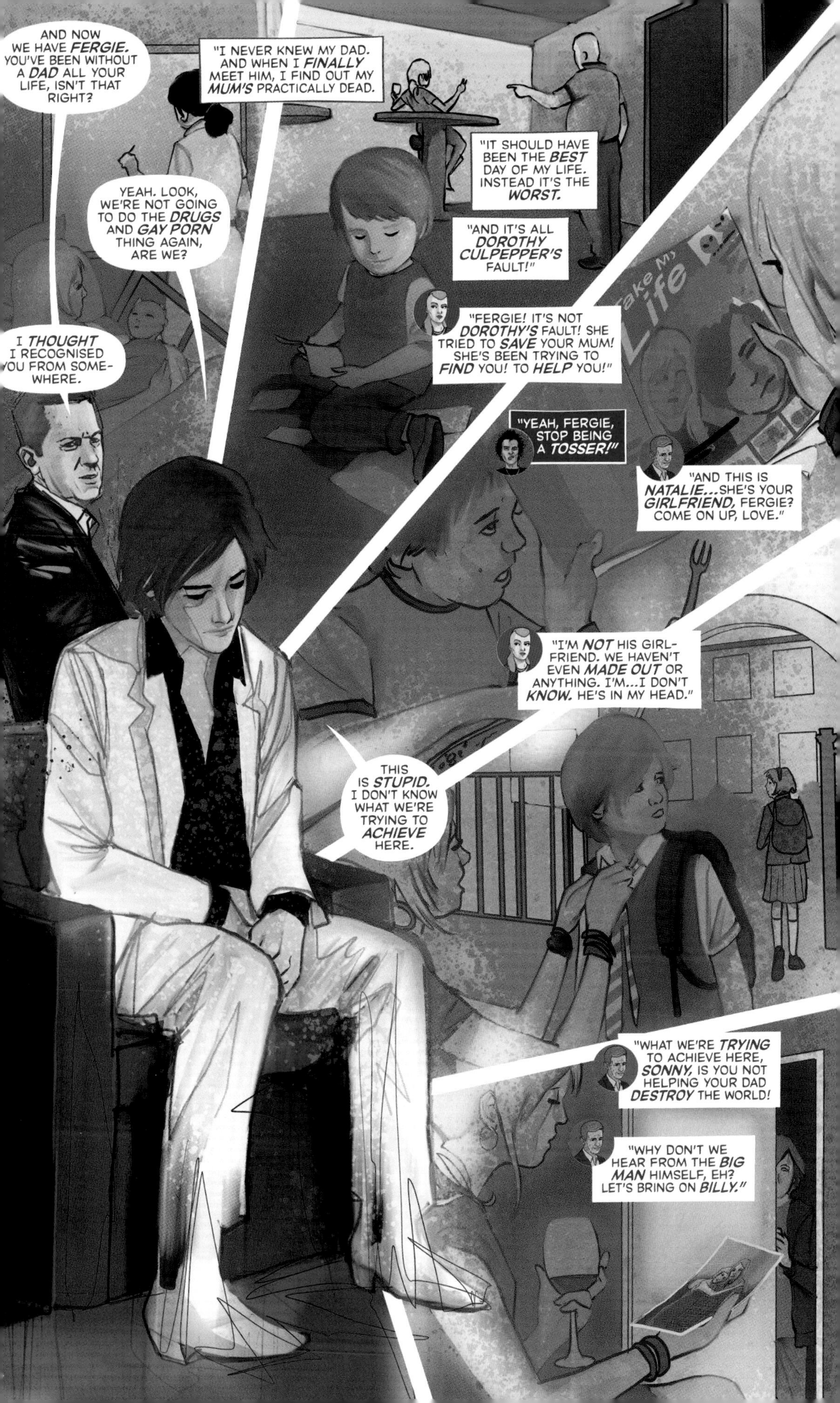
AND NOW WE HAVE FERGIE. YOU'VE BEEN WITHOUT A DAD ALL YOUR LIFE, ISN'T THAT RIGHT?
"I NEVER KNEW MY DAD. AND WHEN I FINALLY MEET HIM, I FIND OUT MY MUM'S PRACTICALLY DEAD.
"IT SHOULD HAVE BEEN THE BEST DAY OF MY LIFE. INSTEAD IT'S THE WORST.
"AND IT'S ALL DOROTHY CULPEPPER'S FAULT!"
YEAH. LOOK, WE'RE NOT GOING TO DO THE DRUGS AND GAY PORN THING AGAIN, ARE WE?
I THOUGHT I RECOGNISED YOU FROM SOMEWHERE.
"FERGIE! IT'S NOT DOROTHY'S FAULT! SHE TRIED TO SAVE YOUR MUM! SHE'S BEEN TRYING TO FIND YOU! TO HELP YOU!"
Take My Life
"YEAH, FERGIE, STOP BEING A TOSSER!"
"AND THIS IS NATALIE...SHE'S YOUR GIRLFRIEND, FERGIE? COME ON UP, LOVE."
"I'M NOT HIS GIRLFRIEND. WE HAVEN'T EVEN MADE OUT OR ANYTHING. I'M...I DON'T KNOW. HE'S IN MY HEAD."
THIS IS STUPID. I DON'T KNOW WHAT WE'RE TRYING TO ACHIEVE HERE.
"WHAT WE'RE TRYING TO ACHIEVE HERE, SONNY, IS YOU NOT HELPING YOUR DAD DESTROY THE WORLD!
"WHY DON'T WE HEAR FROM THE BIG MAN HIMSELF, EH? LET'S BRING ON BILLY."

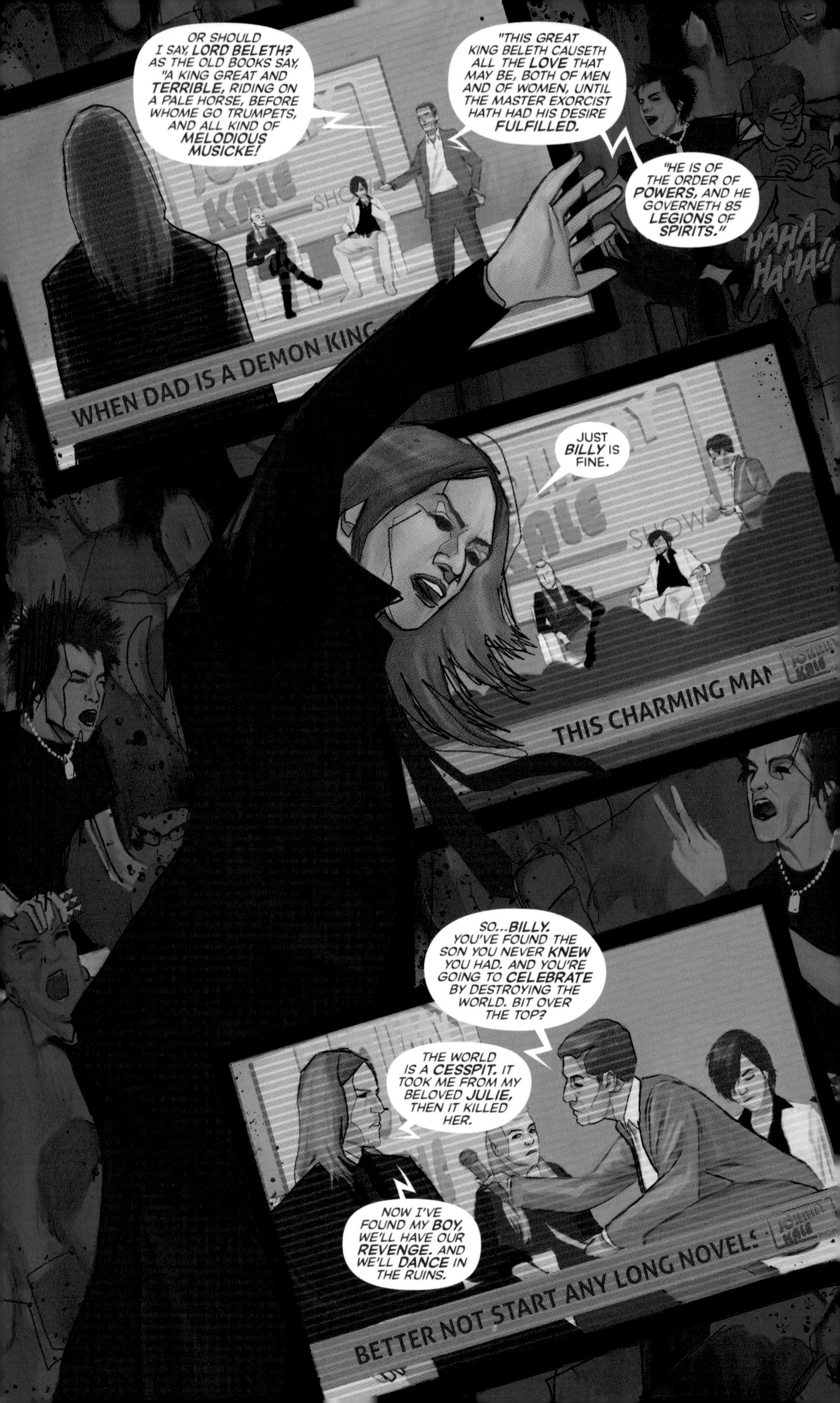
OR SHOULD I SAY, LORD BELETH? AS THE OLD BOOKS SAY, "A KING GREAT AND TERRIBLE, RIDING ON A PALE HORSE, BEFORE WHOME GO TRUMPETS, AND ALL KIND OF MELODIOUS MUSICKE!
"THIS GREAT KING BELETH CAUSETH ALL THE LOVE THAT MAY BE, BOTH OF MEN AND OF WOMEN, UNTIL THE MASTER EXORCIST HATH HAD HIS DESIRE FULFILLED.
"HE IS OF THE ORDER OF POWERS, AND HE GOVERNETH 85 LEGIONS OF SPIRITS."
HAHA HAHA!!
WHEN DAD IS A DEMON KING
JUST BILLY IS FINE.
THIS CHARMING MAN
SO...BILLY. YOU'VE FOUND THE SON YOU NEVER KNEW YOU HAD. AND YOU'RE GOING TO CELEBRATE BY DESTROYING THE WORLD. BIT OVER THE TOP?
THE WORLD IS A CESSPIT. IT TOOK ME FROM MY BELOVED JULIE, THEN IT KILLED HER.
NOW I'VE FOUND MY BOY, WE'LL HAVE OUR REVENGE. AND WE'LL DANCE IN THE RUINS.
BETTER NOT START ANY LONG NOVELS

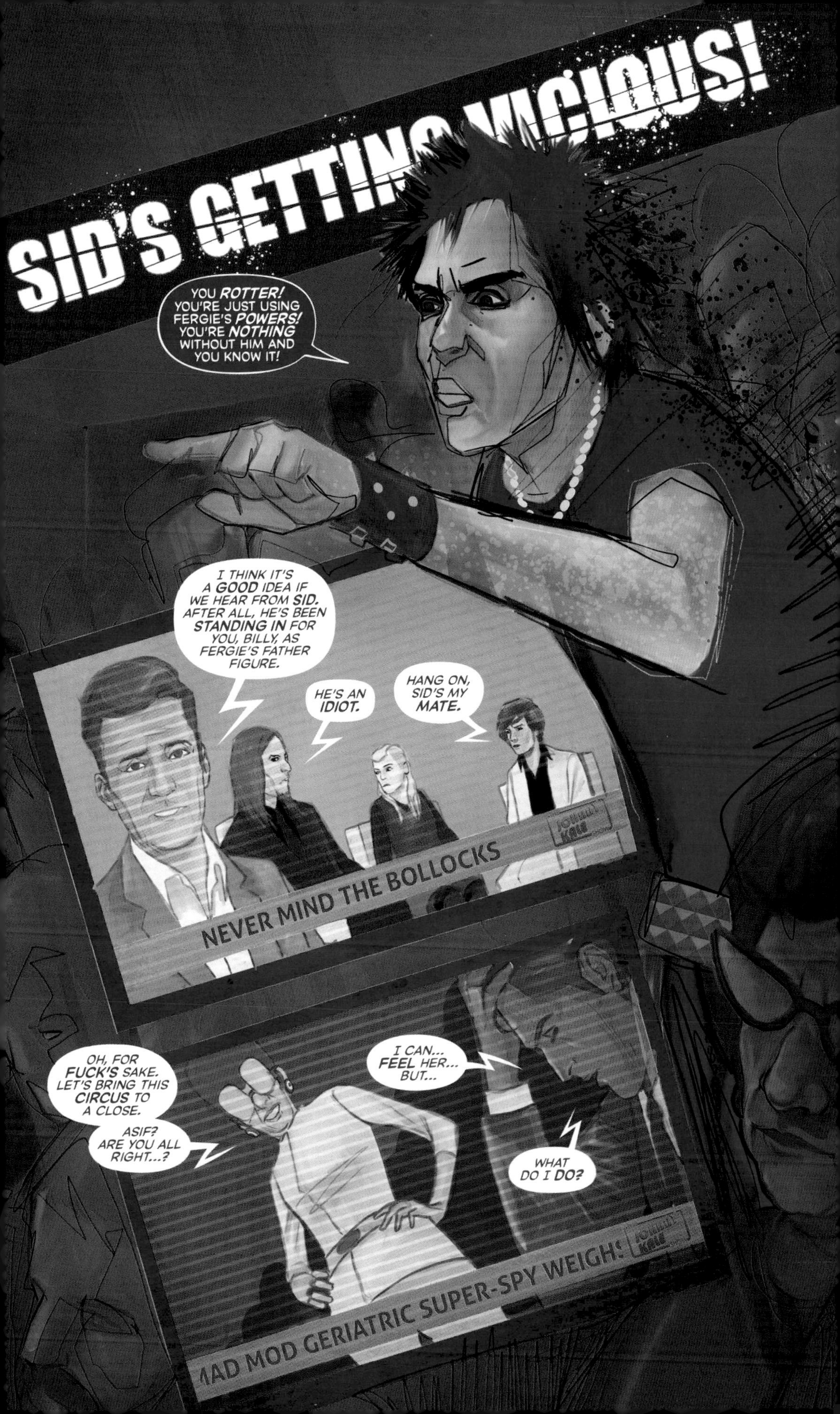
SID'S GETTING VICIOUS!
YOU ROTTER! YOU'RE JUST USING FERGIE'S POWERS! YOU'RE NOTHING WITHOUT HIM AND YOU KNOW IT!
I THINK IT'S A GOOD IDEA IF WE HEAR FROM SID. AFTER ALL, HE'S BEEN STANDING IN FOR YOU, BILLY, AS FERGIE'S FATHER FIGURE.
HE'S AN IDIOT.
HANG ON, SID'S MY MATE.
NEVER MIND THE BOLLOCKS
OH, FOR FUCK'S SAKE. LET'S BRING THIS CIRCUS TO A CLOSE.
ASIF? ARE YOU ALL RIGHT...?
I CAN... FEEL HER... BUT...
WHAT DO I DO?
MAD MOD GERIATRIC SUPER-SPY WEIGH!

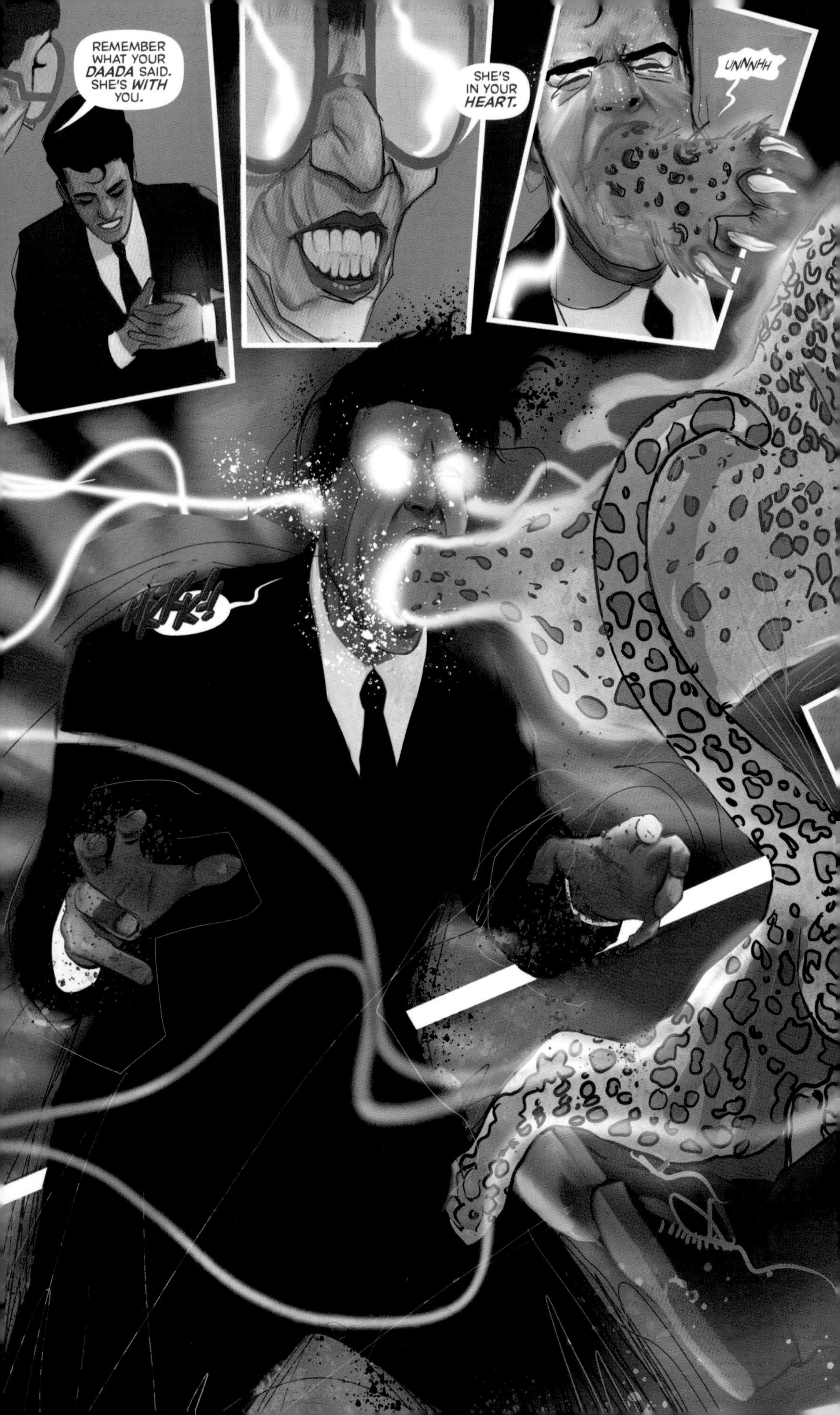
REMEMBER WHAT YOUR DAADA SAID. SHE'S WITH YOU.
SHE'S IN YOUR HEART.
UNNNHH

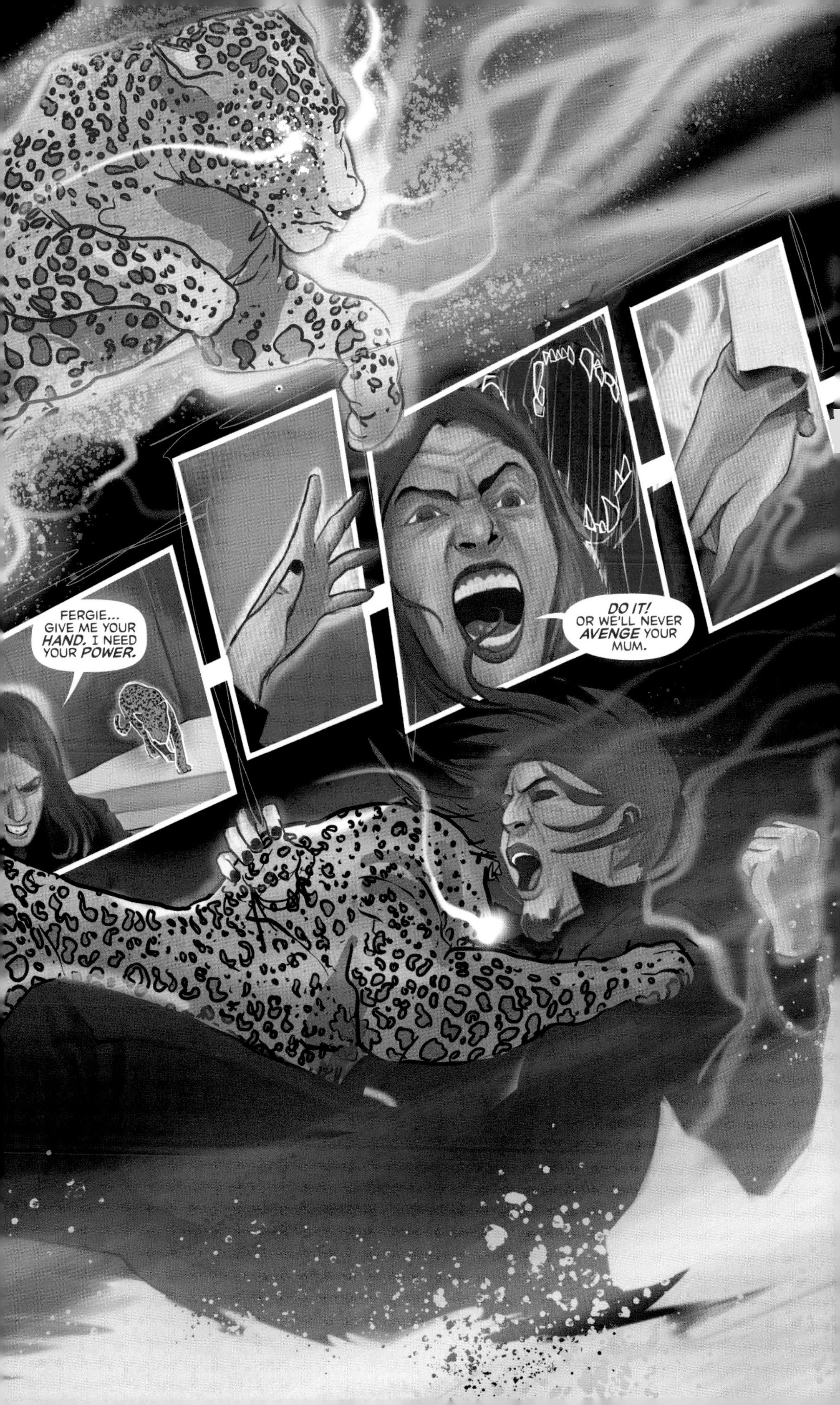

FERGIE... GIVE ME YOUR *HAND.* I NEED YOUR *POWER.*
DO IT! OR WE'LL NEVER *AVENGE* YOUR MUM.

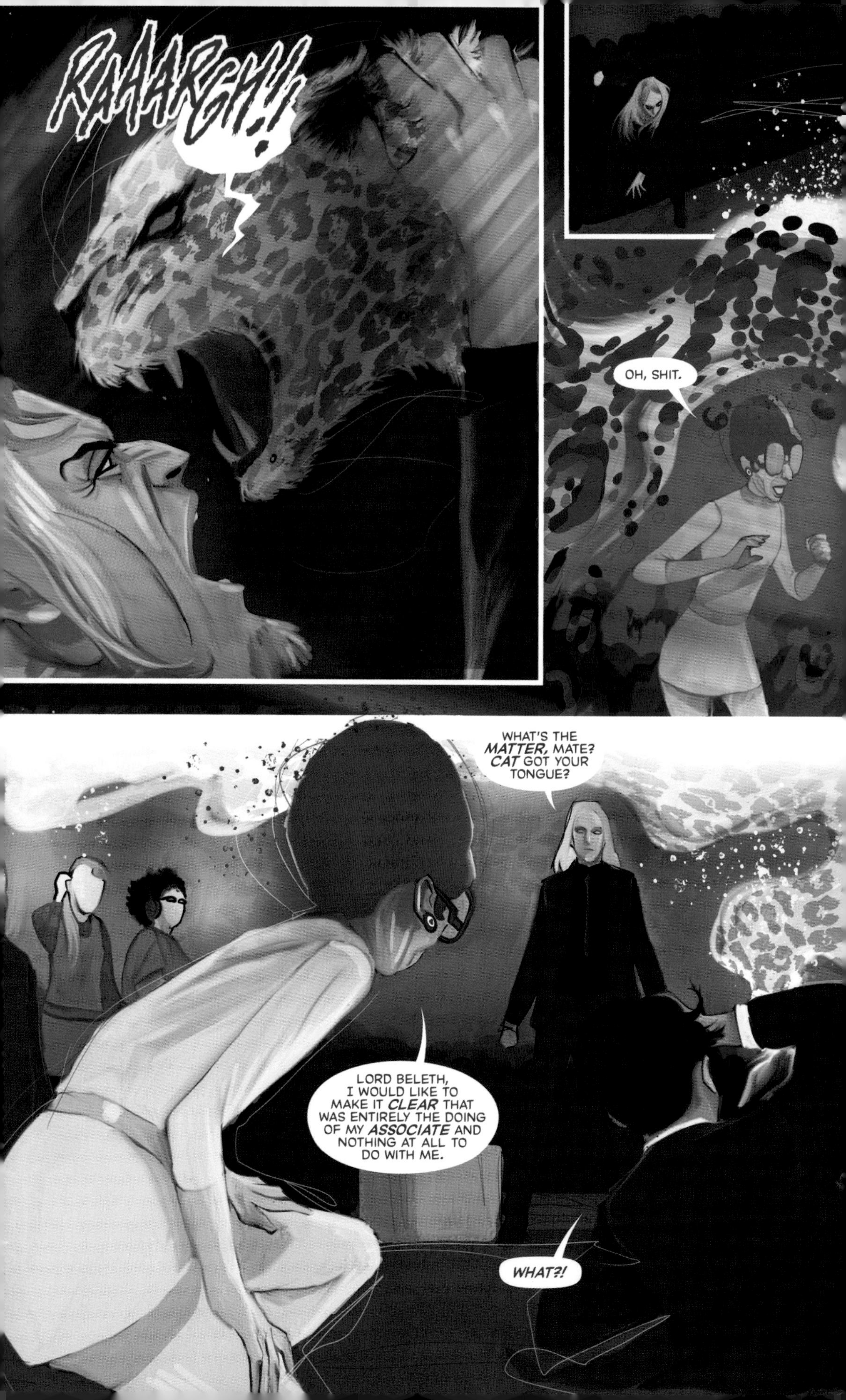
RAAARGH!!
OH, SHIT.
WHAT'S THE MATTER, MATE? CAT GOT YOUR TONGUE?
LORD BELETH, I WOULD LIKE TO MAKE IT CLEAR THAT WAS ENTIRELY THE DOING OF MY ASSOCIATE AND NOTHING AT ALL TO DO WITH ME.
WHAT?!

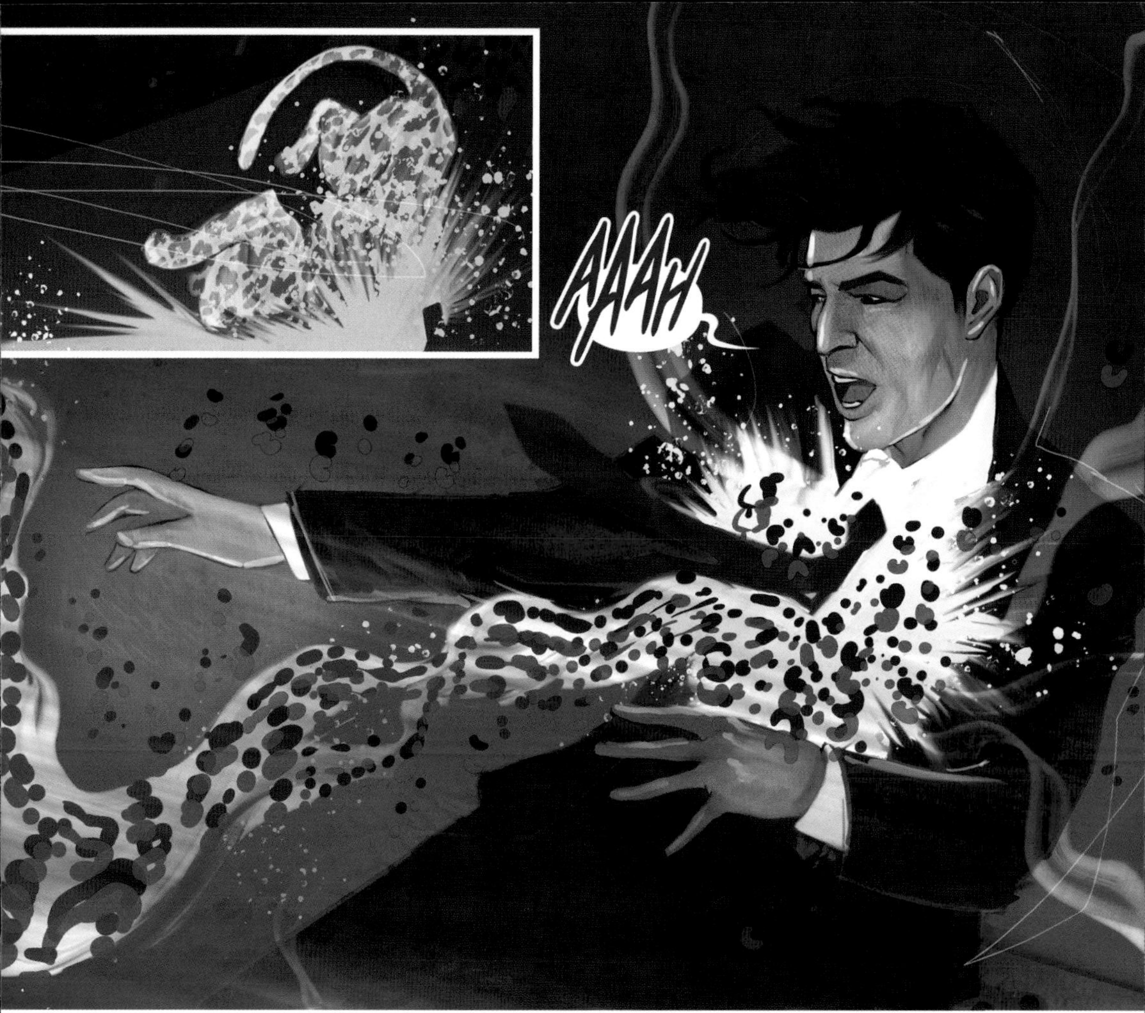
AAAH

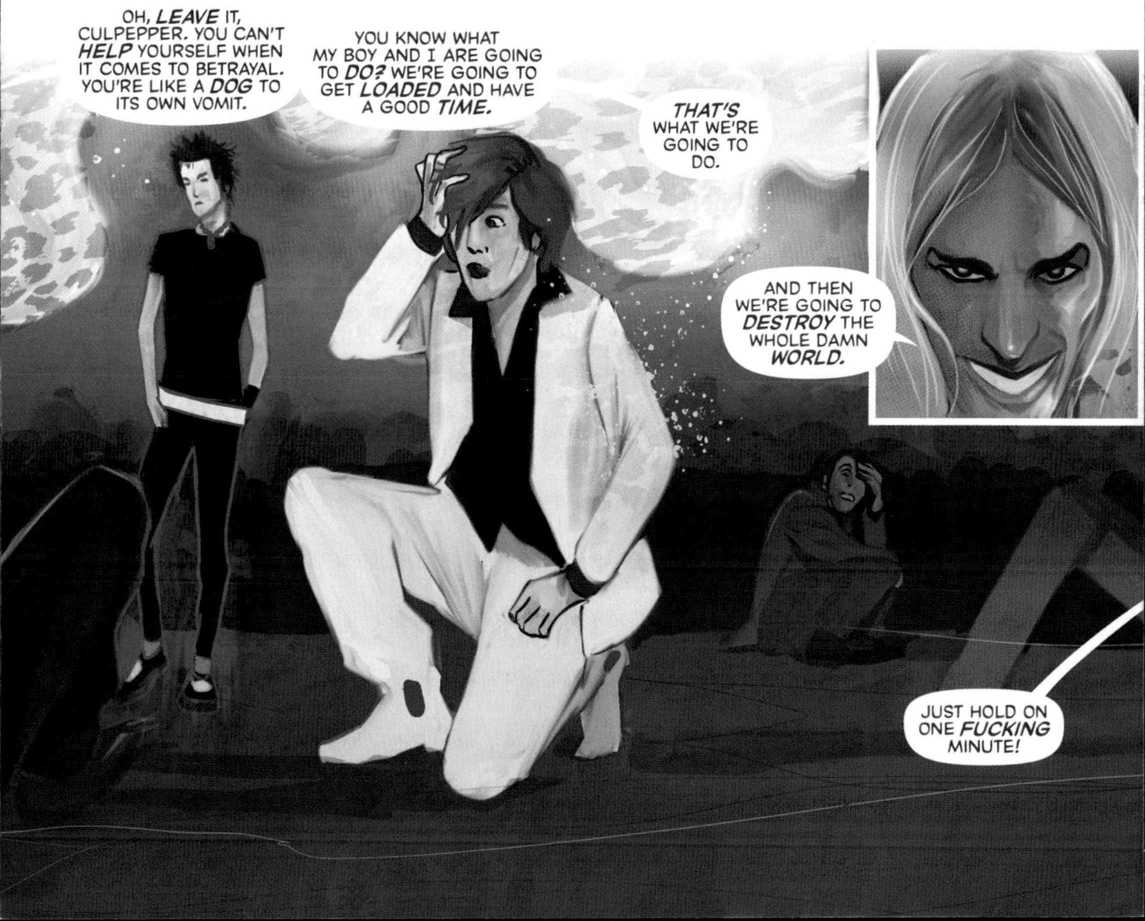
OH, LEAVE IT, CULPEPPER. YOU CAN'T HELP YOURSELF WHEN IT COMES TO BETRAYAL. YOU'RE LIKE A DOG TO ITS OWN VOMIT.
YOU KNOW WHAT MY BOY AND I ARE GOING TO DO? WE'RE GOING TO GET LOADED AND HAVE A GOOD TIME.
THAT'S WHAT WE'RE GOING TO DO.
AND THEN WE'RE GOING TO DESTROY THE WHOLE DAMN WORLD.
JUST HOLD ON ONE FUCKING MINUTE!

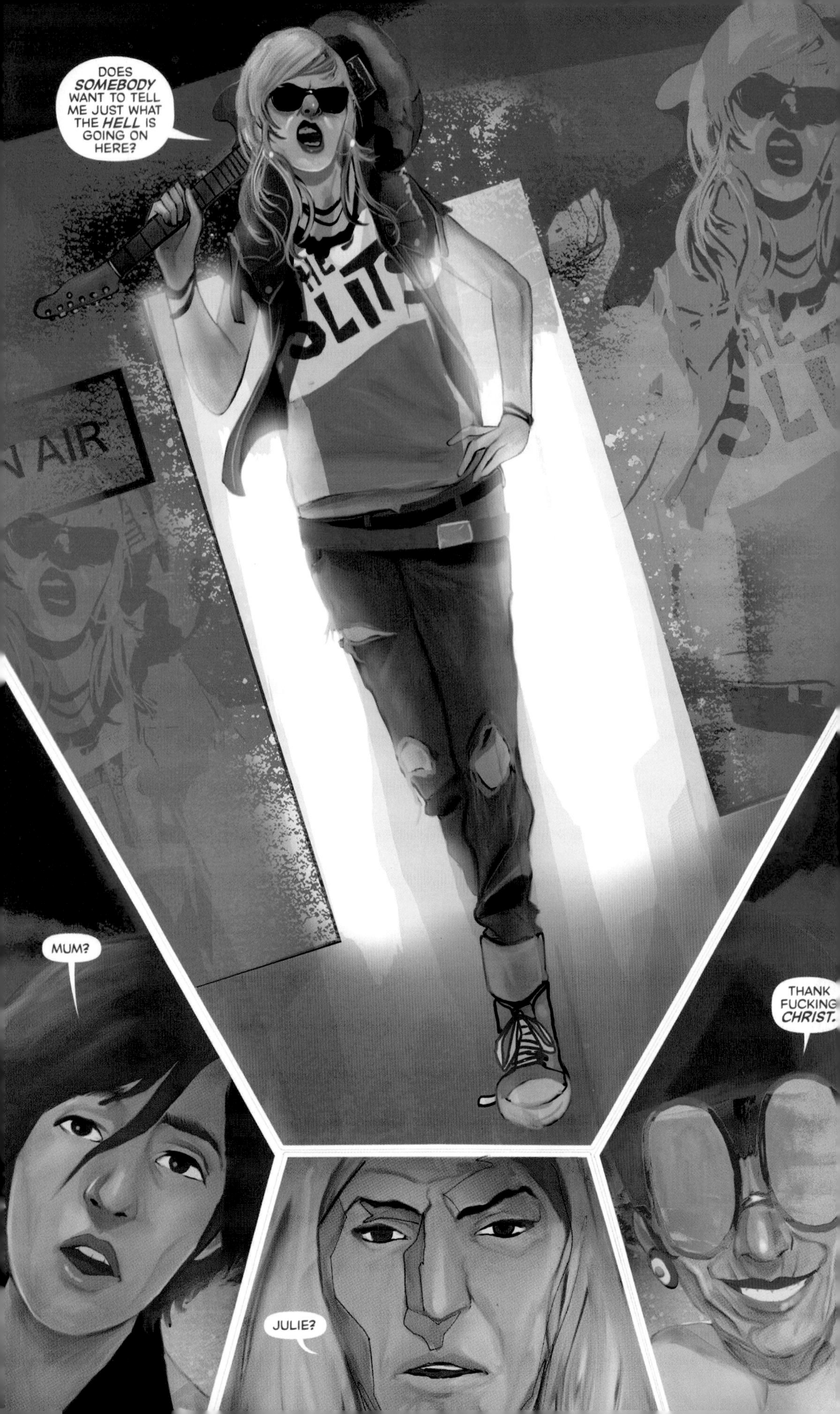
DOES *SOMEBODY* WANT TO TELL ME JUST WHAT THE *HELL* IS GOING ON HERE?
THE SLITS
ON AIR
MUM?
JULIE?
THANK FUCKING *CHRIST.*

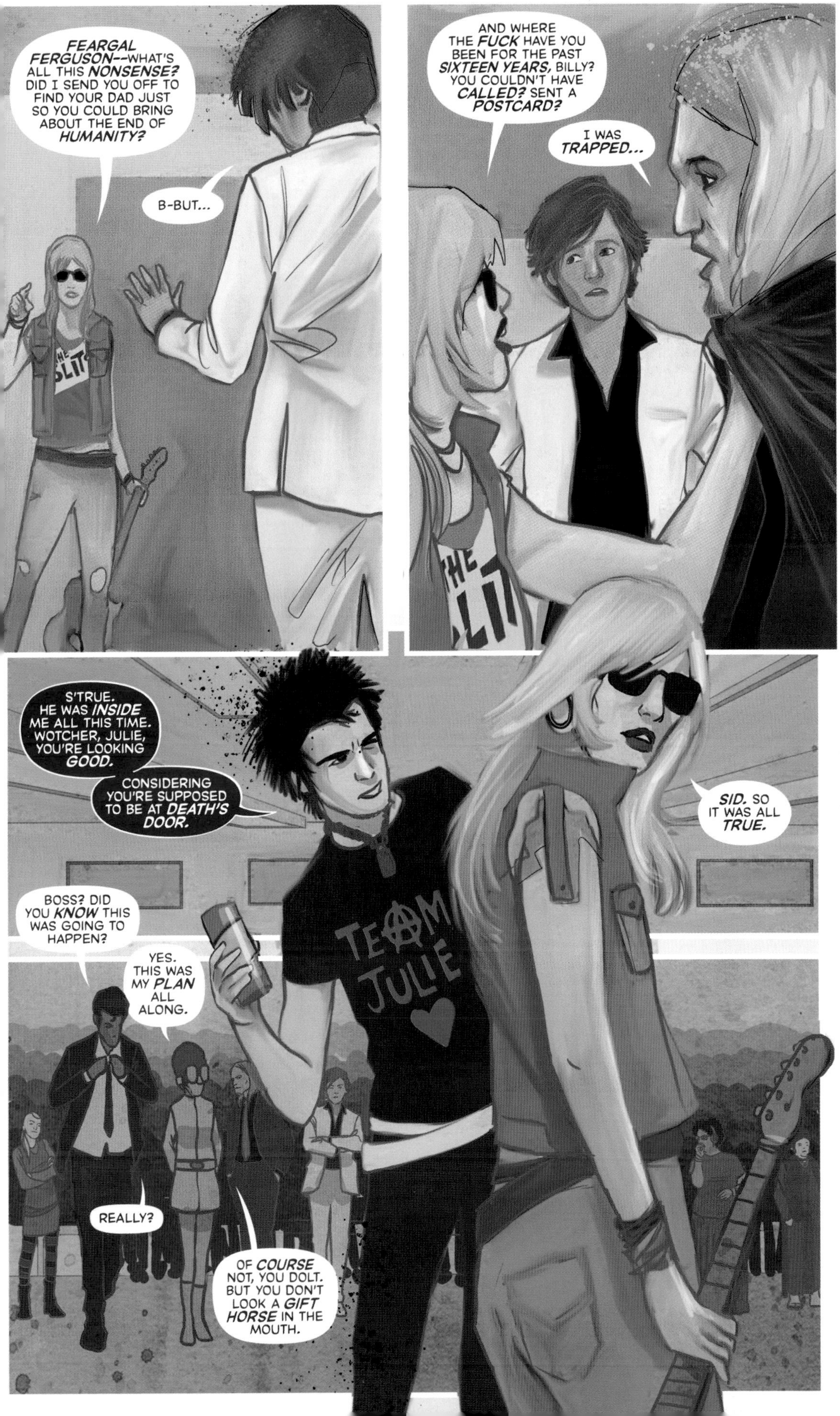
FEARGAL FERGUSON--WHAT'S ALL THIS NONSENSE? DID I SEND YOU OFF TO FIND YOUR DAD JUST SO YOU COULD BRING ABOUT THE END OF HUMANITY?
B-BUT...
AND WHERE THE FUCK HAVE YOU BEEN FOR THE PAST SIXTEEN YEARS, BILLY? YOU COULDN'T HAVE CALLED? SENT A POSTCARD?
I WAS TRAPPED...
S'TRUE. HE WAS INSIDE ME ALL THIS TIME. WOTCHER, JULIE, YOU'RE LOOKING GOOD.
CONSIDERING YOU'RE SUPPOSED TO BE AT DEATH'S DOOR.
SID. SO IT WAS ALL TRUE.
BOSS? DID YOU KNOW THIS WAS GOING TO HAPPEN?
YES. THIS WAS MY PLAN ALL ALONG.
REALLY?
OF COURSE NOT, YOU DOLT. BUT YOU DON'T LOOK A GIFT HORSE IN THE MOUTH.
TEAM JULIE

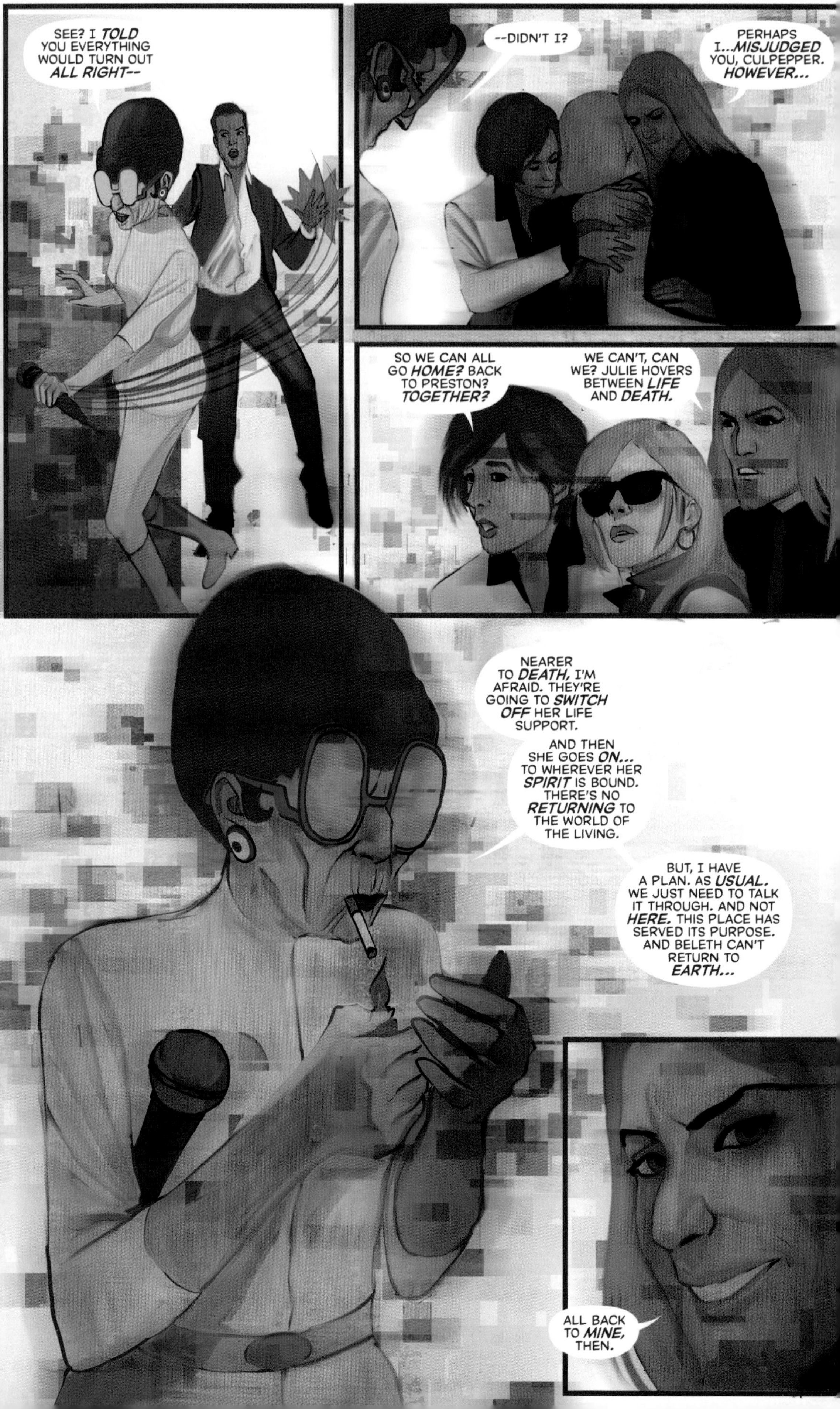
SEE? I TOLD YOU EVERYTHING WOULD TURN OUT ALL RIGHT--
--DIDN'T I?
PERHAPS I...MISJUDGED YOU, CULPEPPER. HOWEVER...
SO WE CAN ALL GO HOME? BACK TO PRESTON? TOGETHER?
WE CAN'T, CAN WE? JULIE HOVERS BETWEEN LIFE AND DEATH.
NEARER TO DEATH, I'M AFRAID. THEY'RE GOING TO SWITCH OFF HER LIFE SUPPORT.
AND THEN SHE GOES ON... TO WHEREVER HER SPIRIT IS BOUND. THERE'S NO RETURNING TO THE WORLD OF THE LIVING.
BUT, I HAVE A PLAN. AS USUAL. WE JUST NEED TO TALK IT THROUGH. AND NOT HERE. THIS PLACE HAS SERVED ITS PURPOSE. AND BELETH CAN'T RETURN TO EARTH...
ALL BACK TO MINE, THEN.

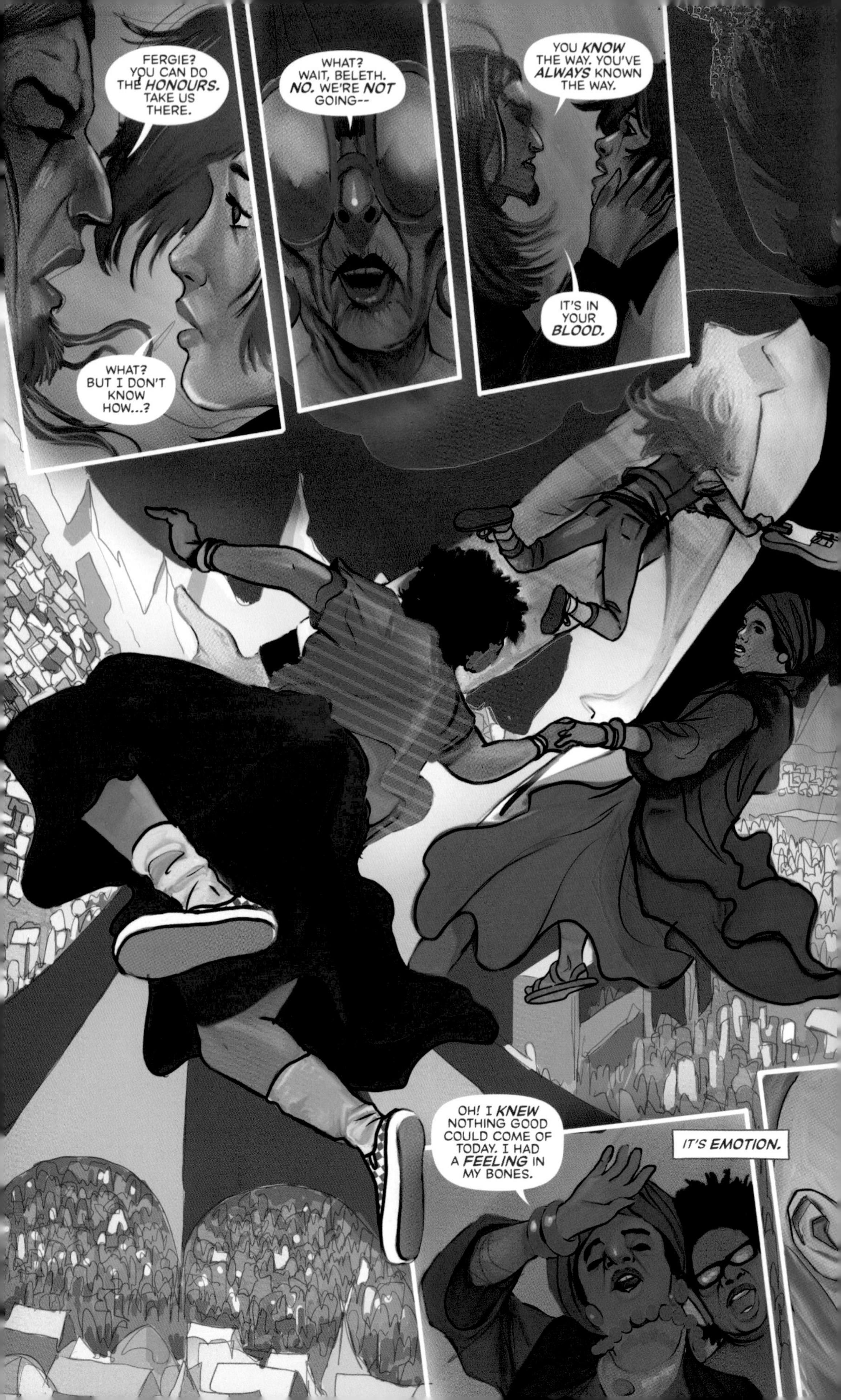
FERGIE? YOU CAN DO THE HONOURS. TAKE US THERE.
WHAT? BUT I DON'T KNOW HOW...?
WHAT? WAIT, BELETH. NO. WE'RE NOT GOING--
YOU KNOW THE WAY. YOU'VE ALWAYS KNOWN THE WAY.
IT'S IN YOUR BLOOD.
OH! I KNEW NOTHING GOOD COULD COME OF TODAY. I HAD A FEELING IN MY BONES.
IT'S EMOTION.

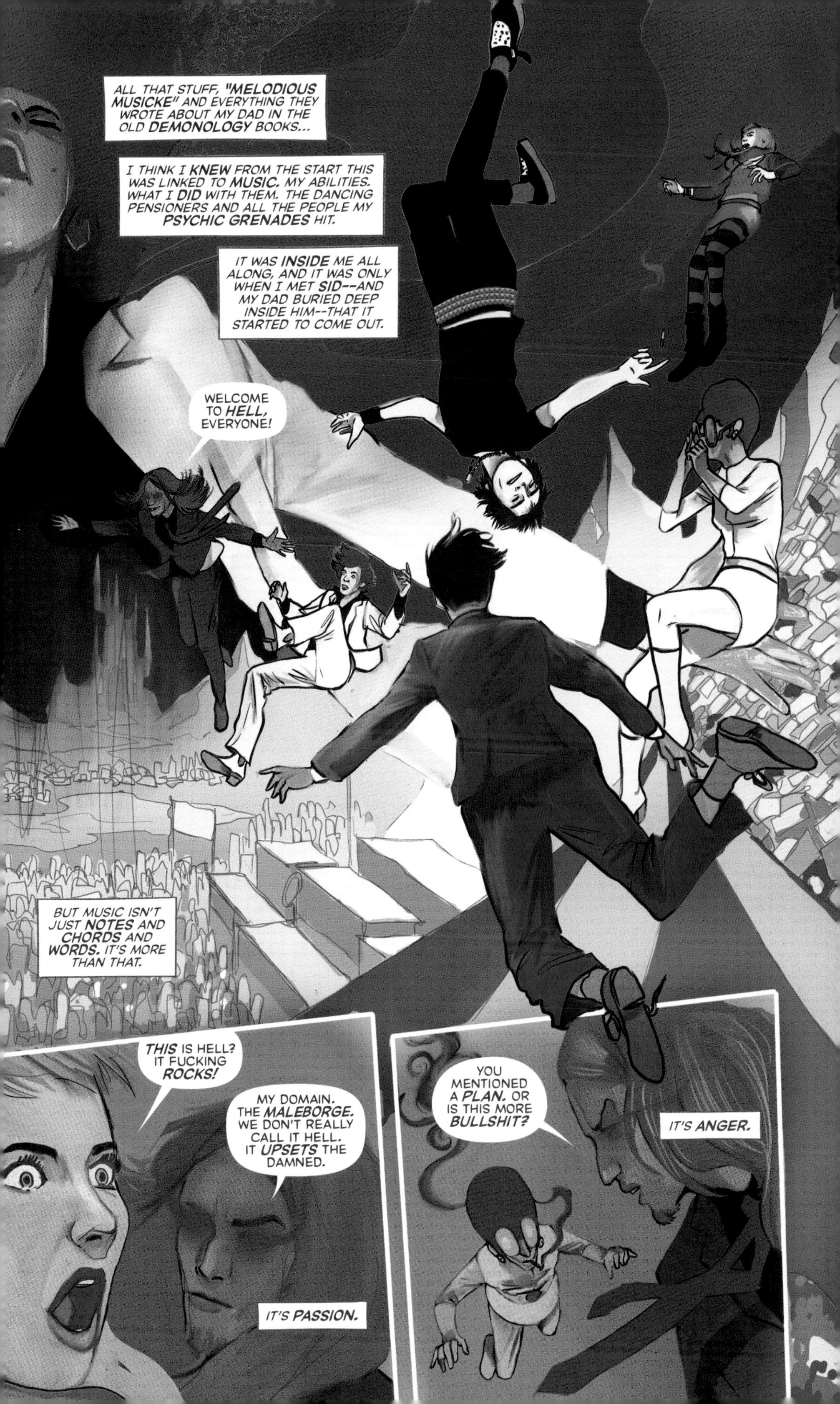
ALL THAT STUFF, "MELODIOUS MUSICKE" AND EVERYTHING THEY WROTE ABOUT MY DAD IN THE OLD DEMONOLOGY BOOKS...
I THINK I KNEW FROM THE START THIS WAS LINKED TO MUSIC. MY ABILITIES. WHAT I DID WITH THEM. THE DANCING PENSIONERS AND ALL THE PEOPLE MY PSYCHIC GRENADES HIT.
IT WAS INSIDE ME ALL ALONG, AND IT WAS ONLY WHEN I MET SID--AND MY DAD BURIED DEEP INSIDE HIM--THAT IT STARTED TO COME OUT.
WELCOME TO HELL, EVERYONE!
BUT MUSIC ISN'T JUST NOTES AND CHORDS AND WORDS. IT'S MORE THAN THAT.
THIS IS HELL? IT FUCKING ROCKS!
MY DOMAIN. THE MALEBORGE. WE DON'T REALLY CALL IT HELL. IT UPSETS THE DAMNED.
IT'S PASSION.
YOU MENTIONED A PLAN. OR IS THIS MORE BULLSHIT?
IT'S ANGER.

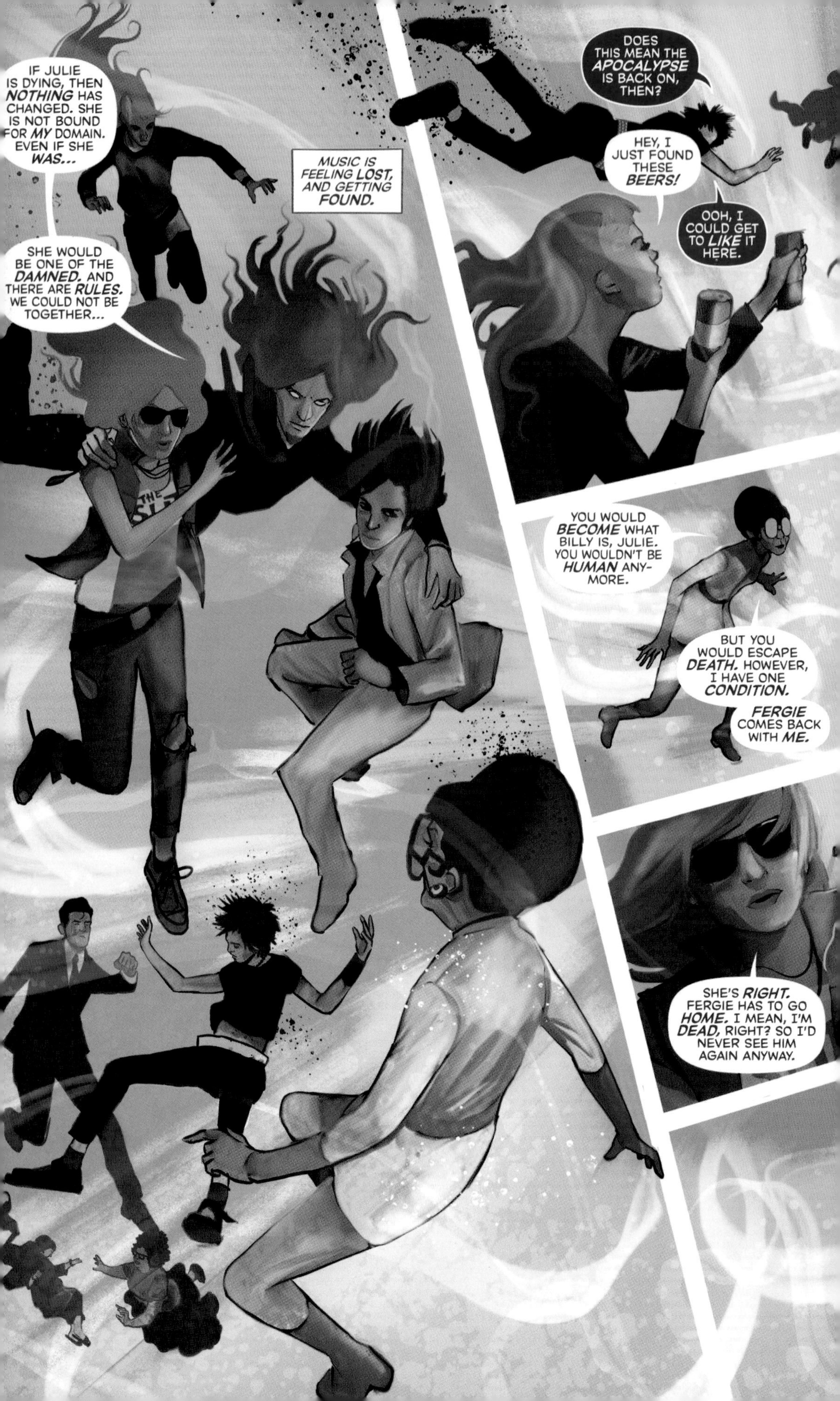
IF JULIE IS DYING, THEN NOTHING HAS CHANGED. SHE IS NOT BOUND FOR MY DOMAIN. EVEN IF SHE WAS...
SHE WOULD BE ONE OF THE DAMNED. AND THERE ARE RULES. WE COULD NOT BE TOGETHER...
MUSIC IS FEELING LOST, AND GETTING FOUND.
DOES THIS MEAN THE APOCALYPSE IS BACK ON, THEN?
HEY, I JUST FOUND THESE BEERS!
OOH, I COULD GET TO LIKE IT HERE.
YOU WOULD BECOME WHAT BILLY IS, JULIE. YOU WOULDN'T BE HUMAN ANY-MORE.
BUT YOU WOULD ESCAPE DEATH. HOWEVER, I HAVE ONE CONDITION.
FERGIE COMES BACK WITH ME.
SHE'S RIGHT. FERGIE HAS TO GO HOME. I MEAN, I'M DEAD, RIGHT? SO I'D NEVER SEE HIM AGAIN ANYWAY.

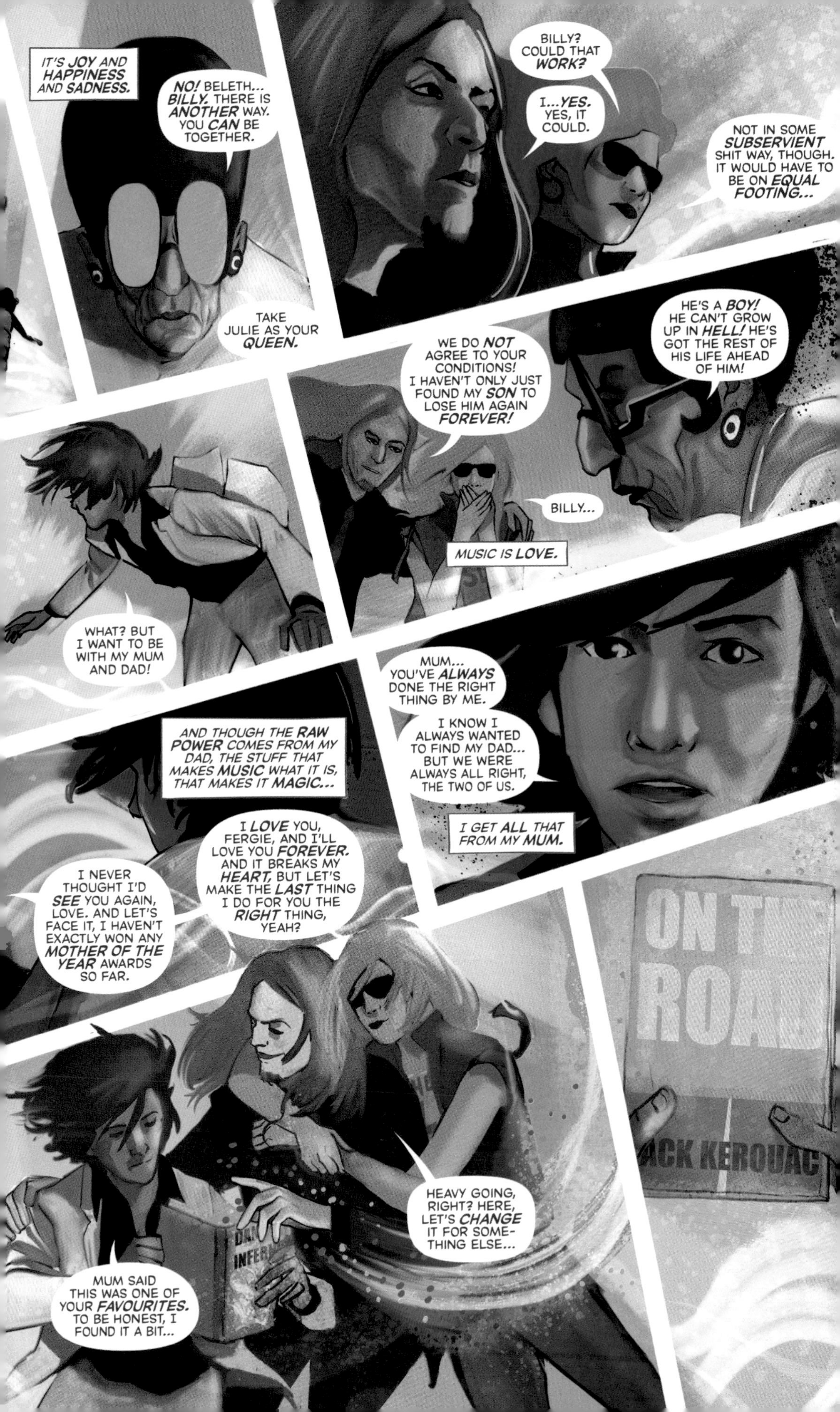
IT'S JOY AND HAPPINESS AND SADNESS.
NO! BELETH... BILLY. THERE IS ANOTHER WAY. YOU CAN BE TOGETHER.
TAKE JULIE AS YOUR QUEEN.
BILLY? COULD THAT WORK?
I...YES. YES, IT COULD.
NOT IN SOME SUBSERVIENT SHIT WAY, THOUGH. IT WOULD HAVE TO BE ON EQUAL FOOTING...
WE DO NOT AGREE TO YOUR CONDITIONS! I HAVEN'T ONLY JUST FOUND MY SON TO LOSE HIM AGAIN FOREVER!
HE'S A BOY! HE CAN'T GROW UP IN HELL! HE'S GOT THE REST OF HIS LIFE AHEAD OF HIM!
BILLY...
MUSIC IS LOVE.
WHAT? BUT I WANT TO BE WITH MY MUM AND DAD!
MUM... YOU'VE ALWAYS DONE THE RIGHT THING BY ME.
I KNOW I ALWAYS WANTED TO FIND MY DAD... BUT WE WERE ALWAYS ALL RIGHT, THE TWO OF US.
I GET ALL THAT FROM MY MUM.
AND THOUGH THE RAW POWER COMES FROM MY DAD, THE STUFF THAT MAKES MUSIC WHAT IT IS, THAT MAKES IT MAGIC...
I NEVER THOUGHT I'D SEE YOU AGAIN, LOVE. AND LET'S FACE IT, I HAVEN'T EXACTLY WON ANY MOTHER OF THE YEAR AWARDS SO FAR.
I LOVE YOU, FERGIE, AND I'LL LOVE YOU FOREVER. AND IT BREAKS MY HEART, BUT LET'S MAKE THE LAST THING I DO FOR YOU THE RIGHT THING, YEAH?
MUM SAID THIS WAS ONE OF YOUR FAVOURITES. TO BE HONEST, I FOUND IT A BIT...
HEAVY GOING, RIGHT? HERE, LET'S CHANGE IT FOR SOME-THING ELSE...
ON TH
ROAD
ACK KEROUAC

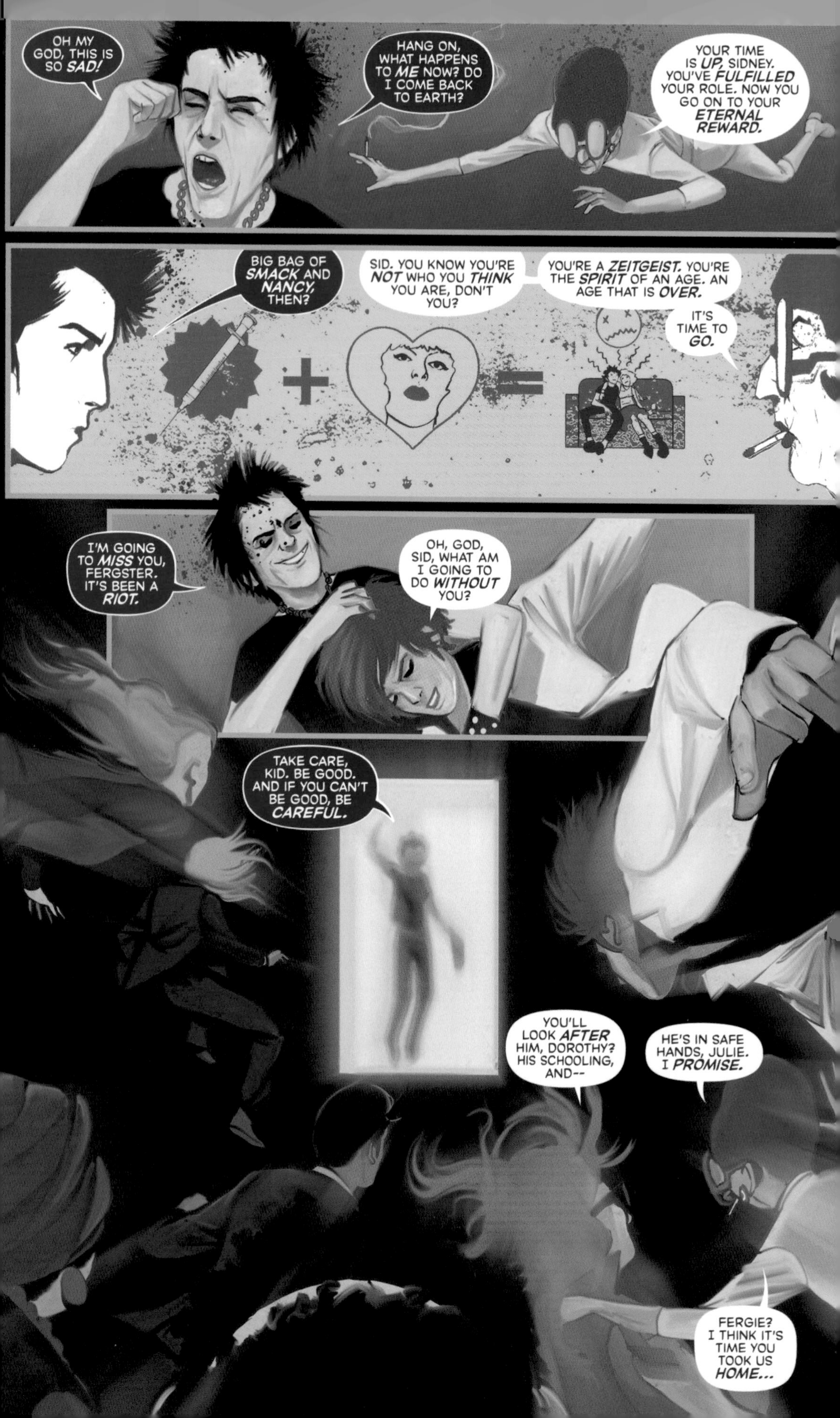
OH MY GOD, THIS IS SO SAD!
HANG ON, WHAT HAPPENS TO ME NOW? DO I COME BACK TO EARTH?
YOUR TIME IS UP, SIDNEY. YOU'VE FULFILLED YOUR ROLE. NOW YOU GO ON TO YOUR ETERNAL REWARD.
BIG BAG OF SMACK AND NANCY, THEN?
SID. YOU KNOW YOU'RE NOT WHO YOU THINK YOU ARE, DON'T YOU?
YOU'RE A ZEITGEIST. YOU'RE THE SPIRIT OF AN AGE. AN AGE THAT IS OVER.
IT'S TIME TO GO.
I'M GOING TO MISS YOU, FERGSTER. IT'S BEEN A RIOT.
OH, GOD, SID, WHAT AM I GOING TO DO WITHOUT YOU?
TAKE CARE, KID. BE GOOD. AND IF YOU CAN'T BE GOOD, BE CAREFUL.
YOU'LL LOOK AFTER HIM, DOROTHY? HIS SCHOOLING, AND--
HE'S IN SAFE HANDS, JULIE. I PROMISE.
FERGIE? I THINK IT'S TIME YOU TOOK US HOME...

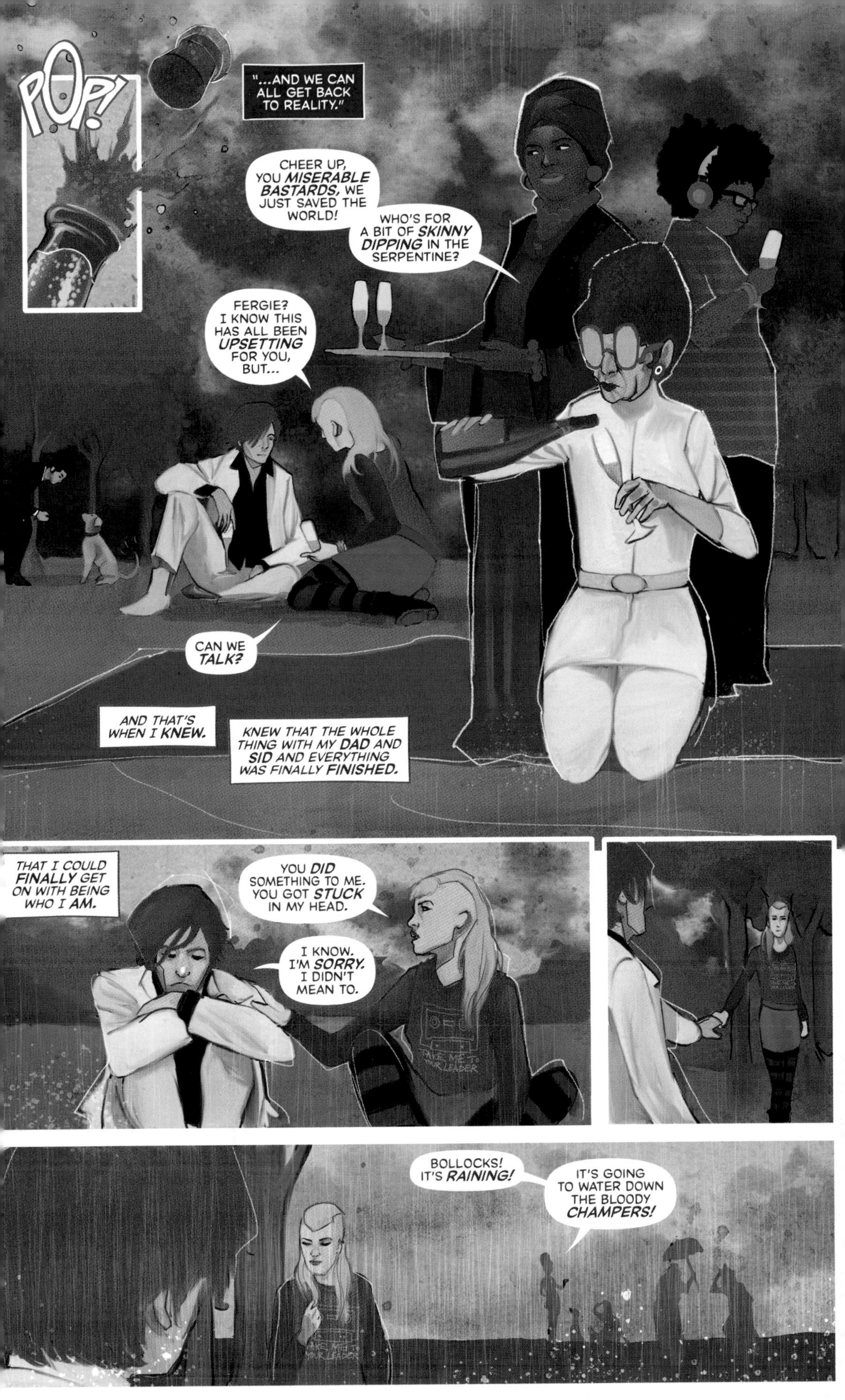

POP!
"...AND WE CAN ALL GET BACK TO REALITY."
CHEER UP, YOU MISERABLE BASTARDS, WE JUST SAVED THE WORLD!
WHO'S FOR A BIT OF SKINNY DIPPING IN THE SERPENTINE?
FERGIE? I KNOW THIS HAS ALL BEEN UPSETTING FOR YOU, BUT...
CAN WE TALK?
AND THAT'S WHEN I KNEW.
KNEW THAT THE WHOLE THING WITH MY DAD AND SID AND EVERYTHING WAS FINALLY FINISHED.
THAT I COULD FINALLY GET ON WITH BEING WHO I AM.
YOU DID SOMETHING TO ME. YOU GOT STUCK IN MY HEAD.
I KNOW. I'M SORRY. I DIDN'T MEAN TO.
TAKE ME TO YOUR LEADER
BOLLOCKS! IT'S RAINING!
IT'S GOING TO WATER DOWN THE BLOODY CHAMPERS!

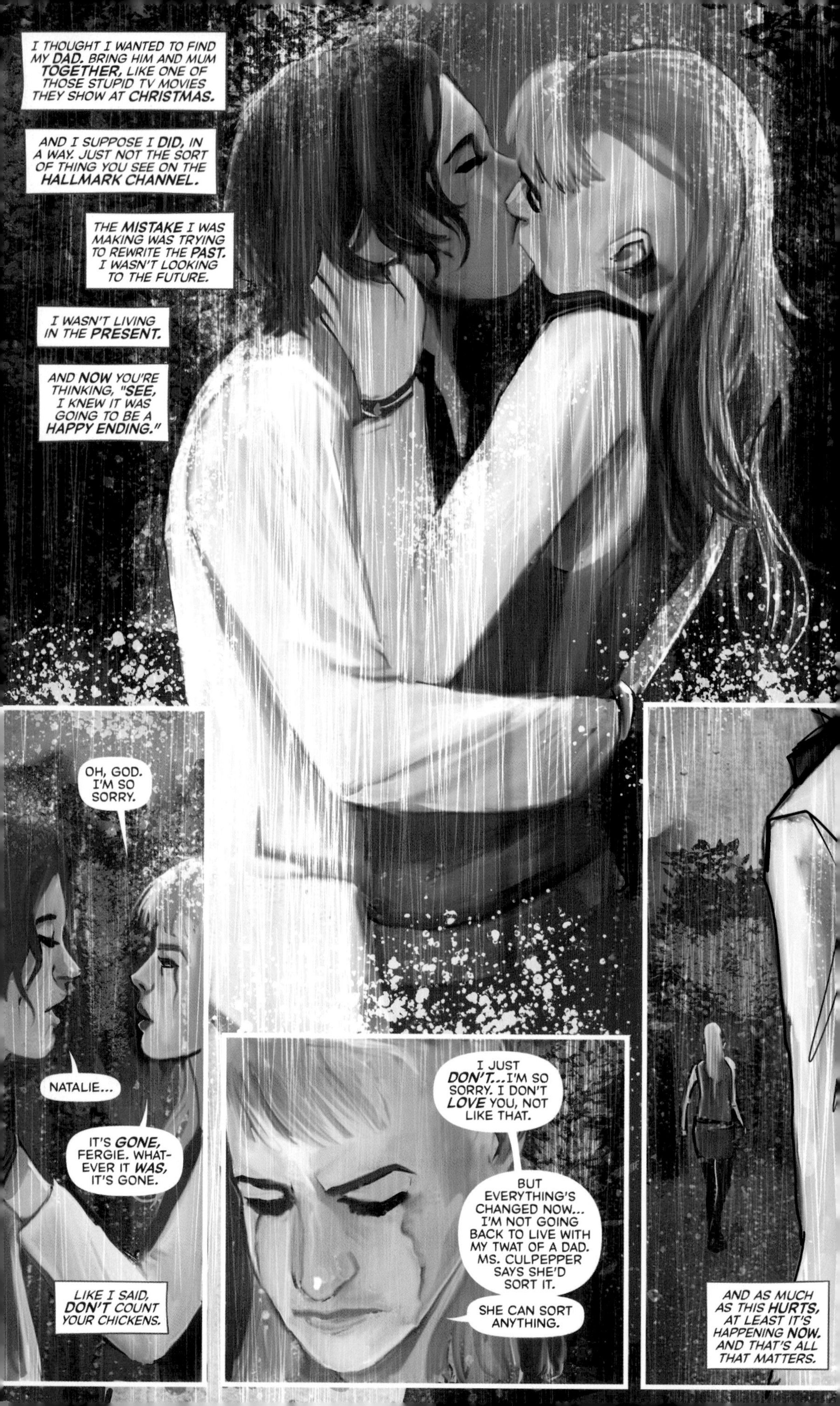

I THOUGHT I WANTED TO FIND MY DAD. BRING HIM AND MUM TOGETHER, LIKE ONE OF THOSE STUPID TV MOVIES THEY SHOW AT CHRISTMAS.
AND I SUPPOSE I DID, IN A WAY. JUST NOT THE SORT OF THING YOU SEE ON THE HALLMARK CHANNEL.
THE MISTAKE I WAS MAKING WAS TRYING TO REWRITE THE PAST. I WASN'T LOOKING TO THE FUTURE.
I WASN'T LIVING IN THE PRESENT.
AND NOW YOU'RE THINKING, "SEE, I KNEW IT WAS GOING TO BE A HAPPY ENDING."
OH, GOD. I'M SO SORRY.
NATALIE...
IT'S GONE, FERGIE. WHATEVER IT WAS, IT'S GONE.
LIKE I SAID, DON'T COUNT YOUR CHICKENS.
I JUST DON'T...I'M SO SORRY. I DON'T LOVE YOU, NOT LIKE THAT.
BUT EVERYTHING'S CHANGED NOW... I'M NOT GOING BACK TO LIVE WITH MY TWAT OF A DAD. MS. CULPEPPER SAYS SHE'D SORT IT.
SHE CAN SORT ANYTHING.
AND AS MUCH AS THIS HURTS, AT LEAST IT'S HAPPENING NOW. AND THAT'S ALL THAT MATTERS.

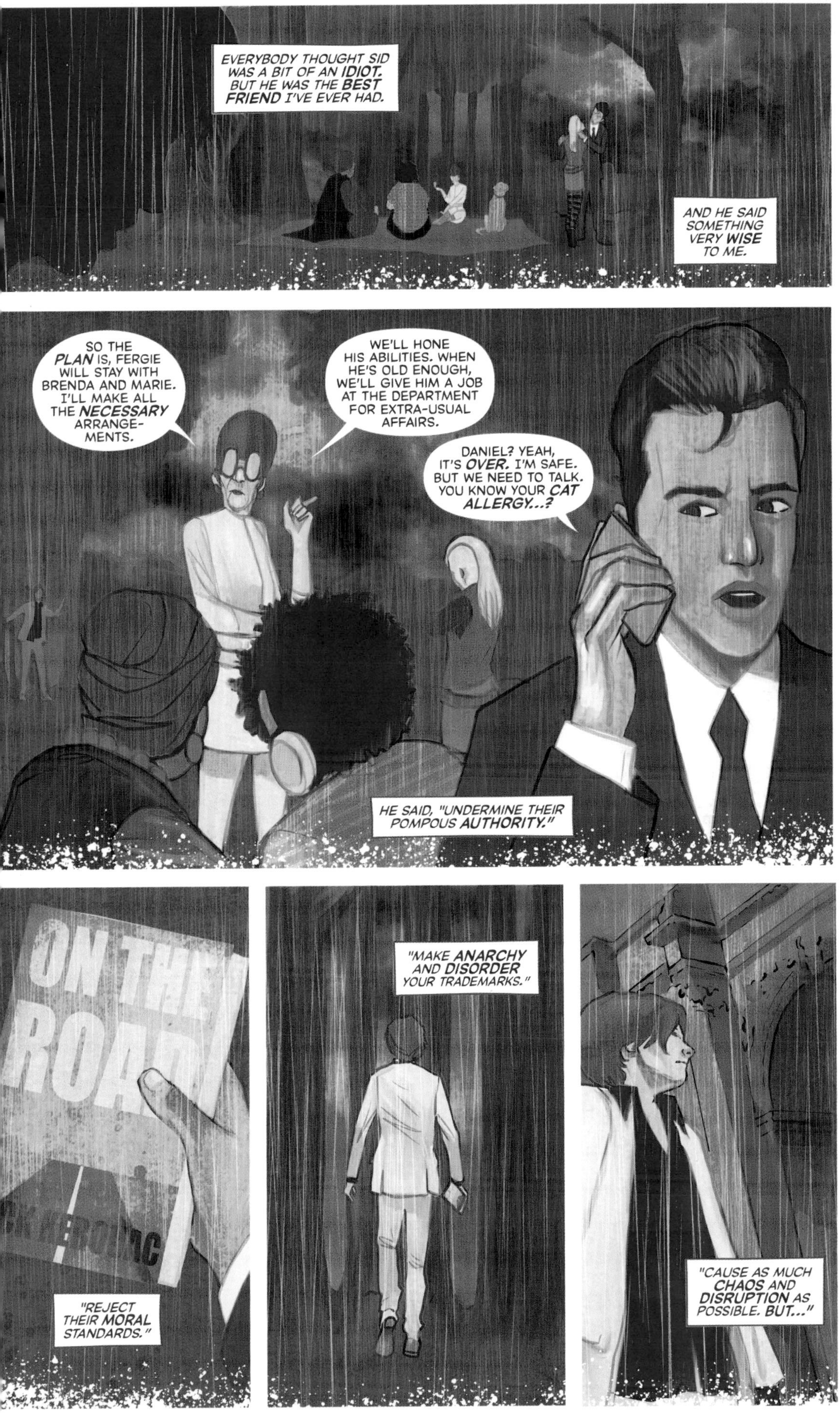
EVERYBODY THOUGHT SID WAS A BIT OF AN IDIOT. BUT HE WAS THE BEST FRIEND I'VE EVER HAD.
AND HE SAID SOMETHING VERY WISE TO ME.
SO THE PLAN IS, FERGIE WILL STAY WITH BRENDA AND MARIE. I'LL MAKE ALL THE NECESSARY ARRANGE-MENTS.
WE'LL HONE HIS ABILITIES. WHEN HE'S OLD ENOUGH, WE'LL GIVE HIM A JOB AT THE DEPARTMENT FOR EXTRA-USUAL AFFAIRS.
DANIEL? YEAH, IT'S OVER. I'M SAFE. BUT WE NEED TO TALK. YOU KNOW YOUR CAT ALLERGY...?
HE SAID, "UNDERMINE THEIR POMPOUS AUTHORITY."
ON THE ROAD
"REJECT THEIR MORAL STANDARDS."
"MAKE ANARCHY AND DISORDER YOUR TRADEMARKS."
"CAUSE AS MUCH CHAOS AND DISRUPTION AS POSSIBLE. BUT..."

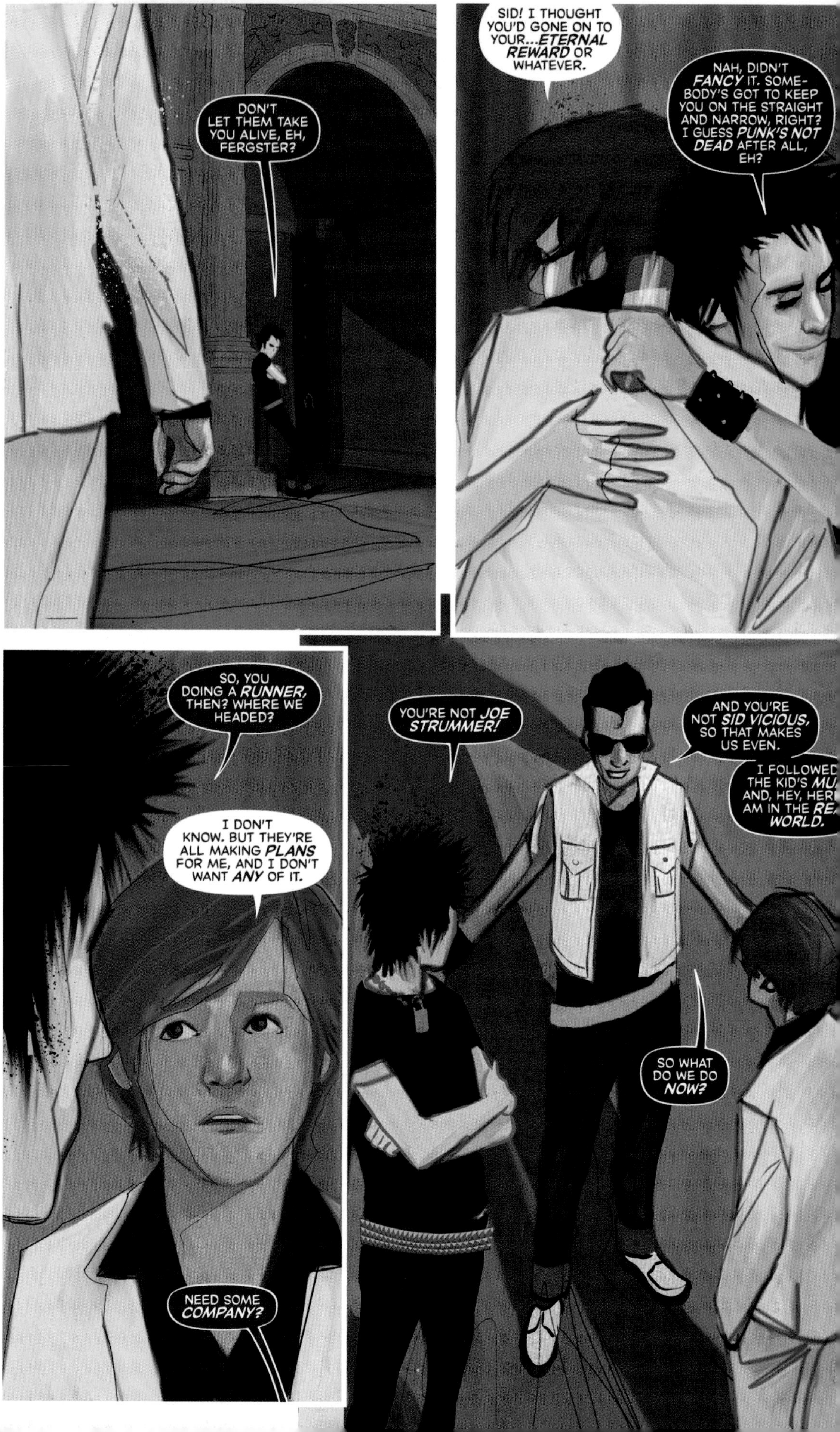
DON'T LET THEM TAKE YOU ALIVE, EH, FERGSTER?
SID! I THOUGHT YOU'D GONE ON TO YOUR...ETERNAL REWARD OR WHATEVER.
NAH, DIDN'T FANCY IT. SOMEBODY'S GOT TO KEEP YOU ON THE STRAIGHT AND NARROW, RIGHT? I GUESS PUNK'S NOT DEAD AFTER ALL, EH?
SO, YOU DOING A RUNNER, THEN? WHERE WE HEADED?
I DON'T KNOW. BUT THEY'RE ALL MAKING PLANS FOR ME, AND I DON'T WANT ANY OF IT.
NEED SOME COMPANY?
YOU'RE NOT JOE STRUMMER!
AND YOU'RE NOT SID VICIOUS, SO THAT MAKES US EVEN.
SO WHAT DO WE DO NOW?

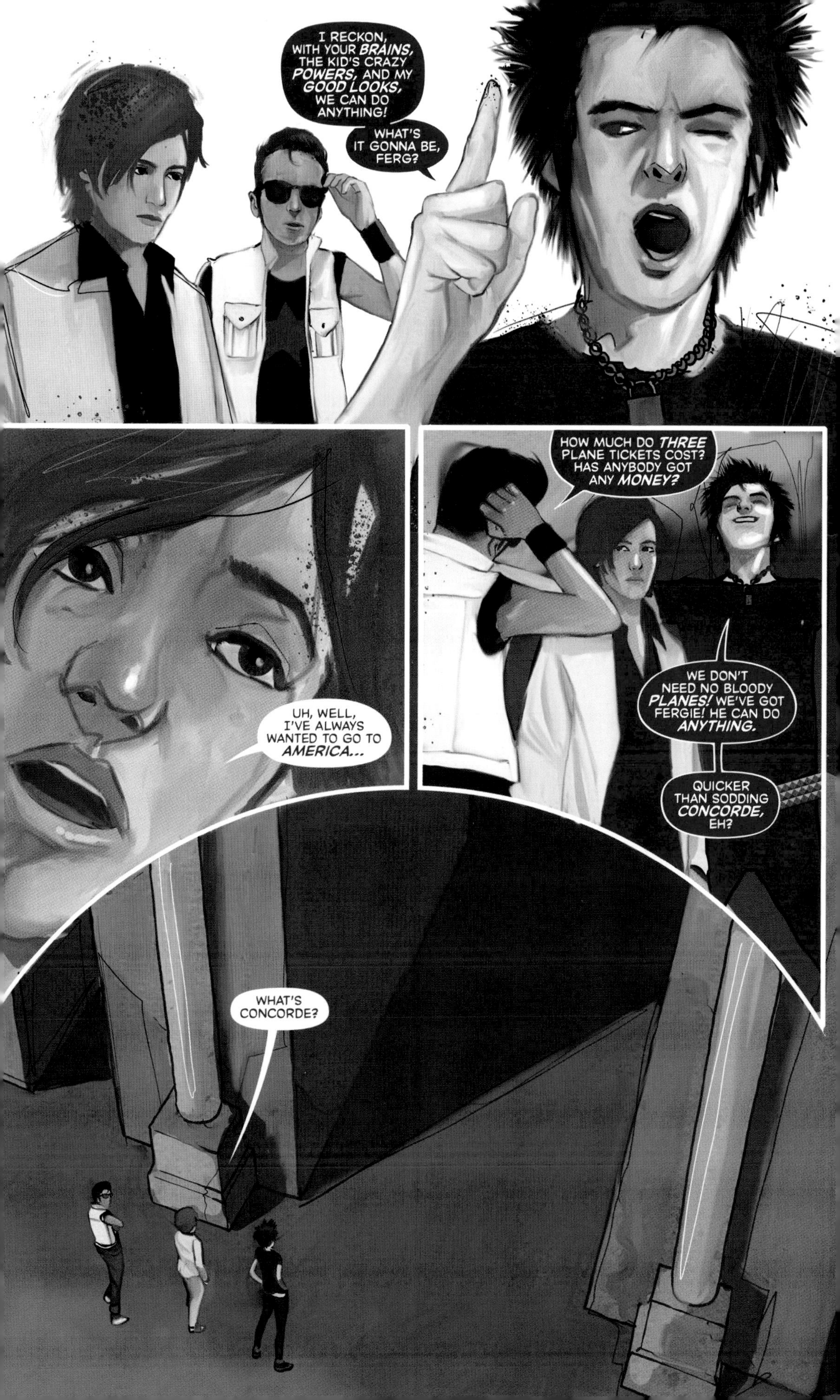

I RECKON, WITH YOUR *BRAINS,* THE KID'S CRAZY *POWERS,* AND MY *GOOD LOOKS,* WE CAN DO ANYTHING!
WHAT'S IT GONNA BE, FERG?
UH, WELL, I'VE ALWAYS WANTED TO GO TO *AMERICA...*
HOW MUCH DO *THREE* PLANE TICKETS COST? HAS ANYBODY GOT ANY *MONEY?*
WE DON'T NEED NO BLOODY *PLANES!* WE'VE GOT FERGIE! HE CAN DO *ANYTHING.*
QUICKER THAN SODDING *CONCORDE,* EH?
WHAT'S CONCORDE?

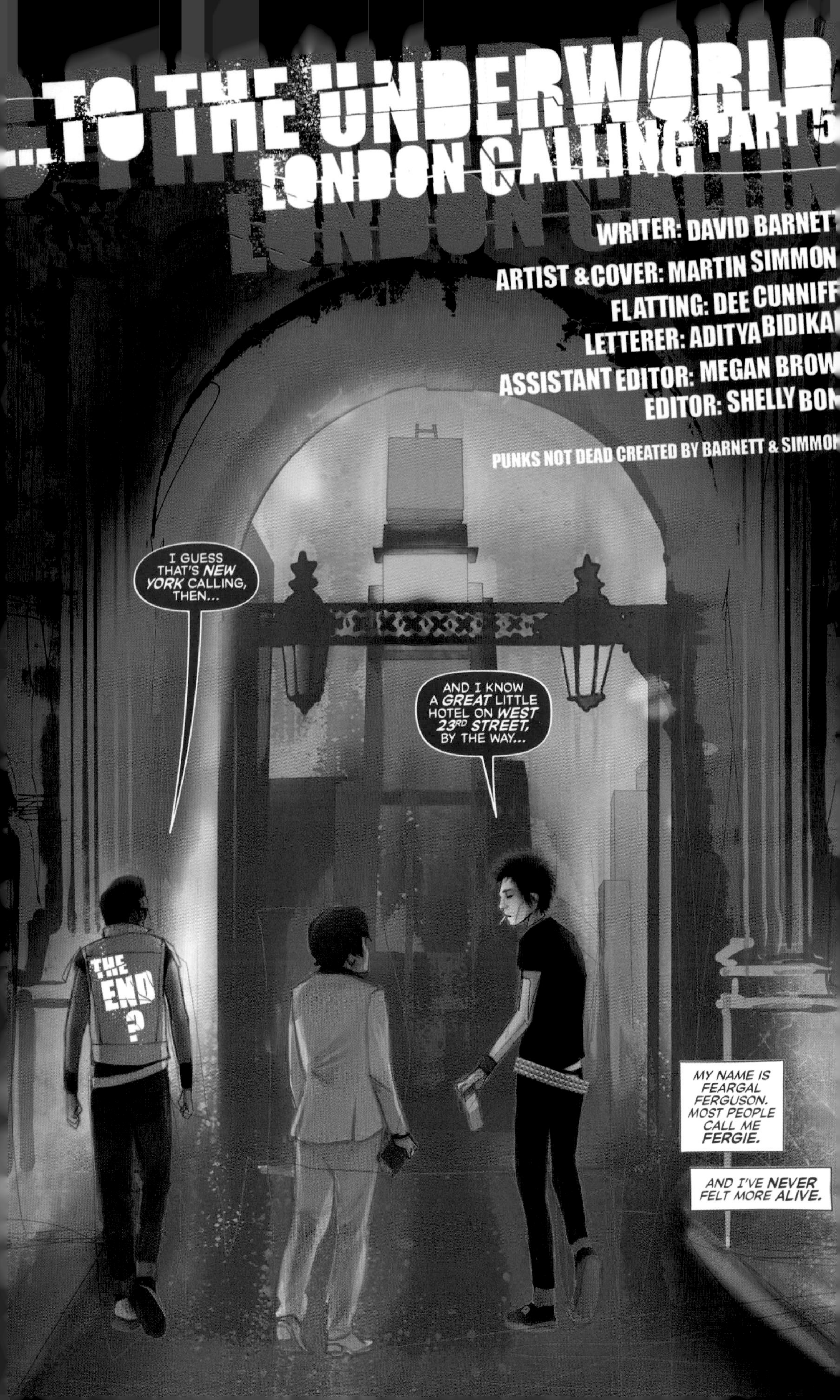

...TO THE UNDERWORLD
LONDON CALLING PART 5
WRITER: DAVID BARNET
ARTIST & COVER: MARTIN SIMMON
FLATTING: DEE CUNNIFF
LETTERER: ADITYA BIDIKA
ASSISTANT EDITOR: MEGAN BROW
EDITOR: SHELLY BO
PUNKS NOT DEAD CREATED BY BARNETT & SIMMO
I GUESS THAT'S NEW YORK CALLING, THEN...
AND I KNOW A GREAT LITTLE HOTEL ON WEST 23RD STREET, BY THE WAY...
THE END?
MY NAME IS FEARGAL FERGUSON. MOST PEOPLE CALL ME FERGIE.
AND I'VE NEVER FELT MORE ALIVE.

POST PUNK

SUPPLEMENTARY MATERIALS

PUNKS NOT DEAD: LONDON CALLING #1 cover by Martin Simmonds

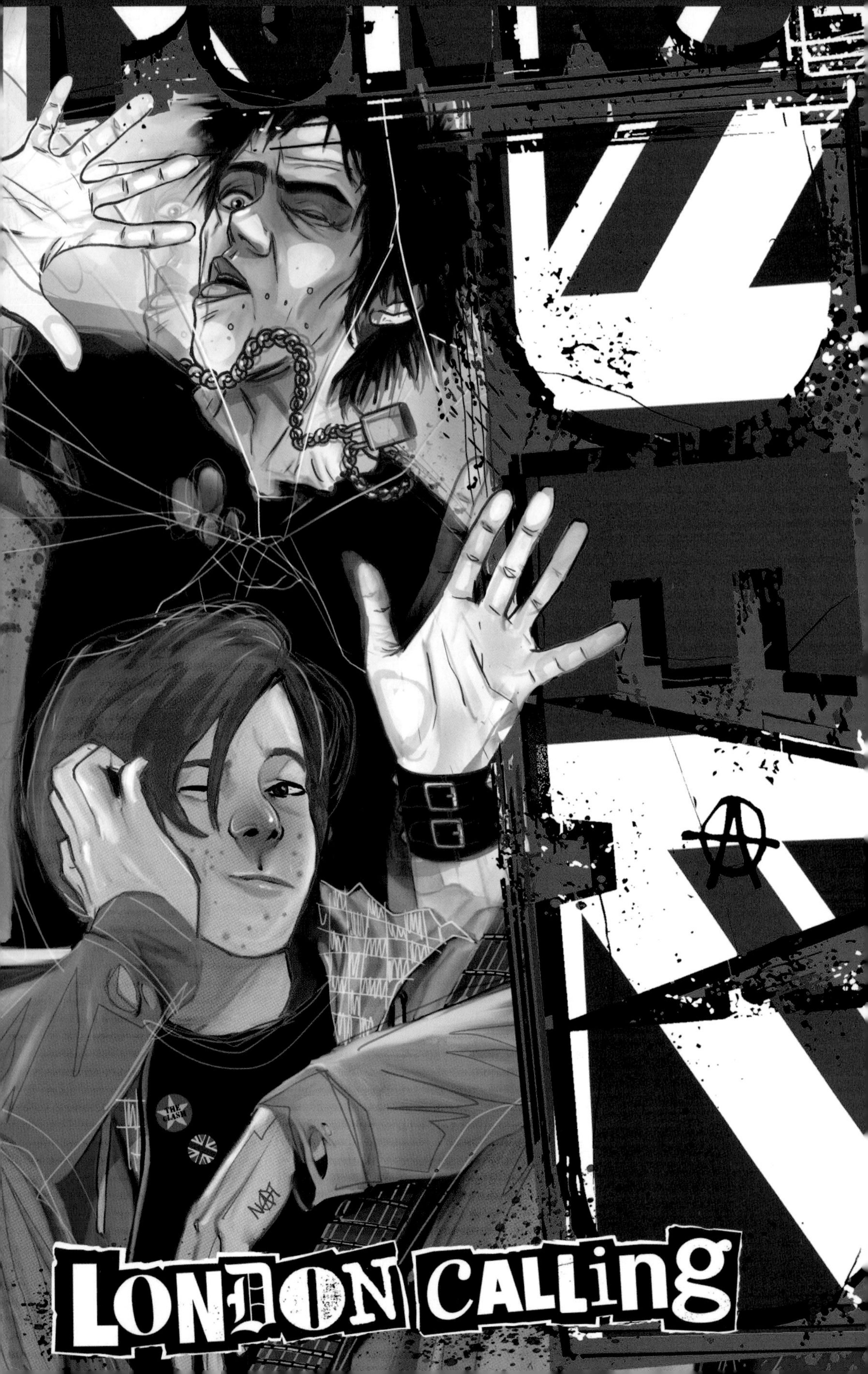
THE CLASH
LONDON CALLING

PUNKS NOT DEAD: LONDON CALLING #1 retailer incentive cover by Rafael Albuquerque

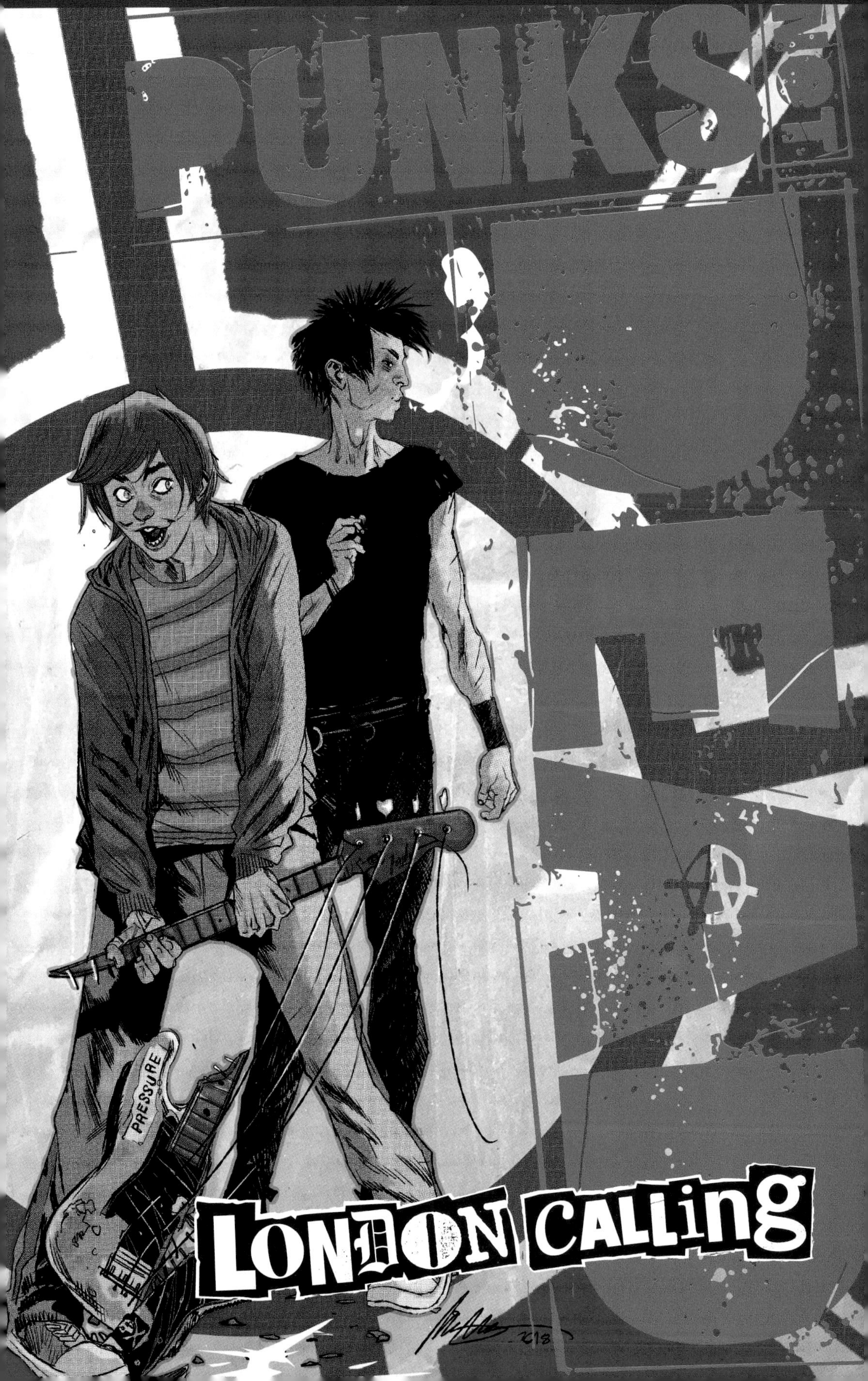

PROCESS BY MARTIN SIMMONDS

1 First, I thumbnail the pages based on David's script. I work on a very small scale at this stage, eight or nine thumbnails to a page. I'm aiming to get well-balanced and interesting layouts, making sure I'm telling the story as clearly and effectively as I can. It's important to place the ballooning on each page as well, as this helps to inform the composition. This stage is one of the most time consuming for me, as a lot of the heavy lifting is done here — page design, composition, pacing, storytelling, character acting etc. I tend to make my thumbnails fairly detailed, as I find this makes life much easier as I progress through the stages.

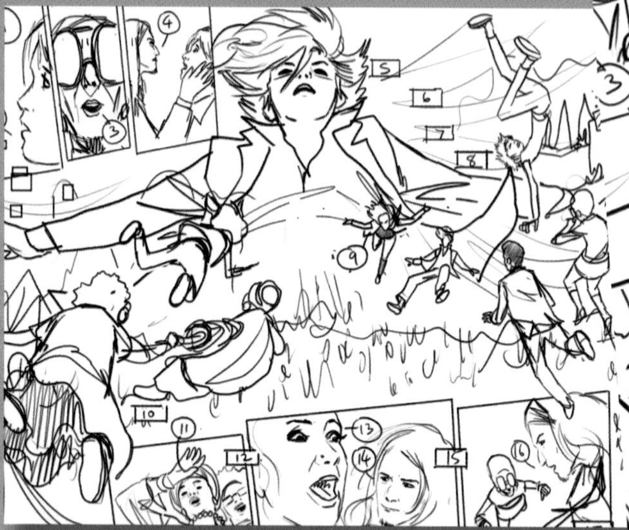

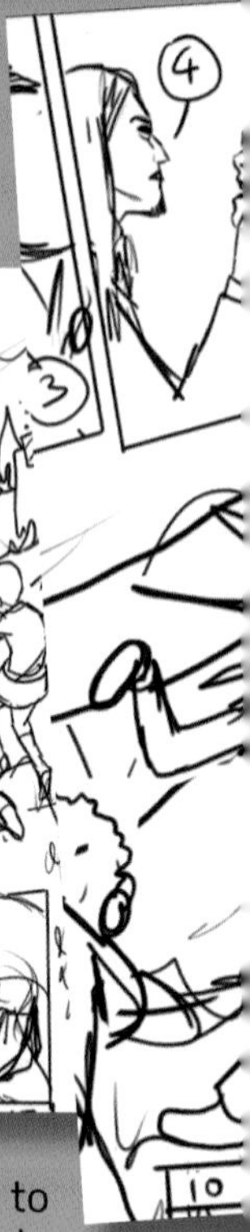

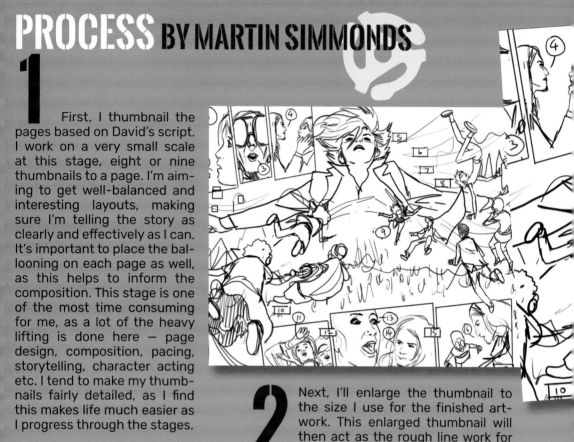

2 Next, I'll enlarge the thumbnail to the size I use for the finished artwork. This enlarged thumbnail will then act as the rough line work for me to work on top of.

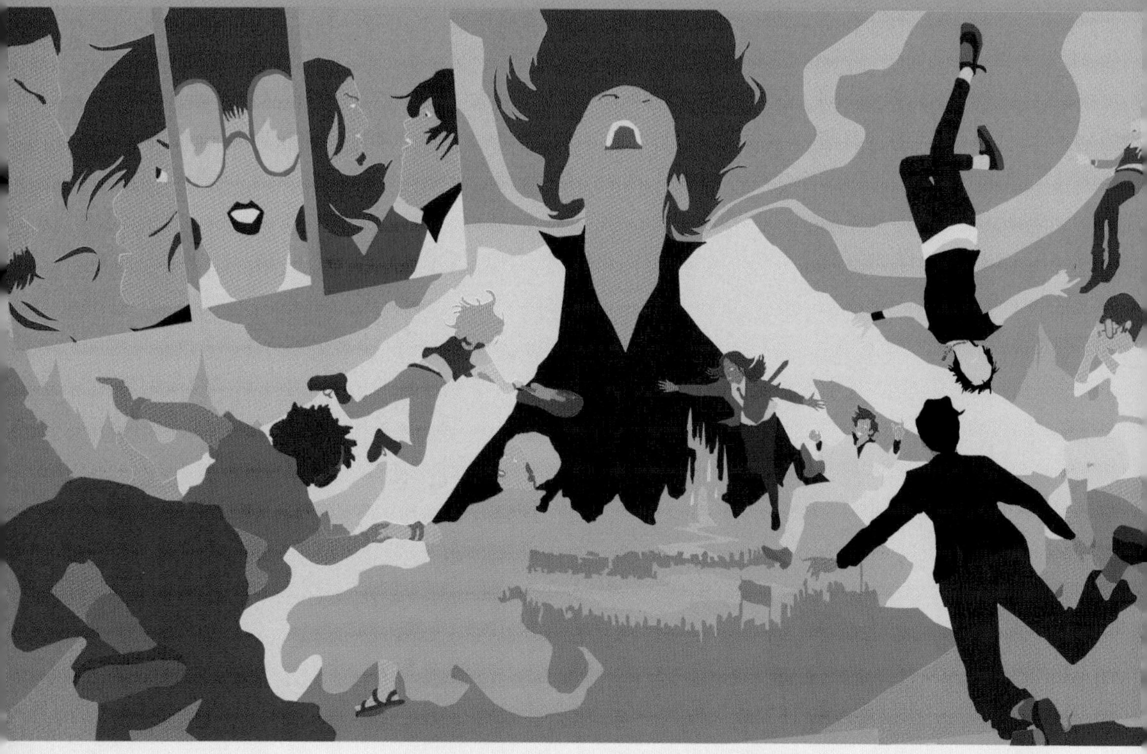

4. Dee (Cunniffe) will fill in all the areas with flat colour (known as flatting). This allows me to isolate areas of colour quickly which I can then adjust as needed. Here's what the flats look like without the linework on top.

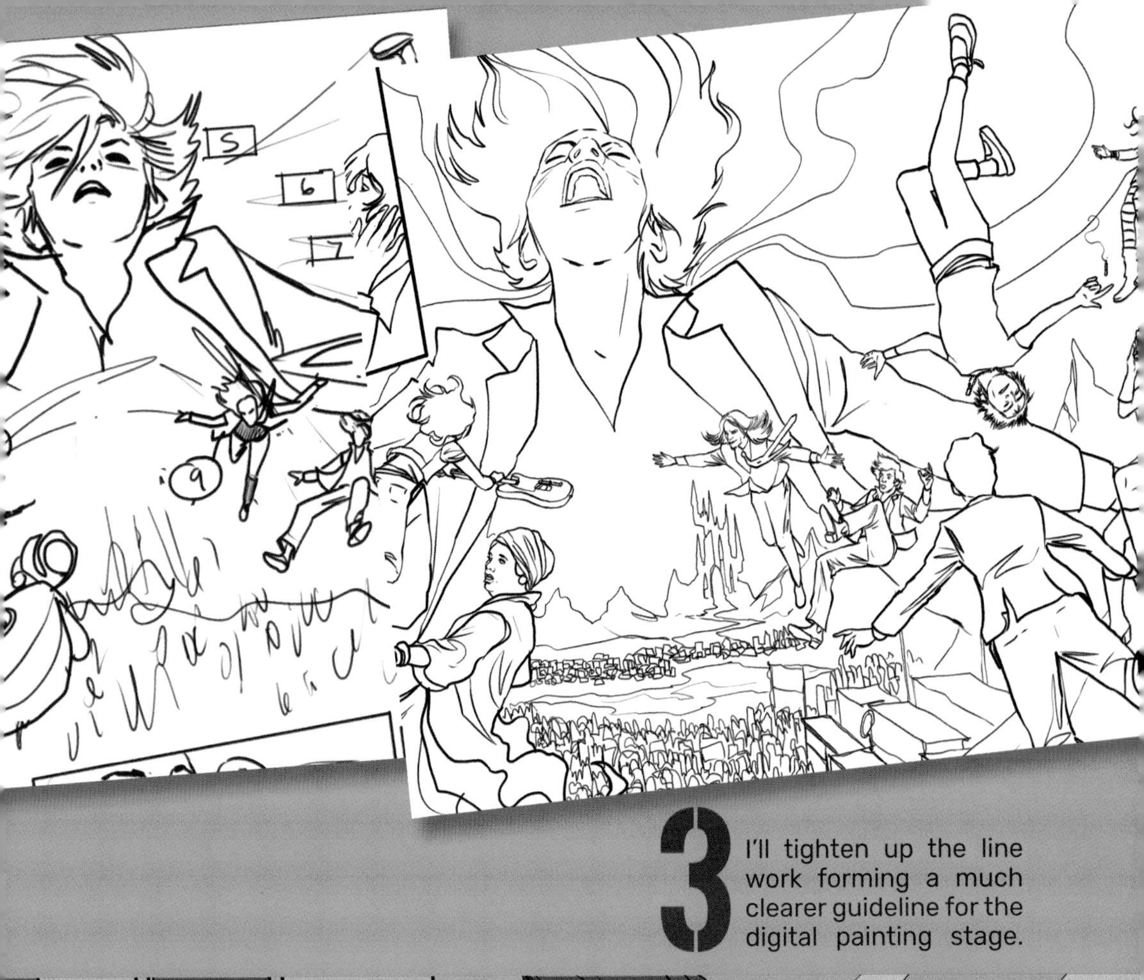

3

I'll tighten up the line work forming a much clearer guideline for the digital painting stage.

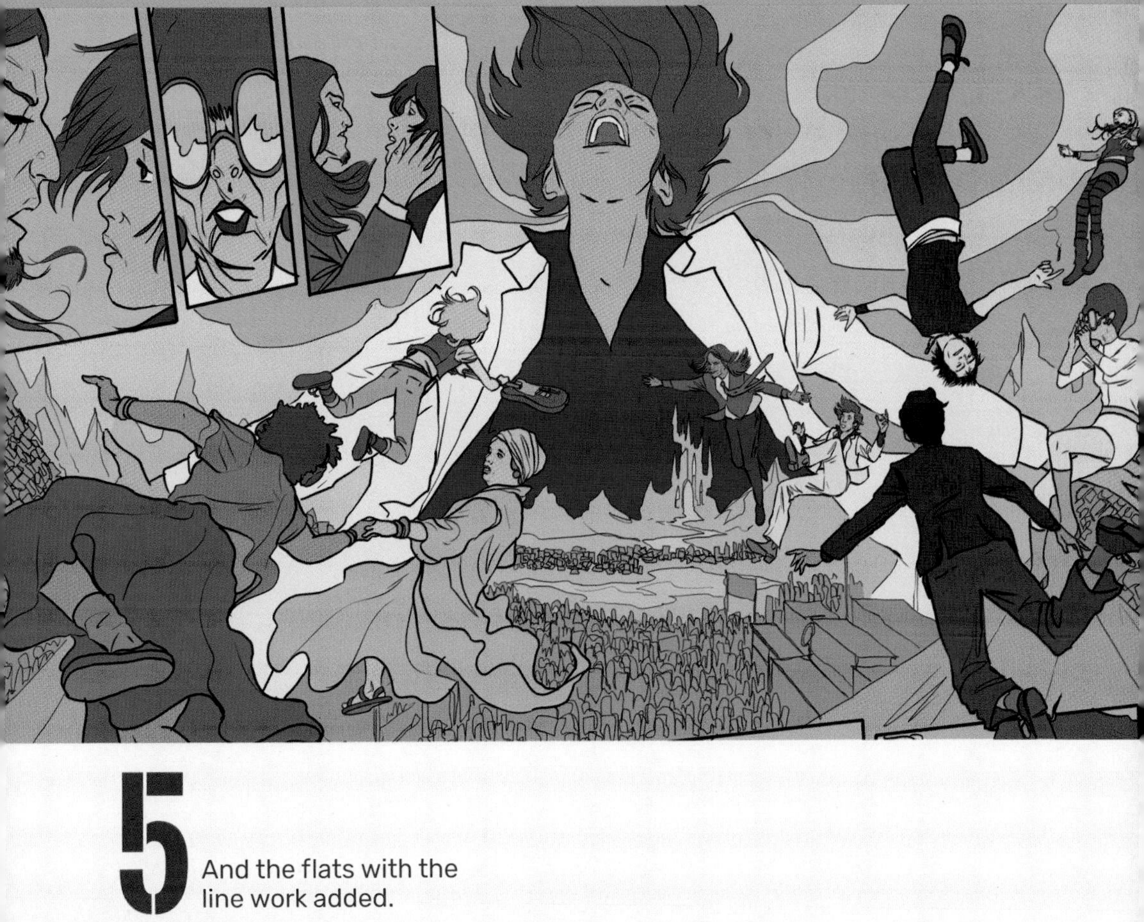

5

And the flats with the line work added.

6

Once the flats are all adjusted to the correct colours, I'll add in hand-painted textures, paint in areas of light and shade, and add additional colour details and patterns. This stage is a lot of fun, and where I'll experiment with the overall feel of the page.

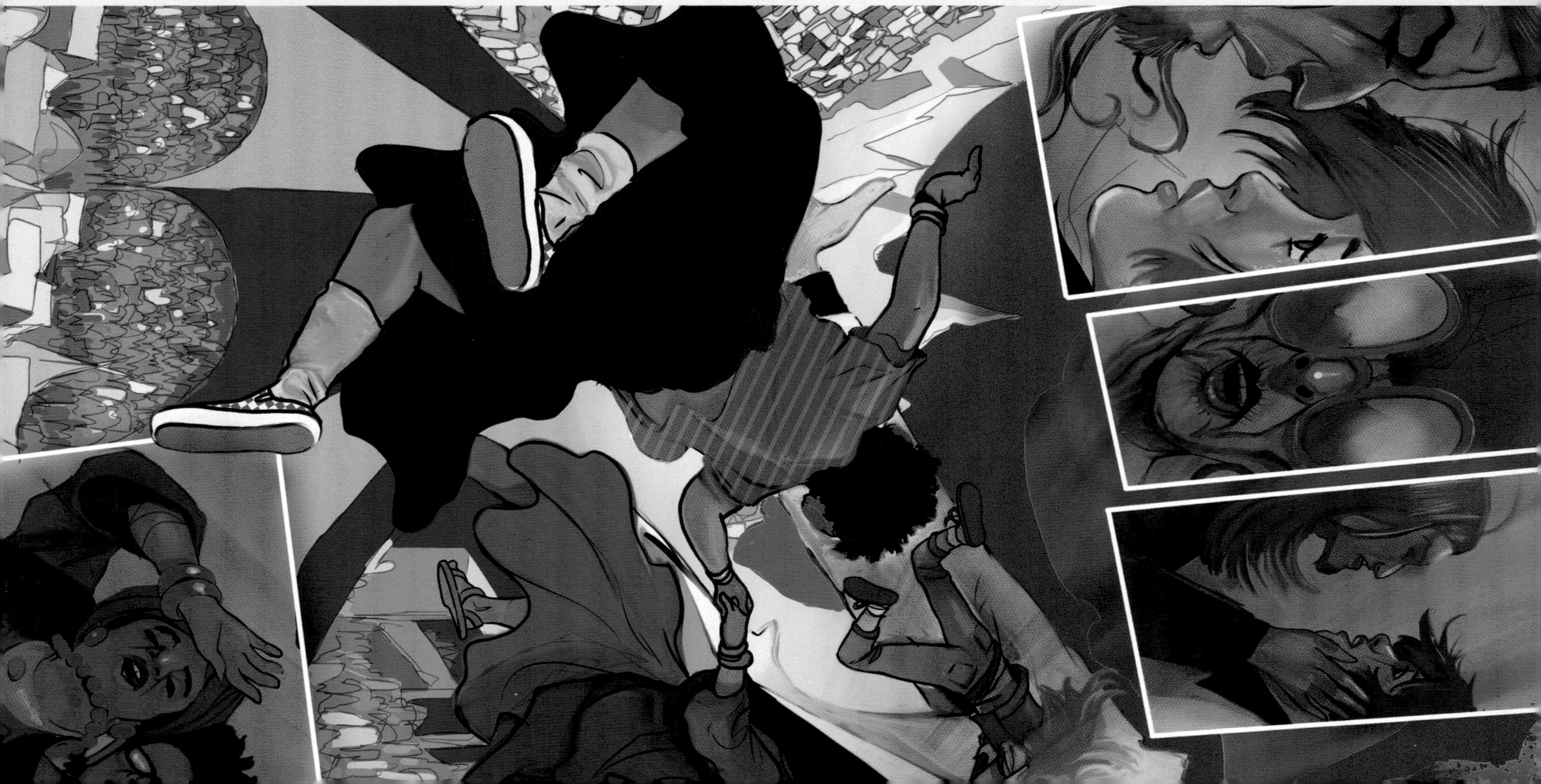

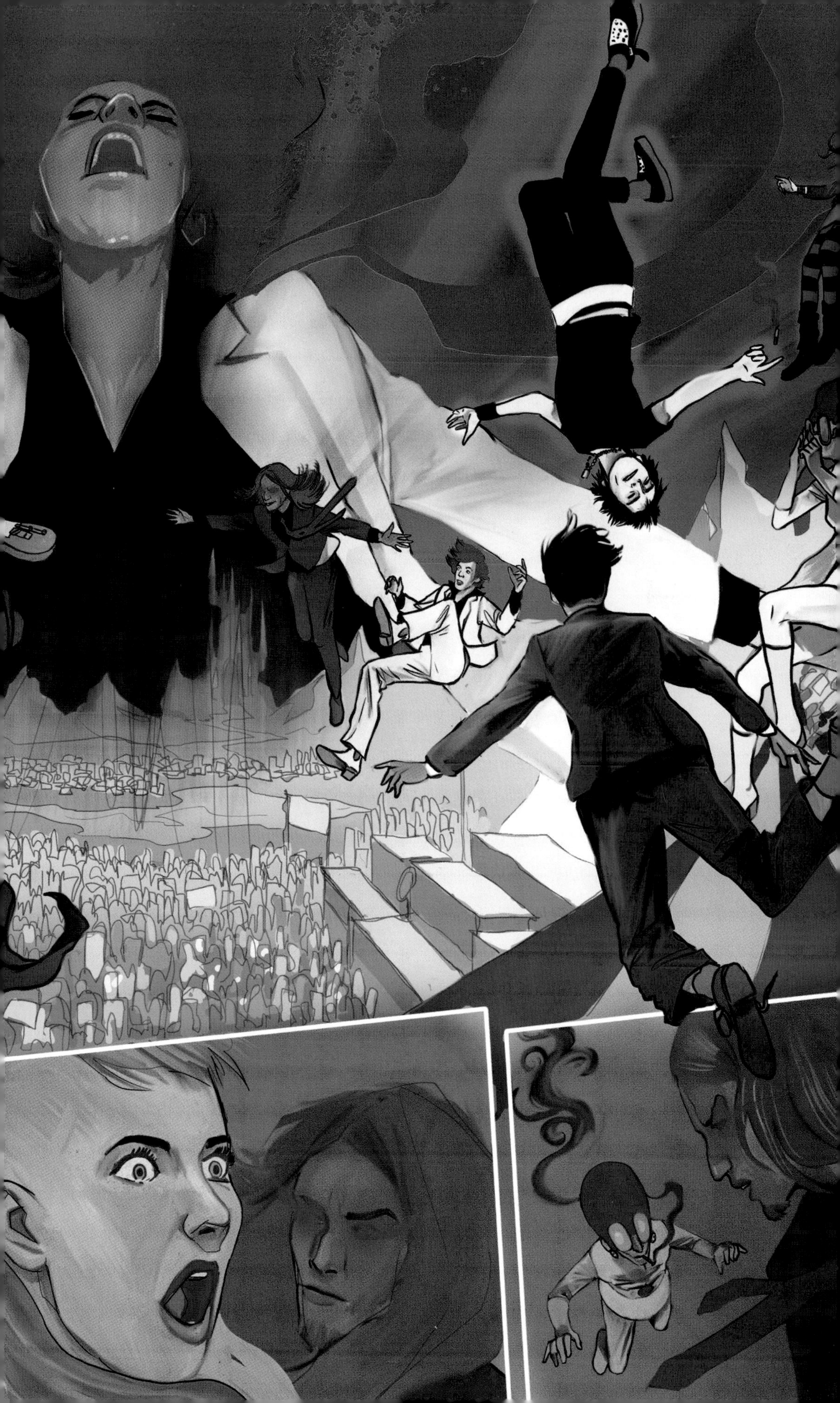

StagE CrEw

DAVID BARNETT is the writer of **PUNKS NOT DEAD** and **EVE STRANGER** for **Black Crown**, the author of novels including CALLING MAJOR TOM and THINGS CAN ONLY GET BETTER, and a journalist working for a variety of outlets including The Guardian and The Independent. And he still finds time to toss it off on twitter at @davidmbarnett

MARTIN SIMMONDS is a comic artist and co-creator (along with David M. Barnett) of **PUNKS NOT DEAD** for IDW's **Black Crown** imprint, and **Friendo** (with Alex Paknadel) for Vault Comics. Martin is also contributing artist to Marvel's **The Immortal Hulk** by Al Ewing and Joe Bennett, and series cover artist for Marvel's **Quicksilver: No Surrender**, and **Jessica Jones**. Previous work includes Titan Comics' **Death Sentence: London** (written by Monty Nero), and the self-published **Eponymous,** written by Mike Garley.
@Martin_Simmonds   simmonds-illustration.com

ADI BIDIKAR is **Black Crown**'s esteemed house letterer and the recipient of Broken Frontier's 2017 Best Letterer Award. Based in India, Adi also lettered ASSASSINISTAS, KID LOBOTOMY, **Motor Crush**, and **Grafity's Wall.**
@adityab adityab.net.

DEE CUNNIFFE provided color flats for **PUNKS NOT DEAD** and KID LOBOTOMY. He is an award-winning designer who gave it all up to pursue his love of comics. His coloring credits include **The Dregs, Eternal**, and **Redneck.**
@deezoid

MEGAN BROWN is an Assistant Editor and **Black Crown**'s San Diego connection. When she's not racking up a tab at the **Black Crown Pub**, you can find her at one of the coffee shops around town, perfecting the art of being a struggling writer.
@megan_mb

PHILIP BOND is the logo and publication designer for KID LOBOTOMY and many fine **Black Crown** titles. He is the artist on **EVE STRANGER**, also written by PND's Barnett. <help i am being held hostage at BCHQ and forced to make comics plz send marmite>
@pjbond

GOD SaVe tHE QueeN

SHELLY BOND has been drive to edit + curate comic books crush deadlines and innovate fo over a quarter century. She live in Los Angeles with her husban Philip, their son Spencer, si electric guitars and a drumkit You can follow her editorial sartorial exploits on twitte @sxbond @blackcrownhq and blackcrown.pub

CATALOGUE

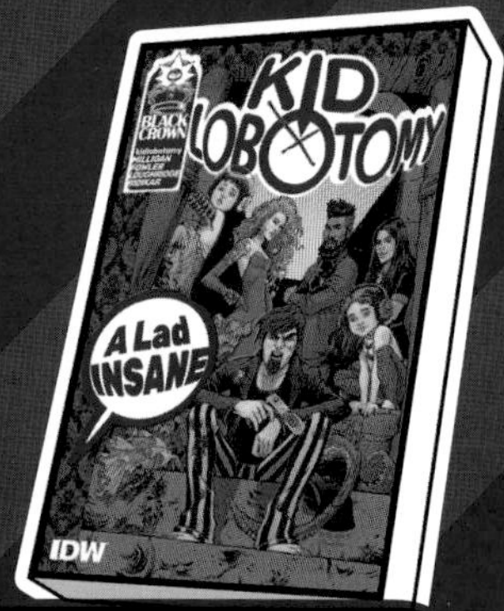
KID LOBOTOMY
A Lad INSANE
IDW

KID LOBOTOMY
Almost Rockstar. Awkward Hotelier. Definitive Madman.
by Peter Milligan + Tess Fowler

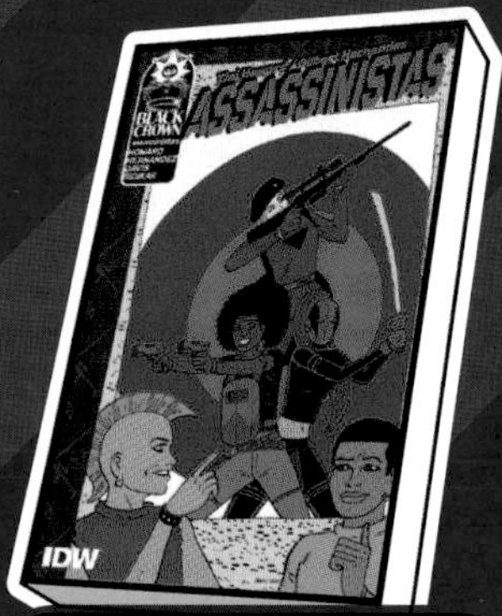
ASSASSINISTAS
IDW

ASSASSINISTAS
Modern Family. Retro Sass. Highly Trained to Kick Your Ass.
by Tini Howard + Gilbert Hernandez

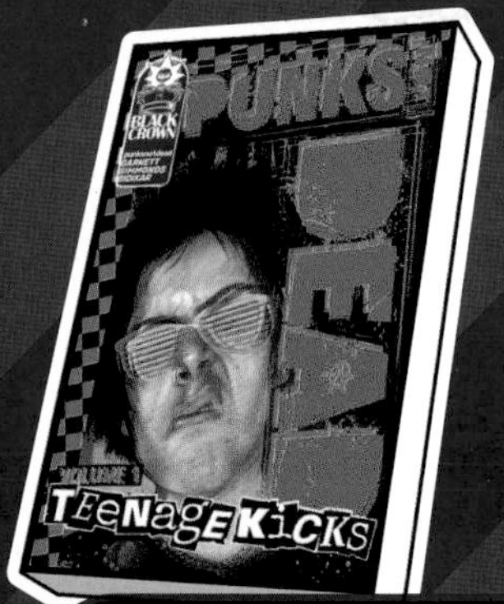
PUNKS!
TEENAGE KICKS

PUNKS NOT DEAD
The Ghost. The Geek. The Geriatric Mod Superspy. Everything & the Bollocks
by David Barnett + Martin Simmonds

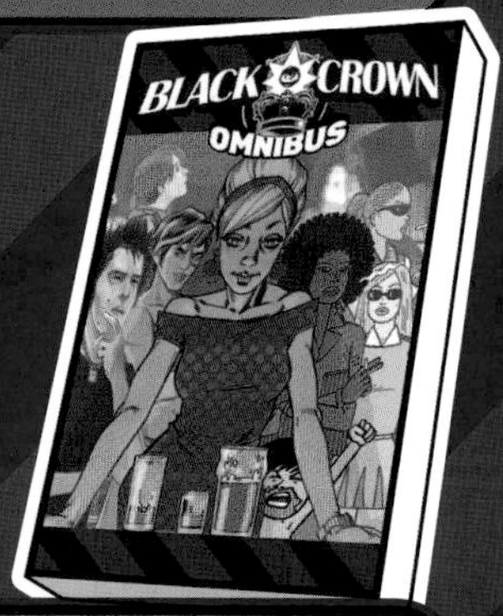
BLACK CROWN
OMNIBUS

BLACK CROWN OMNIBUS
The Compendium of Comics, Culture & Cool featuring Tales from the BC Pub.
by Rob Davis, CUD + others

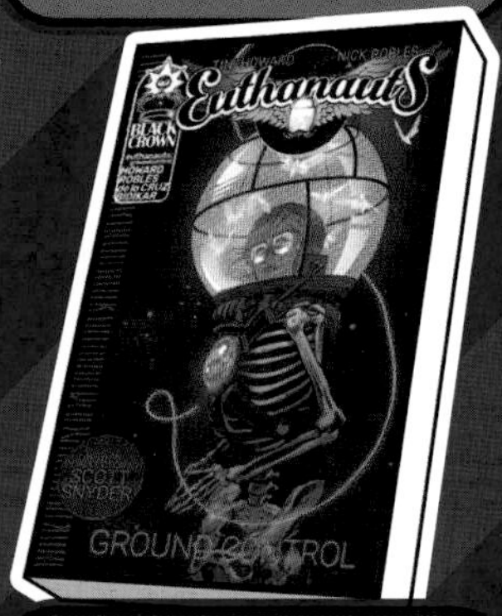
Euthanauts
GROUND CONTROL

EUTHANAUTS
Tethers to the Great Beyond. Psychonautic Mindspaces.
by Tini Howard + Nick Robles

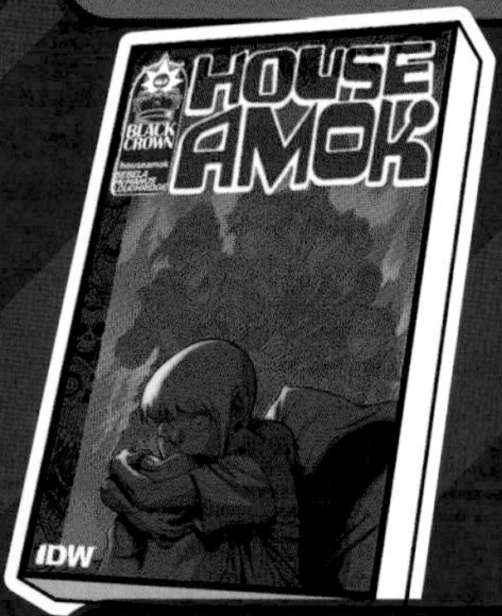
HOUSE AMOK
IDW

HOUSE AMOK
Conspiracy theories come to life. Shared Family Madness & Murder.
by Christopher Sebela + Shawn McManus

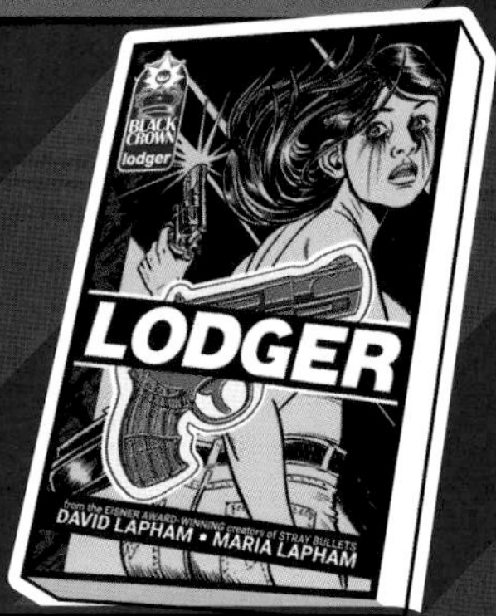
LODGER
DAVID LAPHAM • MARIA LAPHAM

LODGER
A serial killer hides in plain sight as a travel blogger in a game of cat & mouse.
By The Laphams of Stray Bullets

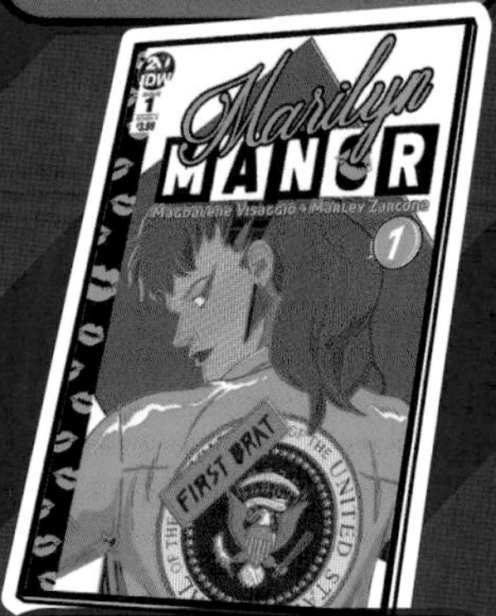
Marilyn MANOR
FIRST BRAT

MARILYN MANOR
It's 1981 and the President's daughter throws a rager in the White House!
by Mags Visaggio + Marley Zarcone

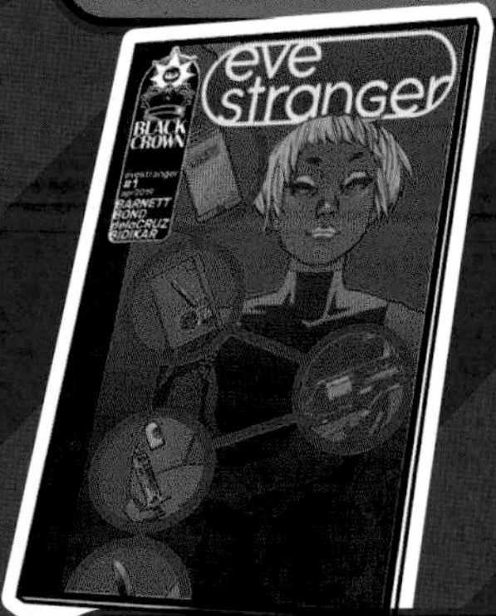
eve stranger

EVE STRANGER
High-Octane Thrills! Weird Science! Doomed Romance!
by David Barnett + Philip Bond

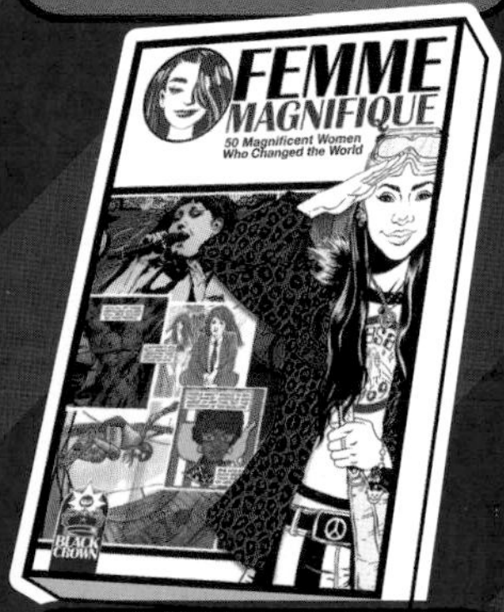
FEMME MAGNIFIQUE
50 Magnificent Women Who Changed the World

FEMME MAGNIFIQUE
A salute to personal icons who shatter ceilings in pop, politics, art & science.
by 100+ A-list writers & artists

#therulingclass

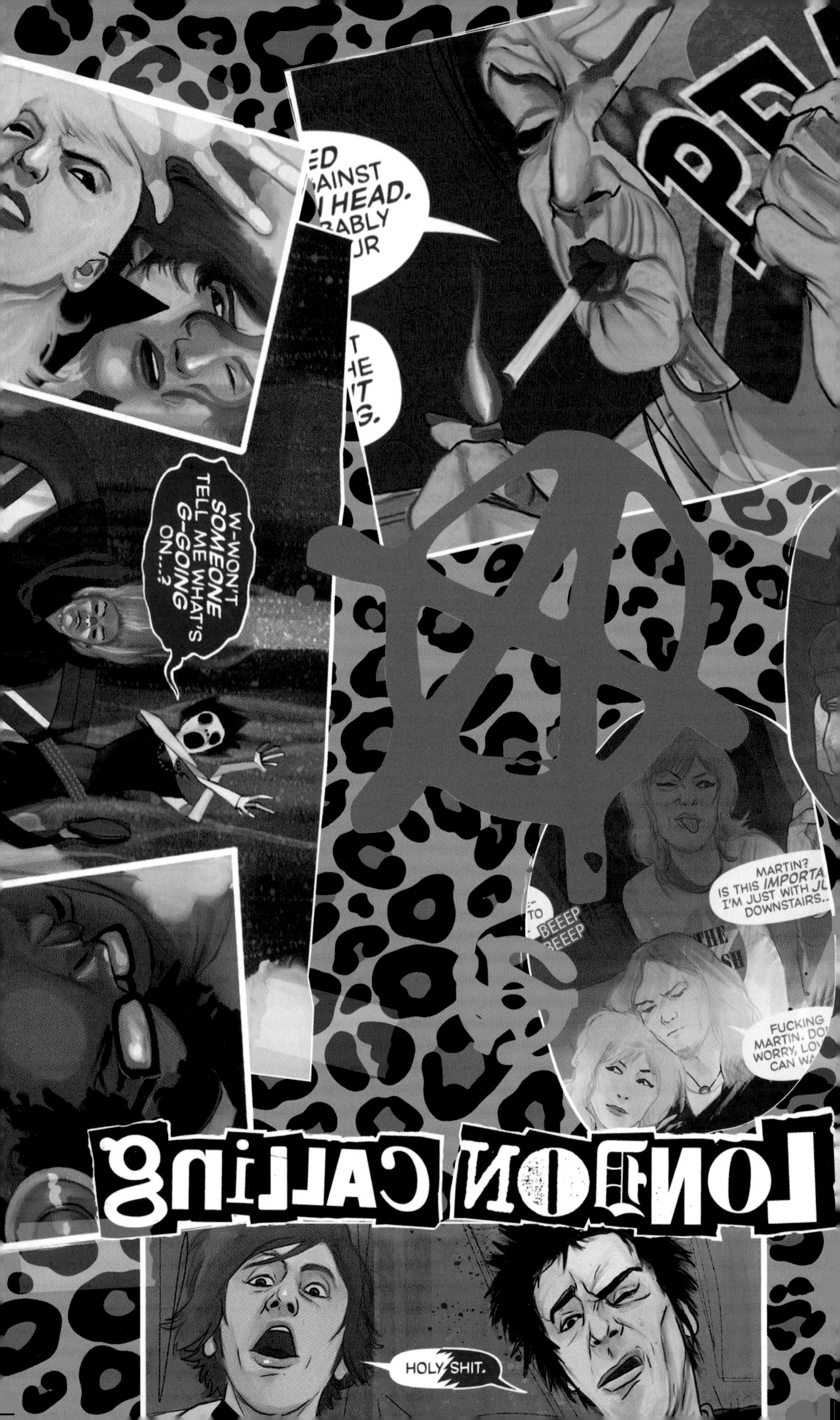
ED AINST HEAD. ABLY UR
W-WON'T SOMEONE TELL ME WHAT'S G-GOING ON...?
MARTIN? IS THIS IMPORTA I'M JUST WITH JU DOWNSTAIRS...
BEEEP BEEEP
FUCKING MARTIN. DO WORRY, LOV CAN WA
HOLY SHIT.